WALKING THROUGH THE VALLEY

D1598467

WALKING
THROUGH
the
VALLEY

AN AUTOBIOGRAPHY

George Woodcock

ECW PRESS

CANADIAN CATALOGUING IN PUBLICATION DATA

Woodcock, George, 1912–
Walking through the valley
ISBN 1-55022-209-0
1. Woodcock, George, 1912-   – Biography.
2. Authors, Canadian (English) – 20th century – Biography.*
3. Historians – Canada – Biography.   1. Title.
PS8545.O6Z53 1994   C818.5409   C94-930596-0
PR9199.3.W58Z477 1994

This book has been published with the assistance of the Ontario
Publishing Centre, the Department of Communications,
The Canada Council, and the Ontario Arts Council.

Design and imaging by ECW Type & Art, Oakville, Ontario.
Printed by Imprimerie Gagné, Louiseville, Québec.

Distributed by General Distribution Services,
30 Lesmill Road, Don Mills, Ontario M3B 2T6,
(416) 445-3333, (800) 387-0172 (Canada), FAX (416) 445-5967.

Published by ECW PRESS,
1980 Queen Street East,
Toronto, Ontario M4L 1J2.

TO MELVILLE SHAW,
*Who gave me the
precious gift of time*

CONTENTS

Introduction

KINDS OF AUTOBIOGRAPHY

The best of autobiographies in my view are those that combine a view of the world with a portrait of the artist; in other words, the artist in his landscape rather than in his study; *plein air* in prose. This is the approach I followed in my two earlier volumes of memoirs, *Letter to the Past* and *Beyond the Blue Mountains*. I shall continue to follow it in the present book, though the approach will vary as I move through what I regard as the four elements of autobiography, the elements that distinguish it within the broader field of narrative writing, and mark it off, though never very decisively, from fiction. These elements are memory, documentation, reflection, and confession.

Memory is undoubtedly the most important, and it is most vitally expressed in those fortunate times when associations work and the Proustian reconstructions of the past take place. I can perhaps illustrate what I mean by a personal tale.

A few years before I started writing *Letter to the Past*, I was back on the same schedule of sixteen-hour days of complicated work that had led to my first heart attack in 1966. Once again the mind and body alliance took control, and I went into amnesia for a period of about eight hours. My wife, who had been out for the day, found me with a bewildered look on my face, saying: "I've lost my memory!" And indeed when she cross-examined me I could remember only things that had taken place at least ten years before. The rest was blank.

A young locum appeared, checked to make sure I had not suffered a stroke, and declared it was due to stress, though what had caused the stress neither he nor I could determine with any precision; I had just been doing too many things at once. However, he prescribed a couple of days of complete rest in bed, and a shot of whisky every two hours to keep me serene. It worked admirably. Within two or three hours I suddenly had a vivid vignette in my mind of an incident in India the preceding autumn. We were driving in the Punjab on the road from Pathankot to Delhi, and suddenly we met, coming in the opposite direction, a company of the Sikh fanatics who call themselves Nihangs in commemoration of the suicide squads in the old Sikh armies. Clad in shining breastplates and brilliant blue turbans, armed with shield and sword and spear, some with long white beards and others hardly more than boys, they clattered along on their horses (some on bicycles!), followed by a baggage train of oxcarts guarded by sturdy spearmen on foot. Other memories of India and of that journey gathered around this original image, and then yet other clusters began to form independently and to coalesce, so that at the end of two days and numerous shots of Ballantines, I had my past put together like a vast jigsaw puzzle. My past, that is to say, except the eight hours when I was in amnesia. I have no idea even now what I did or what happened to me during that period. It was rather like the effect of getting drunk on absinthe. Then I had lost immediate awareness but perhaps not the whole of consciousness, for I and my companion had been able to convey ourselves, presumably on our own wavering legs, from the place in Soho where we had taken the drink to the square in Belgravia where, leaning against the railings, we came back — somewhat sicker for the experience — to a sense of ourselves and the world, and all returned in our minds except that time of intoxication when we might have done murders for all we knew.

In the same way, my memory spontaneously arranged itself in associative clusters, accessible and willing, when I began to write *Letter to the Past*, my first autobiography. Except for the first chapter about infancy, which I wrote largely from remembered hearsay, that book depended mainly on personal memory. Apart from a few old photographs (my family was never highly camera-conscious) and some letters of my teens that a friend kept, I had almost no documentation until the late 1930s — my own middle twenties — when I began to publish here and there and kept letters from the interesting people I met, more because I regarded them as curiosities than because I thought I would use them or sell them, both of which I finally did.

So, as I wrote *Letter to the Past*, it was memory that inspired me, as astonishingly present as it must have been to Proust when he wrote *In Search of Time Lost*, welling up months on end, with little premeditation, as I sat down at my typewriter and wrote my daily thousand words or so.

It was ordered memory for — as Proust observed — the mind had clearly been unconsciously at work on it, creating beforehand the pattern

I would not perceive as I lived it, the pattern of which one is rarely aware — unless one has a maniacal sense of destiny and direction — while one is living the events. Memory arranges, there is no doubt, and in this it resembles true history whose aim is to give shape to the chaos of the past. Even if the order sometimes appears artificial, it is comprehensible, which the discordant facts themselves are not. Perhaps this is what most distinguishes mankind from other living beings, a sense outside instinct of a meaning and a pattern of their lives within time, whether collective or individual. It was there already in that mysterious great-uncle of ours, Neanderthal Man, and it never went away. We cannot accept the chaos and the accident of the natural world, and so we enclose it with meaning. Whether the meaning or the pattern exists is disputable. Can we give shape to our past any more than we can do to our future? The only real difference — and it is the difference between the harmless and the harmful — is that while the actual events exist to fit into the pattern of our past and present and give it an essential reality, the pattern of our future is inevitably a vacuum that, if we dwell on it too long, as the determinists and futurists have done, may become inhabited by the malign forces generated by the totalitarians. We remember to our profit; we anticipate to our peril.

My experience is that a live memory, cultivated over the years, rarely falsifies in any major way. Its patterns inevitably simplify the past; but unless one is mentally disturbed, the most important elements are faithfully retained, and delivered back not distorted but often enhanced as those of Proust were when he wrote his great novel. Memory, in my experience, rarely lets one down on important matters, and rarely lets one off.

This is why I suspect intelligent people who claim to have lost their past or part of it, and then to have rediscovered it, like the Canadian novelist who wrote a book claiming to have "suddenly remembered" in adulthood a childhood in which her father (safely dead and unable to defend himself) had forced her into sexual intercourse. Freud of course established his method on such lapses and recoveries of recollection, but the method was dubiously successful, owing largely to Freud's proneness to fantastic interpretations — he was much more an artist manqué than a scientist — and the hidden past is now so much out of vogue that the heirs of Freud resort as much to chemicals as the couch.

All I can say about my own memories is that I have rarely found them false — checking them when I could with my contemporaries and with whatever documents exist — and then only in detail. What has happened to them lies rather in the areas of selection and enhancement. The memory does not wait for us consciously to pick out the people, the incidents, the themes that are important for a life. The autobiographer may personally think he is performing this act of selection, but in fact it has been done for him, and in normal minds the memory's choices are good. These, one knows by the conviction with which one accepts them, are indeed the important elements of one's past.

But in this kind of memory process, the recovery of lost time as Proust would call it — the act of involuntary associative memory as distinct from the voluntary memory that comes from *willing* to know the past — there are two factors that have to be taken into account, the factor of unconscious selection and the factor of enhancement that largely complement each other. The memory selects unconsciously, choosing among the events those that are most appropriate to retain: those, as Jung was probably right to insist, that are linked with the motions of the unconscious and the great archetypal patterns. On that level, presumably, our memory and our personal myth are identical. We remember that which will give weight and depth to our self-image.

But as it selects, the memory also enhances, as Proust shows in his remarks on revisiting and finding that the place revisited is so much different from and inferior to the place remembered. I had revisited London since our departure to Canada, and found that sufficiently disappointing, though when I had gone for a day to my boyhood town of Marlow, its serene Georgian centre seemed little changed. But I had not gone back to the Chiltern countryside or to Shropshire, which were the two main foci of my memories; I seriously considered returning to them, but a sense of caution held me back. I decided to bear Proust's hint in mind, and write the history of my childhood and adolescence almost entirely from memory, the memories appearing in their ordered sequence.

It may not have been in every detail literally accurate, for memory's addiction to making patterns tempts it to omit the duller facts and to eradicate the more interesting sequence of events. For example, readers have sometimes commented on the lack of dark detail in the description of the worst eleven years, from 1929 to 1940, when I worked in an environment reminiscent of Gissing, the head offices of the Great Western Railway in London. Here I think it is a matter of two kinds of memory conflicting, for I still have a notable recall of the office work aspect of that period, and if I were asked, could easily talk for half an hour, albeit with distaste, on the office looking down on the sleazy hotels of whore-infested Westbourne Terrace in which I worked with ten other clerks, all men. I could give thumbnail descriptions of the men themselves, recall their coarse sex-obsessed talk and their recollections of the Great War, in which all but one had taken part, though they had been sheltered as railway troops established around the Suez Canal and were always more imperilled by the venereal diseases spread by the tarts of Port Said than by German or Turkish attacks.

But all this had been lived unwillingly and received by my consciousness unwillingly, which is why it has always remained in the area of voluntary memory, the recollection of times when one exists rather than lives and harbours memories like grudges. There was no inner command to dwell on such matters as I wrote, so I left them undescribed.

Yet at the same time I was living a quite different life from that of the office and the trains that took me there. I was discovering London, the great city then at the end of its prime, tramping miles at every lunch hour, going on evenings to the theatre and to concerts and especially to the ballet which then had a high flourishing at both Covent Garden (the Ballets Russes reincarnated under Colonel de Basil) and at Sadlers Wells, and on Saturday afternoons visiting the museums and seeing the French films that in those days were reaching a peak of magic quality with performers like Jouvet and Raimu, like Fernandel and Michel Simon and Arletty. It was the time of holidays spent in un-English lands, in Wales and France, the time when I was exploring the range of cheap foreign restaurants from the French and Italian and eventually Spanish places in Soho to the Chinese eating houses for dockers in Limehouse, all of which would be a prelude to eating in France and Italy, in Spain and ultimately China.

Also, however dismal I may have found it during those years to play my role as an office worker, they were also the vital time of my formation as a writer, years when I developed a personal voice as a poet and in which I moved from universal rejection of my manuscripts to acceptance by leading avant-garde magazines; the years when I began to work in from the edges of the London literary world and to make friendships that have continued to this day, so far as age and death have not ended them. And it was this past that my involuntary memory offered me, each day as I touched the keys, a series of memories, well-patterned and illuminated, and I would feel myself the recording secretary rather than the originator of the whole process. My childhood had been given me in the same way, and these positive aspects of my early life were presented with such a display of the magic of true memory that one early reviewer rightly said: "The prose is so rich in detail that its effect is almost that of a life invented, not remembered."

Perhaps, indeed, it was a frustrated novelist in me that seized on the gifts of memory; Kenneth Rexroth, after all, called his memoirs *An Autobiographical Novel*, and I have often wondered about the real line of vision between fiction and the other forms — autobiography, biography, even history, that give their own arrangements of the past without admitting to being other than the projections of actuality. I have always been concerned with reality which leads one beyond the literal, and still treasure the pleasure I experienced when Matt Cohen once remarked of my *Gabriel Dumont: The Métis Chief and His Lost World*, that it seemed to him an essentially fictive work.

My second volume of autobiography, *Beyond the Blue Mountains*, was much more a book based on documentation, and perhaps that is why I re-read it with less pleasure than its predecessor, which was so much more the product of pure irradiated memory, revealing a world of experience that for me was miraculously reborn.

True, parts of *Beyond the Blue Mountains* were just as memory-dominated, particularly the early chapters describing our arrival on Vancouver Island and the hard first two or three years there. It was a time, as readers of this book may remember, when we lived for months on a precarious edge of poverty, but we managed to surface without accepting gifts or loans except from one special friend; we were never tempted even to think about Welfare. We acquired manual skills which we would never have thought of in our English period, and I kept up a little writing even in those years, so that when we were liberated in 1953 I was at the beginning of a period of literary productivity that has continued for forty years. I think we were also affected by the mores of the people we encountered, who were not inclined to stay very long in any one place, or to regard any job as permanent. And when the memories of that time came back, they were not negative as the memories of the Great Western years had been. They were in recollection triumphant years, when Inge and I proved ourselves in difficult circumstances, and I wrote of them with a joy at least equal with that with which I wrote on my childhood, working with the same sense of the past radiantly recovered.

But the years after 1953, and certainly as far as 1977, when *Beyond the Blue Mountains* came to a tentative end, were years enwrapped in records which it was tempting to use, so that in the end the book became a work of documentation rather than of memory. My time of teaching, though in all it embraced less than eight years, was detrimentally influential in the sense, firstly, that I talked out in lectures at least two good books which, as I do not like to repeat myself, I never wrote, but because I also fell into the academic habit of keeping records, of hoarding away scraps of information on bits of paper like the chits, bundled up since viceregal days, that clog the corridors of Indian government offices.

As a result, with travel diaries, odd notebooks, miscellaneous memoranda and voluminous correspondence I had a plethora of material when I came to write *Beyond the Blue Mountains*, and I believe it loaded the latter part of the book with an excess of detail. I had not allowed the memory to do its necessary sorting work, and I was encouraged in a degree of boasting that produced a tone quite different from the joyful telling of *Letter to the Past*. In its latter chapters, *Beyond the Blue Mountains* now seems to me in a double sense an account: in the sense of a narrative but also in the sense of a balance sheet assuring me and my friends that investing confidence in George Woodcock had not been a bad venture. So, while I am still generally pleased with *Letter to the Past* as a good original statement, I recognize *Beyond the Blue Mountains* as a workmanlike book partly spoilt by an excessive reliance on documentation.

I have since found a simple and remunerative means, known to many writers, of dealing with the excess of documentation. It is to sell one's papers or at a pinch to give them for tax exemptions — to one of the many archives, in universities and elsewhere, who are seeking to build up special collections. It is profitable, since under the Cultural Properties Act one does not have to pay tax on a payment by an approved institution, and at the same time it saves one from being crowded out of basement and attic by the bulk of papers. It is also of use to the intending autobiographer, since it allows him to keep only a few essential documents while clearing the mass of detail that is likely to clog the channels of his memory. The wise man keeps this archive at a distance to save him from temptation. Mine is at Queen's University in Kingston, a good two thousand miles from Vancouver where I live. It is a good place for my biographer to go, but not for me; the crafts are different. So I never visit Kingston, though I have a publisher there (Quarry Press). I did think of going before I started this volume to reacquaint myself with my papers, just as I thought of going back to Shropshire when I wrote *Letter to the Past*, but once again an irresistible caution, masking itself as laziness, prevented my going. So this volume will have a relatively slight armature of documentation, and will rely on recall, which will certainly break out as soon as I begin to think of the events of that recent past which stretches sixteen years from the terminal date of *Beyond the Blue Mountains*.

But before I go ahead with the narrative, there are two other aspects of autobiography to be touched upon at least briefly; the reflective and the confessional modes.

In a sense, every autobiography or memoir that goes beyond a bold and boastful narrative of achievements is a work of many-faceted reflection. The autobiographer reflects on his times, for even the most reclusive of memoirists is generally aware of the drift of his world, and autobiography can well be defined as a literary landscape — a landscape with figures even if one of them is most prominent. This involves an awareness of environment as well as history, and even if he does not stand as a judge of his times, the autobiographer is still a witness.

But his reflections, fed often by travel and reading, can extend to times and worlds beyond his own, and then can reflect on the contingent and absolute values of life. In this way, unlike the self-seeking and self-aggrandizing memoirs of politicians, a genuine autobiography is not an act of egotism or vanity, for it sets the observing eye within its world and produces its own prints of what is observed. Reflection, indeed, is far from self-absorption; it is the release of what one has observed in life.

Confession is another matter. Reviewers often expect one to tell all in the sense of describing one's personal emotional life, and each of my autobiographies received the same criticism — that it failed to portray the whole man because it did not enter into what I would have regarded as tedious intimacies. One reviewer surmised that I had been involved in various liaisons in my bohemian days in London (he was correct in that!). Why did I not describe them?

I am ready to admit (though not confess) that I have been reticent about my intimate relationships, partly from a natural *pudeur*, and partly in resistance to the masculine culture on which I grew up where sexual exploits in which one dominated and used the woman ("possessed" or "had" her as the wording went) were seen as tests of manhood.

My wife shares my *pudeur*, and when I set out to write an autobiography, we agreed that her past before she met me was her own, and that our intimate life was our own and that of our closest friends. The ventures from which we had gained our greatest fulfillment, whether travelling together over much of the world in a lucky age, or in our activities with others helping some of the world's most unfortunate people, we agreed should be part of my autobiographical terrain. Many people knew we had done these things; why we had done them was the interesting question.

In principle I have no difficulties about this reasoned reticence. To "tell all" has never, for aesthetic as much as for personal reasons, been my aim. By the nature of narrative writing, which tames the chaos of existence, every memoir is in some degree selective, if only because it would take up too much of a life to tell that life literally. Still, I grant that in my earlier autobiographies I did — perhaps with excessive primness but also with the thought of not embarrassing others by digging up the corpses of past relationships — present myself as more reclusive and self-absorbed than in real life I have been.

Of course, confession is by definition for sinners, and mainly those who are not ashamed of their sins, which is why criminals, politicians, whores and other amorists proud of their acts offer the most sensational confessions: Casanova's account of himself is highly entertaining, even if the man was despicable. My "sins" exist (who lacks them?), a little adultery long ago, much lying but little theft, and the murder of sundry animals which the amoral code of small boys permitted and which still at times trouble me. The worst faults perhaps are pride and censorious-ness, but there is nothing distinguishing me enough from other men to boast about or even write about, and I would have sounded tame whispering them to a priest in a confessional box.

This book, which will inevitably be more reflective than its predeces-sors, is written out of the repeated encounter with my own mortality. When I wrote my earlier autobiographies I had experienced only one life-threatening sickness. Now I have experienced two more, and Death has become a member of my angelic escort, though up to now a most accommodating one.

I cannot do other than face without optimism my physical condition, which is that of the last age of man in the Sphinx's famous riddle. I go, as it were, on three legs, supporting my arthritic limbs on a neatly carved Garhwali walking stick such as a sahib might have used circa 1910. Repeated attacks have reduced my heart to a remnant and given me, like Heraclitus, a tendency towards oedema (or plain dropsy) which I have to control from day to day with a small battery of pills and other regimens. I am an insomniac who cannot sleep without my nightly narcotic.

Yet I feel this is something to state and then to defy, if not to conquer.

My eyes still function, marvelously in distances where I happily follow the eagle's flight, and my mental activity has never flagged. During the past five years I have written abundantly, and some of it has been my best writing. I still keep fondly in my mind the image of Proust correcting proofs of *Le temps retrouvé* on the eve of his death; I found myself imitating him last summer with the proofs of *Power to Us All* while I was confined to my bed on the very eve of a life-and-death operation. And as I lay in the Vancouver General Hospital then, the impatience I experienced did not relate only to the execrable food (far worse than any prison food I've tasted on my journalistic expeditions) or to the ingrained evasiveness of doctors, but to the upsurge of ideas on those fevered nights that made me long to get home to my study and sit at the desk — even for a minimum time each day — to give them expression.

So much for my condition, of which the reader should be informed, since perhaps it will give a special edge to my memories and judgements. I hope in fact that it will make me more tolerant of others, more understanding of myself and my times. I cannot dismiss the world, which has perpetually fascinated me, until the world dismisses me, and in the meantime I must presume to invert the old Anglican liturgical statement that "In the midst of Life we are in Death" and assert for myself that "In the midst of Death I am in Life." I talk not of the future, but of that past and present in which we somehow tread the verges of true eternity.

So I begin neither with a family history as I did in *Letter for the Past*, nor *in media res* as I did in *Beyond the Blue Mountains*, but looking back from the crumbling peak of old age on the downward path, as it once appeared, which now seems rather like an upward entanglement in the foothills of the unpredictable.

Chapter 1

A LAST LIBERATION

William Hazlitt began one of his essays with the statement that "no young man believes that he shall ever die." There is a sense, I have found, in which old and still active artists also proceed, in their work at least, in the confidence that the future is open, that in a sense they shall never die, even if as men and women they live daily with that awareness of mortality the body will not let them forget.

— *Beyond the Blue Mountains*

My last autobiography, *Beyond the Blue Mountains* (from whose conclusion the above epigraph comes), was published in 1986, but, though at the publisher's insistence I wrote a five-page updating epilogue, its action really came to an end in 1977. I felt at that time that events and one's own mental development must have a period of marination in mind and memory before one could write of them. That is now sixteen years ago, and, sixteen years nearer death, my viewpoint has somewhat changed. Like many people who grow old and have not cast off from their past, I feel the urgency that makes me want to write even of the recent past before it is too late, and also, to see at times my life in panoramic recession.

Perhaps what has distinguished the past sixteen years from previous periods of my life, as I have been transformed from an active man in his sixties to a near-invalid in my early eighties, has been the real freedom in which I have finally been able to work, even though in the last few years it has been physically restricted.

For I realize now, looking back over my eight completed decades, that from the days I left school in 1929 up to 1977, I was involved in institutions or something very like institutions, and depended on them largely for my living. I began with the eleven years working for the Great Western Railway. When I left that in 1940, I involved myself for almost a decade in the anarchist movement, which, though apparently lightly structured and voluntary in its operation, in fact had the orthodoxies and the moral pressures that made it into an institution of its own kind. Like Orwell, I found that a writer cannot further his political ideals by immersing himself in an organized movement, but only as a guerilla fighting in his own terrain.

I broke away from the "official" anarchists, and came to Canada in 1949 on a whim to see the land where I was born, and have stayed here ever since. There was only one way in which I could earn a tiny amount of money from writing; it was through an institution of yet another kind, the Canadian Broadcasting Corporation, and from 1950 to the 1970s I was writing regularly for radio. But in the early years the pickings from the CBC were so scanty that during the 1950s I began seeking work with the universities to establish a reliable basis for living. Without any degrees, I seemed to stand little chance, but in 1954 I was employed for a year by the University of Washington, and offered lasting appointment. Instead I had a year's enforced leave when the United States government refused to let me re-enter the country; it was a then-unrecognized blessing, as it turned out, for the University of British Columbia, now disregarding my lack of a degree which beforehand had hindered them, gave me an appointment with the understanding that I would be able to edit a magazine there, and eventually I did begin to publish *Canadian Literature* under the university's aegis. I gained a large measure of freedom in 1963, when I tendered my resignation since the university refused me a period of unpaid leave so that I might return to India for a short time to deal with aid to the Tibetans. A compromise was worked out by which I should merely edit *Canadian Literature* for half a full professor's salary, tagged as a Lecturer because there was no academic rank of Editor, and free to wander where and when I wished so long as I produced four issues on time a year. This freed me from teaching, an occupation I had come to enjoy as a histrionic extension of myself, but also resented because it made me talk out, without desire for repetition, books that I should have been writing.

But even this last, tenuous connection with an institution in the end began to irk me. I was absorbed by the task of creating *Canadian Literature* and happy to play a notable role in the post-1950s naissance of a genuine Canadian literary tradition. But though I still look proudly on the seventy-odd issues as they stand on their special shelf like Bergotte's novels as Proust displayed them, and regard them as a creation that rivals my books in importance, yet I came to feel after seventeen years that I could not continue the task of giving an original context to the writing of other people. So I resigned to become, at sixty-five, for the first time a writer living entirely by and for his own written works. Other people at the university, notably Basil Stuart-Stubbs, the librarian who headed the University Publications Committee, urged me to stay on, but my sense that it was time to shake off the last and rather pleasant bonds of institution prevailed, and as I hoped — and had intrigued to that end during the committee process that dominated decisions at a university — W.H. New became my successor as editor of *Canadian Literature*.

I left him the material for two issues and then followed the old military code that one doesn't meddle with one's successor's interpretation of the task he has assumed from you. In the event, my trust in Bill was extremely well placed. He has shown a great flexibility in his choice of criticism and poetry, and has demonstrated a talent, which I did not possess, for raising funds, so that his editions of *Canadian Literature* are now almost twice as large as mine, and the journal never seems to stumble on the edge of financial disaster as it did during the last years of my editorship. Moreover, he has shown a power of delegation which I did not possess, for I felt happy only when everything had been chosen by me and checked by me. I have the feeling that I was the right kind of extemporizer to launch the magazine into the cold days of 1959, but Bill has been the appropriate editor for a magazine of proven prestige and tenacity that remains the senior journal of Canadian literary studies.

Though I had long been a strong critic of academia, the university arranged a friendly public parting, with an honorary D.Litt., the strange title (unique in my knowledge) of Lecturer Emeritus, and, what was most important to me, lifelong library privileges.

Canadian Literature through Bill New made its own tribute, for he collected and edited a festschrift entitled *A Political Art* in which voices spoke from almost all periods and many places of my life. From the early days in London during the 1930s and 1940s there were Julian Symons, Roy Fuller and Derek Savage, Kathleen Raine and Denise Levertov. Colin Ward spoke for my anarchist past, Robert Heilman for my brief American interlude teaching at the University of Washington, and Mulk Raj Anand and Bhalchandra Rajan were there to commemorate my long association with India and Indians. The people of the visual arts appeared in force: Jack Shadbolt, Gordon Smith and Arthur Erickson, John Korner, Alistair Bell and Bob Steele, and P.K. Page in her painterly persona of

P.K. Irwin. Mo Steinberg, Donald Stephens and Bill New himself were reminders of my loose but lasting relation with the English Department at UBC. Most numerous were the Canadian writers with whom *Canadian Literature* had drawn me into such inspiring contact: Margaret Laurence, Jack Ludwig and Ramsay Cook, Naïm Kattan, George Bowering and Tom Marshall, Seymour Mayne and John Robert Colombo. Finally, Ivan Avakumovic, by then my friend for thirty years and collaborator in books on Kropotkin and the Doukhobors, ended the volume with a pretty complete bibliography of my writings. It was a moving record of friendships and associations, made even more pleasing by the care that the fine Victorian printer, Dick Morris had taken with the design and printing of the book, and by the linocut designs which my long-dead friend George Kuthan had made to decorate the early issues of *Canadian Literature*.

Yet my departure from academe did not end without an unseemly squabble. As soon as I left *Canadian Literature*, I decided that it was time to disembarrass myself of the papers, manuscripts, tearsheets and correspondence that dated back to my English days, and in cardboxes and bundles of files were crowding me out of whatever storage space I had. Besides, I knew, since the papers were rich with letters from important figures in the literary world, that I had a resource for which someone would have a use. I put the papers in order, a little astonished at some of the things I found, and guessed their market value, from what I had heard of other people's manuscript sales, at $100,000. Then I decided that they might most appropriately be stored at UBC with which I had been so long associated and which was so comfortably near to home. I began to negotiate with Basil Stuart-Stubbs, the librarian; he wanted the papers, thought the price was reasonable and believed he had the funds available; all we had to do was agree on an independent evaluator.

However, he had to pass the proposal before the incumbent president of UBC, a psychologist named Doug Kenny, who like most psychologists had very little idea of the way the minds of normal people work during negotiations.

Kenny's immediate response was the old academic ploy of creating a committee; the matter would be taken out of Basil's hands. The committee consisted of a dean I had always despised and often quarreled with, plus the heads of Economics and Commerce. Appalled by the prospect of my archive being judged by such philistines, I immediately wrote in angry terms to Kenny, challenging the competence of his appointees to judge on literary documents, and declaring that, according to custom, I would negotiate only with a librarian or an archivist. For him to demand anything more was to cast aspersions on the honesty of both Basil and me. I did not even receive an answer to my letter or any kind of acknowledgment. Clearly there was no chance of my papers reposing at UBC.

Not long afterwards, however, Al Purdy told me that he had sold his papers to Queen's University, and suggested I write to the archivist there, Anne MacDermaid, which I did. Her reply was keen. She welcomed the prospect of adding my papers to her collection. Unfortunately she did not have, immediately on hand, the kind of funds that I was seeking, but she would look for a donor. Meanwhile she came with one of the evaluators from the Cultural Properties Board to look at my papers, and after a hard day of searching was pleased with what she found. Soon a suitable donor, an anonymous admirer of my books, was found, and my papers reached Queen's, where I replenish them occasionally as my cupboards fill. And as I have said, distance from, rather than proximity to, my papers now seems a tolerable and even desirable situation.

There was one interesting consequence of this situation. As Purdy's and Woodcock's letters were now in the same archive, George Galt hit on the idea of making a book out of them. Al and I both agreed, and, after some setbacks, *The Purdy-Woodcock Letters* eventually appeared in 1988, published by ECW PRESS.

It seems to me a strange even if rather appealing document, I rather primly editorial in the beginning, but later expanding into geniality and a great number of subjects — personal, literary, erudite; Al always the same, expansive, colloquial, as well-read as his vast book collection suggests. I don't know whether this book solves the puzzle many people have found in our friendship, since our public styles are so different. But we have in fact a great deal in common, our autodidacticism, our poor childhoods, our distrust of academe, and of course the affection and personal trust without which no friendship can flourish. We meet so rarely, and yet we understand each other and cherish our differences.

★ ★ ★

If my liberation from academia in 1977 was of my own seeking, my freeing from broadcasting work at the same period was much less willing. Between my first talks for the CBC in 1949 and my continuing work for the corporation as late as the mid-1970s, I had written several hundred talks — literature, travel, history, polemics — and prepared scores of plays and historical documentaries and dramatic adaptations — even a libretto for an opera called *The Bridesnip*, for which the Canadian composer Robert Turner wrote the music. It was in one sense wasted time, for the ordinary radio talk or even radio play is among the most ephemeral forms of literature, performed once or at best twice, and then relegated to the archives; even there it was not safe, for the tapes of a whole series of historical plays I wrote during the Centennial year were wiped by a hostile CBC employee. Yet in this respect I was probably better off than most writers for radio, since my literary repute enabled me to publish at least four of my plays, and one was put on stage, though disastrously performed, by an amateur theatre. I could also sometimes turn a talk into an article, and very often passages from my talks found their way into my books, particularly my travel books, and then the effort was doubly paid. In itself work for the CBC provided a fair proportion of my income for almost twenty years. And my vanity, I admit, would be touched when cultured matrons enthusiastically listened to my talks and called me "The Man with the Golden Voice."

But undoubtedly what I gained in the long run from my years of writing for radio was a vivification of my writing style. The material I produced for the microphone may not have been easily publishable in its raw form, for substance — as distinct from interest — was not generally required. But the composing of prose for oral delivery in itself helped to create my own mature individual style by breaking down the wooden palings of my early rather didactic prose, and substituting a fluent, conversational and largely colloquial manner together with a power of condensing facts into a restricted space (most of these scripts were 13½ minutes which in the end I attained at first go) and yet somehow increasing their significance by the process. One of the reasons why I lament the decline of broadcasting writing as a literary form (however fragile and transient) in Canada is that few younger writers are able to experience the unique discipline of radio writing at its best. I do not include television writing; there I found the perpetual war between image and word intolerable, imagist though I am by poetic instinct.

I did not have to abandon the CBC in order to devote myself to the career of writing prose and verse for print and perpetuity which I now recognized as my true vocation. The CBC of its own accord abandoned me and most of the other serious radio writers, when it began to follow a policy of centralization and vulgarization, hastened by galloping bureaucratization. When I first began to write for Canadian radio, in 1949, there were busy regional stations (none more busy than Vancouver) that not only produced their own programmes using local writers and actors, but also contributed items to the famous national network shows of that period like *Wednesday Night* and *Critically Speaking*.

Among the works I prepared for Vancouver producers like Gerald Newman, Robert Chesterman and Don Mowatt, apart from my original plays which I wrote entirely for Gerald, were translations from Racine and Molière, adaptations for radio of works like Otway's *Venice Preserved*, Synge's *Playboy of the Western World*, and Evgeny Zamyatin's *We*, but also historical documentaries on subjects like the Indian Mutiny, the Spanish Civil War and its English participants, the Great Exhibition of 1851, and the career of Mozart's great librettist, Lorenzo da Ponte, which was given a rich musical flavour by the zeal with which the producer Robert Chesterman and the musician Hugh McLean sought out the compositions of Mozart's contemporaries on which da Ponte had worked, and assembled singers and musicians to perform them. The recording was an extraordinary occasion, and it typified the moments of sheer joy that could come from good radio work. Such tasks challenged one's erudition, stimulated one's ideas, and exercised one's prose. It was an important formative phase in my development as a writer.

But by the time I gave up editing *Canadian Literature*, my work for the CBC had virtually come to an end, and mostly through changes in policy in the corporation itself. On the one hand, the mounting centralization destroyed the old regional stations as active originators of programmes, and resulted in the creation of an immense career-oriented bureaucracy which became obsessed with ratings and the need to compete for listeners with the commercial network. This led to a kind of distorted populism, and the CBC systematically tried to eliminate everything "élitist" from its programmes. I, and most of the other writers I knew, were regarded as part of the "élite," and the very kind of things we could do best — talks and documentaries and challenging plays — were virtually taken off the air, while the other programmes were downgraded in the hope of capturing the audiences of the commercial stations. The results were predictably disastrous. Not only did the CBC abandon its cultural and educational programmes, and, by destroying the regional networks, abdicate its original mandate of creating understanding between Canadians of all regions. In the event it also lost a loyal audience of people oriented towards the arts and the intellectual life, the guardians of a country's mythos, while its organizers lacked the skills to produce the kind of vulgar entertainment that would attract the junk-eaters who listened to or watched the products of the commercial networks. The Americans have always done better in that field.

Those who valued the original role of the CBC in fostering the arts and the intellectual life in Canada did not let this go entirely unprotested. Indeed, one of the chapters towards the end of my *Beyond the Blue Mountains* tells how with friends and fellow writers I helped to organize the Committee of One Hundred in Vancouver in the hope of changing the situation. But Trudeau and his jackal Pelletier had already set their minds on a kind of fake populism that confused arts with entertainment, and as always the CBC followed the politicians. In retrospect, I see the slow corruptive decay of the CBC as one of our major national tragedies, and a notable cause of our present political, social and cultural malaise.

Still, in 1977 I was not entirely finished with broadcasting; I merely ceased to seek work and was selective when I was offered opportunities, which were diminished by my repute as a trouble-maker. In the period covered by this book I did in fact become involved in a small number of important and interesting programmes.

But I also acknowledge how rarely such things are now done, and how *Ideas*, which that quiet perfectionist Phyllis Webb invented long ago, remains the last beleaguered remnant of the CBC which I once knew, and which my American friends envied, and for which I worked with such zest.

Chapter 2

POEMS AND OTHER EXCURSIONS

Thus, at sixty-five, when most are forced into the dry pasture of retirement, whether they wish it or not, I merely withdrew from certain functions, as editor and broadcaster, in order to spend the greater part of my time on what had always seemed most important to me, the writing of poems and essays and books. Right at the beginning, when I started to write at the age of fifteen, I felt that I was being called to a vocation, and that sense has never left me. I knew then it would be a lifetime task, perhaps with interruptions, and so it has been. When I retired from *Canadian Literature* I was liberating myself, as it were, into the total fulfillment of my calling, and the last sixteen years have been perhaps the most productive period in my life, with more than a score of books written and published, with many literary and occasional essays, a form to which I think I have given a new life, with two major works of translation, and with a few campaigns conducted with my friends to assist threatened animals and human beings. For most of the period, until 1988 when arthritis grounded me, I and my wife continued our long travels, with first journeys to China, to Burma, to Australia, and return journeys to India, New Zealand and continental Europe.

The books that appeared in my first year of liberation were actually written or almost completed by the middle of 1977, and they developed themes that had long preoccupied me. Perhaps they also illustrate rather well the kind of transition I was then completing, of becoming a Canadian writer rather than remaining an English writer. From 1968, when Oxford University Press in Toronto published *The Doukhobors* (by me and Ivan Avakumovic), I had been increasingly appearing with Canadian publishers, large and small, and *The Anarchist Reader*, which Fontana brought out in 1977, was the last of my books to originate in England. My interests, and, what is more important for a writer, my stores of images and my local loyalties became derived from Canada, in the same way as the Welsh Marches of my childhood had been the original locus of my inspiration but were released by re-evoking them in *Letter to the Past.*

The Anarchist Reader was in fact drawn largely from the well of my English past, for it was an anthology of the kind of libertarian texts that had been influencing me since the early 1940s, and with its commentary was really a kind of companion volume to my *Anarchism* of 1962, supplementing the history with contemporary texts, so that the anarchists could be seen to be speaking for themselves. It was an easy task even if it resulted in a substantial book, for I was selecting from the propagandists with whom I had become familiar since I first began to study and write on and, in a shadowy intellectual way, to practise anarchism. It allowed me to exercise my translation skills for the larger works to come, since not only many French writers but even such figures as Bakunin were still available mainly in French. It turned out, coming at a time when interest in anarchism had increased greatly, to be a quite popular book with an international sale.

Peoples of the Coast (1977) was a work of mingled history and lay ethnology. It was the first comprehensive study of the Indian peoples from Alaska down to Cape Flattery, both before and during their period of destructive meeting with the white men. I had become deeply interested in the local cultures when I arrived on Vancouver Island and found the chaotic little museum, stuffed with strange and impressive artifacts, which at that time was crammed into a few basement rooms in the Legislative Building at Victoria. When we were living intermittently at Sooke between 1949 and 1953, I used to take every opportunity, if we visited Victoria, of searching through the crowded glass cases in that crepuscular setting which no art of museumship had tamed, and afterwards I spent much time in collections of Coast Indian art wherever I found them, from the architecturally splendid Anthropological Museum which my friend Arthur Erickson designed at UBC, to the exquisite little museum of Kwakiutl regalia at Cape Mudge, a helical structure filled with unique objects once confiscated by the RCMP at Dan Cranmer's famous defiant potlatch in 1921. Inge and I went to Indian villages where traditional artifacts like totem poles were still in place; our favourite locality, to which we returned often, was the cluster of Gitskan villages on the Skeena River where the carving of poles and the illegal celebration of potlatches had never come to an end, and where in Hazelton the Indians had reconstructed as a museum one of their typical villages, which they called "Ksan" and filled with the dance and potlatch regalia they had kept and treasured. We also attended Indian ceremonials such as the Salish spirit dances in the Cowichan area, which showed the notable recent revival of ancient customs, and we would come back laden with gifts as tokens of our witness. Out of this came an empathy, an intuitive and imaginative sense as well as a broad knowledge of this culture so magnificently strange in terms of one's own experience. Jim Christy said that my account of the Salish dances seemed more exotic than anything I had written of distant alien cultures, and I remember an American woman who accompanied us on our trips to the Skeena villages, saying that she had never been in places "so foreign" in all her world travels. And I think she was right, for in India and China and Japan I have always been aware of the cultural links and parallels that the great world civilizations maintain with each other. But the Coast Indian culture was *sui generis* and entirely outside universal patterns.

Peoples of the Coast appeared, well illustrated and well produced by Mel Hurtig, with the University of Oklahoma Press bringing out an American edition, and when it came out it was well reviewed, at least two leading authorities on the Coast Indian cultures praising it highly. But then came the longest, craziest and most patently malicious review I have ever suffered. It appeared in *B.C. Studies*, vast in length — about fifteen pages — and had been concocted rather than written by a group of ethnologists and linguists from the Provincial Museum in Victoria, now developed from a basement treasure house into an elaborate display of modern museumship run by academics. No less than ten soi-disant scholars contributed to this rackety howitzer of a review. (I will not name the ringleader, since he was the son of one of my oldest friends in Canada.)

Their first and principal lamentation was that none of them, and no other academic, had shown the initiative to write a book of this kind, which was patently needed. Now they were chagrined that an "uninformed outsider," as they considered me, had presumed to do what they themselves were incapable of doing. To make it worse, they naïvely said, I was such a good writer that people would read me and presumably be misled. Their actual complaints were either debatable pedantries such as accusing me of not quoting what they thought was my source for a statement when I had actually used another equally valid source. At times they resorted to lies, as when they asserted that a certain anthropologist had read the book for Oklahoma University Press and had recommended changes. This was pure invention on their part, for neither the publishers nor I saw anything but a warm endorsement from the same man; otherwise Oklahoma would not have published.

Generally I do not complain about unfavourable reviews when they are a matter of critical opinion. After all, by the fact of publication one offers one's book openly for consideration, and only ninnies make a fuss about adverse comments. But when one has been misrepresented, and insulted in the process, that is another matter, and I gave in reply a good salvo in *B.C. Studies*, countering each important point and enjoying my skirmish with these petty pedants, none of whom, incidentally, has written that academic counterpart of my book whose absence most of them lamented. It struck me as bizarre that while academic critics in English respect my work even if they do not agree, and academic historians treat me as a writer to be taken seriously, this little clique of museum-bound nonentities should raise such a fuss about trespassing on their territory. Their pettiness finally went to the extent of forbidding the bookshop in the Provincial Museum to stock my book. Criticism in their hands had magnified into censorship. I mention this unpleasant incident as much as anything else for its rarity in my experience. Not that it in the end harmed the book, for, precisely because it was the only one of its kind, it sold well to the right people. I still remember with pleasure a photograph of Margaret Laurence sitting facing the camera with a copy of *Peoples of the Coast* in her lap. It was a quiet positive gesture of solidarity very characteristic of Margaret.

Towards the end of my editorship of *Canadian Literature*, I had been writing poetry again and two collections — one a very slim one — appeared shortly after my departure. In 1977 there was *Anima, or Swann Grown Old*, published by Black Moss Press, and in 1978 *The Kestrel and Other Poems of Past and Present* appeared, published by a little English cooperative press that Roy Fuller had put me in touch with, Coelfrith Press in Sunderland; it became my first book of verse in England since 1943 when *The Centre Cannot Hold* appeared; my later English verse up to 1949 did not appear in an English collection, but had been printed in California by Untide Press, a group of war-resistant poets with whom I had established contact through William Everson, alias Brother Antoninus.

My production of lyrical verse had always been intermittent. From 1949, owing to the moral and mental crisis of Marie Louise Berneri's sudden death, I wrote almost no lyrical verse for almost two decades; I could not at that time even write an elegy on Marie Louise, the best and closest friend I had. But a combination of place and emotional incident brought me back to verse writing. From the middle sixties, Inge and I had made our centre for a spring month (usually May) the little spa of Bad Fussing to which my parents-in-law had retired. It was in the Inn Valley, just over the river from Upper Austria. And there, relaxing into the pastoral scape of wooded hills and lanes lined with blossoming fruit trees, its abundance of wild flowers and birds, its little herds of roe deer grazing on the edges of the dark woods, its small baroque towns and its great empty castles and monasteries, and stirred emotionally by my father-in-law's final illness, I began to write again, elegiac, pastoral and whimsically ironic verse.

Otto was in one aspect an old-fashioned German who loved Goethe and Wagner (both of whom I have always detested) and talked about the "Good Old Kaiser's Days," just as elderly Austrians across the border often spoke nostalgically of "Good Old Franz Josef's Days." But he had a hatred of politicians and during the war had helped Jewish friends to escape from the Nazis. He had been a great hunter and fisherman, but later on, rather like Rod Haig-Brown, he turned to a somewhat protective watcher of wild animals. He had also been a great mountaineer and I remember him, when he was more than sixty, making a great mountain tramp on his own near Meyerhofen and not returning, while we all waited anxiously, until well into the night, drenched to the skin; he had a hot bath, drank a bottle of schnapps, lay down and sweated prodigiously, and awoke at eight fighting fit for the next day's tramps. With his wife Gertrud I got on even better, for there was a good deal of Polish in her that gave her a whimsical wit. We joked a good deal with each other and developed a kind of gallant macaronic way of speech for our elderly flirtations, with words of German, words of English, even tags of French, inextricably mingled.

Alas, when Otto came to realize that his death would not be far away, he never did thoroughly face up to his own mortality, and observing his emotions and experiencing my own feelings about him released me from the silence caused by the death of an even more loved person, and when I began to write again I had shed both the awkward political radicalism and the curiously conservative formalism that had marred my verse, as well as that of others, during the 1930s and the 1940s. Some of these new poems found their way into *Notes on Visitations*, which Anansi published in 1975, and more of them into *The Mountain Road*, which Fred Cogswell brought out at his Fiddlehead Press in 1980, and into the *Collected Poems* that appeared in 1983.

The Kestrel and Other Poems started off with a selection of my English poems from 1935 to 1949, and continued with a batch of new poems from 1974 to 1978. It had an odd kind of unity dominated by the spirit of the later poems. Out of my earlier poems I picked either nature verses or poems about human doom — the general doom of mankind, which as the war magnified into Hiroshima had depressed me greatly. It was the kind of selection I would not make today, but it was consistent at the time with my preoccupation with individual dooms, which, with a background of nature poems mostly set in Bavaria, formed the substance of the 1970s sequence. I wrote a gently parodic tribute to W.H. Auden, and an elegiac sonnet on the California terrorist Nancy Ling Perry, one of the more grotesque products of the New Left, in which I considered my relationship as a teacher of anarchism to these "terrible children, comrades, enemies." (Peggy Atwood later picked it for her *New Oxford Book of Canadian Verse*.) And at last I was freed emotionally to write my two elegies on Marie Louise Berneri. The present nearness of Otto's death had released the inhibitions death and grief had first created. I reproduce my favourite among these elegies not solely for its possible qualities as verse, but because for me it is an important autobiographical document. It is called "To Marie Louise Berneri, Twenty-eight Years Dead."

Now I am old,
false-toothed and almost bald,
and ruby-nosed from drink,
all but my mind decayed
and even my mind, no doubt,
clogged up with care and caution.

And you have been dead
almost as long as you lived —
those thirty years of beauty
and incandescent spirit
lost in three decades of absence.
You never did grow old
or felt your mind
lapse out of confidence.

The cause was always unsullied,
our triumph was always assured;
Bakunin had laid the word down;
Kropotkin had proved it by science.
I dreamed of your distant death
the very hour it happened.
You came in another dream
to complain of solitude
in a strange whine like the dead
crowding around Odysseus.

Since then other women
populate my dreams
with their temptations
and denials. You,
whom I loved and grieved
like a self, never appear.

Yet it is as if
you were always there
on the edge of consciousness,
your ideas echoing
in what I write, my thought
still touching yours.

And sometimes when the mind
waking, slips out of gear
and out of time, those years
when we worked together,
mind turning into mind,
seem never ended. The eye
of memory is open
and the vision it denies
when I strive for recollection
is there without willing
and you are as you were
your own short life ago,
laughing within my mind,
prophesying Utopia

within your lifetime, and
filling the hearts of
those who watched you with
rage and happiness.

Utopia has arrived.
You would not recognize
or like it. We are still
hoping for liberation
but do not expect it.

I have been as free as
any man, have succeeded
in all my personal aims,
and yet I have failed
what we both strove for.

Perhaps it was the impossible
and you could have achieved
no more. But you were spared
both failure and success,
their varying corruptions,
and you move in the mind's eye
untouched by the knife of age,
spared by the cancer of doubt.

You are a shade,
  and I still flesh,
yet which of us
  has died?

A large proportion of these new poems were set in Bavaria, concerning natural life and death. Otto was in his own way a histrionic, and it was sad but fascinating to see how his attempts to theatricalize his situation turned eventually into an apprehensive vigilance. I talked of this in a poem entitled "The Wolves Depart."

We have attended too often
the theatre of your dying
when you have cried
all the wolves of the continent,

the gaunt survivors from
Transylvanian forests and
Pyrenean gullies, standing
hungry and fire-eyed
to howl the chorus as you
wept and lamented
the grey next morning
when we would not find
you alive —
and each morning
you greeted us
smiling and
forgetful,

But now the theatre is closed and
the wolves gone
to other hauntings;
it has been established
they are not man-eaters.

I find you
speechless, your eyes
glowing with a dumb wonder,
and feel, as you do,
another predator
silently drawing near
on feline
inescapable
pads.

And in contrast I wrote of life surging upward in the Bavarian spring;
my favourite example of this is the title poem, "The Kestrel."

Kestrel, bird of the middle sky,
I hesitate to address you.
The English poets turned you
into a cliché, Hopkins using you
with intellectual splendour,
Day-Lewis misusing you
with politic dullness.

Yet each day as I travel

this narrow Bavarian road
between dying villages and
see you above the same field
balancing in the lark's air,
every line curved cruelly and
necessary for your special being;
see you balanced, wings vibrating
and then out of your wind hover
plunging to your quarry,
I feel the same elation
I feel when I see horses
racing, manes streaming,
around the confines of paddocks.

Your needs are determined
by need and instinct,
yet joy is created
by your flight, by your standing
in the high air, by that
dizzying fall when your shape
and your motion are one.
Joy is liberation
within one's nature.
It is not flight
from the self.

I watch you and the paradox
of necessity and freedom
exists no more. We act
as we must, racing
in the paddocks of our destinies;
we hover and swoop in the
skies of our possibilities,
and life, like all else, is
finite yet infinite, and
joy takes us out of time
and so into freedom,

and necessity becomes
the ground of our liberation.
Fly on, brave bird
flashing your red splendour
down the rushing air.
Your life is short and
yet your time is
endless.

Anima, or Swann Grown Old, was very different from *The Kestrel*, though like most of my poems it contained a share of nature imagery. I called it a "Cycle," and that was true in more than one way, for the sixteen poems traced out my infatuation — and its decline — for a dramatically beautiful woman with a touch of the saint. First I found her sympathetic in nature, one of those bred north of the Trent like myself, and willing to be friendly, but her kind of dark proud beauty scared me so that I made no overt advances, and eventually the great admiration I had felt for her work among destitute people turned into a rejection of her pietism, which accompanied it. In the end I realized, like Swann in *Swann's Way*, that I had spent a great deal of time suffering — for infatuation can be as painful in its effects as true love — for a woman who (in a different way from Odette) was not my type. I say this merely to give the poems a fitting context, not in the mood of confession, which in any case is impossible, since the dark lady is still alive and, I gather, well.

Anima, published separately in 1977, became a section of my *Collected Poems* (1983), and I think among its contents are some of the best of my short lyric poems. This time, instead of merely making my own choices of poems, I am picking some that other poets liked and praised. Earle Birney, doubtless because he knew what it was to be an old man in love, found a particular charm in "Blaze of Azaleas."

A cold spring day
in the blaze of azaleas.

Walking near your home
I remember
in their wisdom
ancient Chinese

wrote tenderly their
poems of old
men in love.
They understood
the atmospherics of
ripeness and the
cloudy agony
of voiceless
longing.

John Robert Colombo was particularly impressed by my three-liner "The Gist of a Sonnet," of which he said (I write from memory) that I had achieved in a tiny space what had taken other poets many lines.

Dark lady, you are
eating my heart out
with teeth of silence.

For myself, I would pick the poem "Bone and Skin," which in 1980 Doug Fetherling would include in *The George Woodcock Reader*. It was about the occasion when the dark lady suffered a hard bereavement, and suddenly — and temporarily — we seemed equal and accessible to each other, friends in misfortune.

Sorrow
has whittled you
to the bone and skin
of lasting,
worn at your black
and frightening beauty,
made you accessible.

As you run up the steps
offering to my kiss
instead of your face
that mask
of an incredible nun,
whose great eyes
look through

and beyond
and yet include
me in their vast pain,
I know there has been
a change in the weather
of love.
I am too old
to expect what
I desired with
such dumb terror
but know the tenderness
of touching
solitudes
and I accept,
granting romantic dogma
that the best love
is satisfied
never.

This period of poetic activity continued into the early 1980s. In 1980 Fred Cogswell published in his Fiddlehead Press series a brief collection called *The Mountain Road*, for which my old friend Molly Bobak did a fine flamboyant cover design of crimson poppies among black foliage. It did not contain a great deal of new material, for many of its items had already found English readership in *The Kestrel* and now became available to Canadian readers. But among those few new poems was one to which I am attached because it commemorated a friendship I valued, with A.J.M. Smith. In the later years of his life, Smith's critical flair had been reactivated by the appearance of *Canadian Literature*, and he often wrote for the magazine, but my poem to him — "The Dream" — did not refer to the editor-contributor side of our relationship.

It all seemed very natural.
There was I, squatting
beside the border, dusty smell of
summer weeds on my hands, and you
stepping along the lawn, young
as I had not known you.

I thought you were mad, saying
you had come to see my river! You liked
that sort of thing, you said, pointing
over the lawn. It was then I wondered
if *I* were crazy. There it ran
cutting the lawn like a clear
new knife, a river
in miniature, glassy over
polished stones.

   I bent, dipped
my hand, licked the sweetness;
dipped again, lifted my cupped
palms towards you. You
were gone. I let the water
drip to the brown grass. The stream
flowed on.

What did it mean? Perhaps no more than my gratitude to an older poet who had given me some of the waters of Helicon and then was "gone." Smith died shortly afterwards.

About this time, for no evident reason, I began to have vivid dreams of the kind I recorded in my poem to Smith, and I was astonished with the narrative quality they displayed. Some of them I picked out and arranged in small prose fictions, and others became poems. This kind of dream epiphany, always revealing something that at least appears of special importance in my life or thoughts, has continued ever since, distinguished by great visual colour and clarity, and always approaching the parable in its effect, which is clearly influenced in most cases by my studies of Buddhist thought and Jungian psychology.

A little while after the publication of *The Mountain Road*, I began to discuss with Robin Skelton, who was then the chief editor of Sono Nis Press, the idea of a collection of all my significant poems, among which I thought of including some of my shorter dream narratives in prose.

Skelton was then editor of the *Malahat Review* which he had founded, the only really Canadian international magazine of literature, and a poet, like me, who had started his career in England, so that he tended to understand my early poetry, written in an English milieu, more than a Canadian writer might do. In fact, he had published in *Malahat* a batch of poems of the late 1950s that had come to light in the house of an aunt with whom I had spent a short time after my mother's death in 1940. When I met Skelton, with his immense bird's nest of a beard, his fingers crowded with occult rings, and the tetragrammatical sign in bronze hanging on his chest (the regalia of the witch and healer), he said to me, "Warts and all, we are assuming?" and "Warts and all," I agreed. He did at first object to including the prose pieces, but after I had taken them out, he reinserted them when the book was brought out by Sono Nis Press, now owned by the printer Dick Morriss with whom I had worked for years (and even more years with his father Charlie before him) on *Canadian Literature*.

The principal result was a handsome-looking book (Dick had done me proud with design and printing) which poets and librarians tend to buy, rather than the general public. The second, disturbing accompaniment of the book's publication was that as soon as it appeared, I ceased to feel the urge to write poetry and produced none for about five years. The only explanation I can offer is my choice of the word *Collected*; I see now the wisdom of other poets who have classed what is virtually a *Collected* as a *Selected*. There is not the air of finality which makes the muse relax with a sense of task achieved that comes with a *Collected*, the poems of a career, as it were. However, the muse did eventually shake off her sleep towards the end of the 1980s.

Chapter 3

BIOGRAPHICAL EMPATHY

I am not in any sense of faith, practice or philosophy a religious man. Childhood experiences with evangelical preachers and teachers nourished my doubt rather than my belief and made me an infant sceptic, as I have told in *Letter to the Past*. I have indeed been attracted at times by the aesthetic aspects of Western religions, the paintings of El Greco, Tintoretto and their kind, the splendid theatricals of good High Anglican liturgy, the poetry of the King James Bible and the Book of Common Prayer, those founts of literary English. I have been attracted to Asian movements like Buddhism and Taoism, not for their religious content, which in each case seems a later dilution, but for their ethical and philosophical aspects, so well interpreted by the present Dalai Lama, who figures in the contemporary world for his widespread ethical presence rather than for his leadership of a single sect of Tibetan Buddhists. Indeed, if I am not a religious man, I have tried to be a moral man, tempted always by natural wickedness, rather than a moralist.

Since I detest absolutes of any kind, I have never called myself an atheist, and though I sometimes let myself be called an agnostic, in fact I sustain a kind of deist belief, since I find the world so marvellous and intricate and splendidly patterned even in its chaotic and malign aspects (the splendour of the tiger's beauty and its pitilessness) that I cannot accept as anything less than absurd the atheist proposition that all this happened mechanically, without an inspiring consciousness. That, as Schelling once pointed out, seems as foolish as the fundamentalist theism that credits the task to a personal, transcendental god derived ultimately from Yahweh, the local deity of a collection of wandering Middle Eastern herdsmen.

I do not believe in the transcendental being Blake called "Old Nobodaddy Aloft," but I do believe in the immanence of a kind of universal consciousness, which is evolutionary though not necessarily progressive, and of which the consciousness of every living being is a part, as a deciduous leaf is part of a tree. But just as it is not given to the leaf — doomed to fall as we are doomed to die — to know the whole tree, so it is impossible for us to know the universal spirit entirely; as Buddha said in other words, we may as well abandon the idea of doing so and get on with the business of living in harmony with other living beings who are part of the whole.

This does not mean that I am uninterested in what are called religious experiences. I have had too many intermittent "psychic" experiences to doubt the assertions of mystics without necessarily accepting their explanations. Ecstasy is possible for most human beings, but it is too easy to induce by artificial, chemical means, for us to accept it as more than a phenomenon of the mind, differing in intensity perhaps, but not in kind, from the "inspiration" that directs the poet, the musician, the painter. It exists among peoples with no organized religion, like the shamanists of the Pacific North West Coast and the Arctic, as much as it does among those enthusiasts, usually suspected of heresy but later canonized, who strive for personal ecstasy within organized churches.

I had given some expressions to these views in my book on Aldous Huxley, *Dawn and the Darkest Hour*. Perhaps this was why I was approached by two young clergymen, one of them the vicar of an Anglican church in the Vancouver area, and the other a lecturer at St. Michael's College, a Catholic seminary attached to the University of Toronto. They invited me to write an essay on Thomas Merton, the Trappist monk who was also a well-known poet, for a conference they were organizing. I did not know much of Merton, I told them. I did not know whether I would find either sympathy or empathy for either him or his work. I was in no real way a religious man. These arguments left them persistent. I was a good critic. I was a fellow poet. Moreover, in whatever I had written on Buddhism, I had shown an interest which Merton shared with me, and also an understanding of ways of religious experience that I did not follow.

In the end I was not so much convinced as challenged by their arguments, and I agreed to their proposal with the qualification that the work I might do on Merton, if I took the trouble of reading his work and absorbing its intent, was likely to be a book rather than a brochure, and that we should do our collective best to find publishers. We were successful. Douglas & McIntyre in Vancouver and Farrar, Strauss, Giroux in New York shared in commissioning it.

The book was written, published in 1978, and astonishingly well received, particularly in the circle of Merton's admirers. Brother Patrick Hart, for example, one of Merton's fellow monks at the Trappist Abbey of Gethsemani, described it as "absolutely a first rate work, situating Merton as a poet within the context of his monastic vocation. [Woodcock] handles his subject with great sensitivity and insight, and his interpretation of Merton's poetry is positive and critical in the best sense of the word."

I do not habitually quote reviews just because they are favourable, but for some kind of light they may throw on my work, and I think Hart does make an important point when he talks of me as "situating Merton as a poet within his monastic situation." I did in fact begin with Merton's poems and sought out the way of life from which they emerged. In the process I realized that there was a certain division between Merton's role as a priest within an elaborate monastic structure, and the passion for solitude that in the end so strangely contrasted with his world-wide reputation and links. I detected two strains among his work, "poetry of the desert" and "poetry of the choir," and in the process I came to an understanding of the man, far though his beliefs had been from mine, that astonishes me now when I read the book again fifteen years after it appeared.

The reading in fact led me to some reflections on the nature of biography, in general and in relation to my own work. What draws a biographer to his subject? I have heard it suggested by the advocates of reincarnation that a biographer's subjects are the people he has been in past lives. But the existence of brilliant biographical studies by near contemporaries of their subjects is sufficient to discredit that theory.

Nevertheless, when one discounts the pseudo-biographies written by mediocrities to earn money or to support the sensational career of some popular hero or powerful man, it seems to me that true biographies are written in the context of the biographer's strong feelings about his subject; none is written without emotion.

The feeling may be antipathetic, and in this direction one meets the great debunking biographies, from Lytton Strachey's *Queen Victoria* onwards. Sympathy, I think, occurs more often than antipathy; I see it as the drawing towards someone whose ideas or nature resemble one's own, to whom one can say, "Mon semblable! Mon frère." Most of my biographical and semi-biographical works have been of this kind — lives of the anarchists like William Godwin, Pierre-Joseph Proudhon, and the book I did with Ivan Avakumovic on Peter Kropotkin; or of maverick writers like Oscar Wilde and Aphra Behn; or my intellectual biographies of friends like George Orwell and Herbert Read, and my small book — a tribute to childhood enthusiasm — on the great field naturalist Henry Walter Bates.

But there were two books that did not fall within the area of similarity and sympathy between the writer and the subject, but in the third category of biography which I am proposing, that of empathy, which involves the imaginative entering into the nature of somebody whose personality and ideas and way of life differ sharply from one's own. In sympathetic biography one is enlarging the self. In empathetic biography one is embracing The Other.

My first book of this kind was *Gabriel Dumont: The Métis Chief and His Lost World.* I admired Dumont as a rebel; I realized how his historic importance had been overshadowed by the image of the martyr Riel. I also found an attractiveness in the communal life of the Métis, whom he led so well. But I also realized the life, the feelings, the thoughts of the brilliant and capable illiterate Dumont in no way resembled my own. He came from a more Homeric setting than mine as a European-oriented intellectual. Yet by an act of empathy, induced by the sheer grandeur of the man, I entered into his life with the necessary imagination. My own feelings about the task were shown in a sonnet that I wrote to celebrate the book's ending.

A year I have lived the most of my mind with you,
Acting your deeds as best I can, thinking your thoughts, and
Now I stand back, take your dark presence in my view,
And realize that though we say goodbye, easy hand
In hand, like companions ending a long hard journey,
We are still strangers, you from your world where
Violence is what happens in the natural daily way
Between animals and men; I from the rare
Interlude of a time where peace has been a fragile
Possibility in a few favoured places for a few.
But what is the echo I feel compellingly ring
In my ear as you bow sardonically into your defile
Of dark death? What does it tell me I share with you?
Is it, fierce stranger, that freedom is a word
      our hearts both sing?

There was no such celebration when I finished *Thomas Merton*, yet I realize that though the book does not have the frame of action which made *Gabriel Dumont* as well read among French as English Canadians, I had nevertheless, by my intense reading of Merton's books, succeeded in entering into his mind in a way that even his monastic colleagues found admirable. As persons I doubt if we would have found much affinity. To some of his ideas I remain far from sympathetic. But there was a sufficient modicum of common interests — poetry and Eastern religious philosophies (rather than religions in my case) — that provided a stepping stone from which empathy could operate and temporarily allow me to see and understand Merton's vision. I still regard my book as something atypical of my general inclination as a writer, a kind of sport, yet not at odds with one basic motive of my writings which critics have identified — and I agree — as curiosity. My curiosity was being challenged when I agreed to write the book, and this carried it through to the end, teaching me a great deal in the process, including a disinclination to concern myself further with saintly figures. The tension between my empathy and my scepticism had been too great.

Chapter 4

POPULAR AND SERIOUS HISTORY

My withdrawal from *Canadian Literature* did not mean that I was abandoning my interest in Canadian writing or in Canada itself considered — as Kildare Dobbs once suggested — as a society rather than a nation. I wrote of Canada on various levels, the popular and what some of my critics have called the élitist, but always, I think, with the same clarity and care of the language. Part of my creed as a man of letters is that I must develop the craftsmanly skills that can be used in all circumstances, from writing a fund-raising appeal for Tibetan refugees to compiling a learned history backed by the knowledge of a lifetime, or an operatic libretto, or a probing work of criticism. What distinguishes the popular writing is that it is not so much *on* as *of* the surface, about life as it is visible to large numbers of persons. Such writing, if it is to be well done, makes as great demands on one's craftsmanship as any other, and can indeed result in work that is of general importance, as well as being written with an intent to popular readership, like — for example — Wells's *Outline of History*.

There is of course one mercenary advantage to popular writing; if one picks the right lifestyle magazines whose editors wish to create a sophisticated image for their presentations, then articles can be written without compromising one's standards in any way, and at the same time one can earn a great deal more than through publishing in academic journals and literary little magazines. Such accommodations are virtually necessary in a country like Canada if one wishes to escape or avoid the mental tyranny of academic employment.

I shall have more to say about my involvement with magazines when I come to the 1980s. Immediately, I am concerned with a group of books I wrote at the turn of the decade at the suggestion of Mel Hurtig, the Edmonton publisher who had already brought out my *Gabriel Dumont,* and who had once suggested that I be editor of his *Canadian Encyclopedia*, one task I found too daunting and declined.

Some time during the late 1970s Mel had approached me with an interesting collection of largely unfamiliar photographs of well-known Canadians from the nineteenth and early twentieth centuries — political leaders, fur traders, soldiers, commercial entrepreneurs, native leaders, ecclesiastics, artists — a cross-section of Victorian and Edwardian society in British North America as people at that time perceived it. My task was to write a text for each photograph in such a way that what appeared would not be merely a series of brief biographies, but would also convey the sense of a whole time and place that was encased within them. I decided to call it *Faces from History: Canadian Portraits and Profiles*; it appeared late in 1978 and sold well. As a result of its success, Mel invited me to put together a further book of the same kind, to be called *100 Great Canadians*, and to include figures from the present as well as the past. He assigned me an editor to help me gather the photographs, and so there appeared a kind of undeclared history of Canada represented by its most striking personalities, which by no means exclusively meant the political and official personalities, for the rebels Louis Riel, Gabriel Dumont and Poundmaker were all there as well as Sir John A. Macdonald, and so was a good scattering of painters, writers and musicians, the book ending with the Inuit sculptor Tiktak and the novelist Margaret Laurence, both of whom I knew. I was intent on showing the spirit of a country through its creators and its dissidents as well as its manipulators.

Mel and I followed *100 Great Canadians* with *A Picture History of British Columbia*. It turned out to be a kind of dry run for my later full history of the province, gathering early prints and later photographs, whose lengthy captions, supplemented by a narrative fifty thousand words long, offered a compact but strongly visual look at the development of the province that by now has become my home, my adoptive fatherland.

I enjoyed working with Mel on these popular books, since they involved no vulgarization of style. Apart from satisfying my localist loyalties as a publisher in the West, he was generous and just, invariably, in my experience, settling a dispute between an author and his office in favour of the author. Best of all, he kept his checklists active, promoting his books as long as they were in print, which very few publishers do nowadays. He never remaindered any of my books. Politically he found my strong regionalist beliefs as disturbing as I found his support of strongly centralized government. Yet I have always wished him well in his battles against the Canadian establishment. He has brought back a bit of crusading honour to the role of the politician.

Regionalism was to be an important element in the two less popular historical books I published at this time. *The Canadians* (1979) considered Canada and its people within a regional and confederationist framework, not as a nation-state. Two years later these views were sharpened in the more polemical *Confederation Betrayed* (1981).

The Canadians appeared with Fitzhenry & Whiteside, and was also published by three university presses abroad, Harvard University Press, Athlone Press (of London University) and the press of Queensland University in Australia. It was a book heavily illustrated with contemporary prints and photographs, and dating forward from the first contact between native Canadian peoples and Europeans; it developed the theme that Canada could not be considered in the context of European-style nation-states, which are usually small in area, and, where they work, homogeneous in population. Advocates of centralism and legislative union have always worked against the true genius of Canada, which is plural and regional. The regions, which often correspond with the provinces or territories, are historical entities that, with the exception of Saskatchewan and Alberta, existed as autonomous political units before they joined the confederation of Canada; in most cases they are geographically distinct from each other, and have been populated by such a variety of peoples that the old cant about the two founding races, quite apart from its invidious reflections on the native peoples, has been made meaningless over the past century by the influx of continental Europeans and more recently of people from Asia, Latin America and the Caribbean islands. It is only if we look at Canada as a functioning disunity in political terms and cherish its vitality that we can begin to understand the forces that so improbably hold it together.

I developed this theme in *The Canadians* by following the map of the country from east to west, and showing how regional, geographical and climatic conditions had interplayed with the cultural traditions of the minorities (for by now we are all members of a minority) to produce the unique lifestyles of the regions and to creatively disunify the country.

In *The Canadians* I was defining the true nature, according to my viewpoint, of Canada as a society. And I emphasized how in a world where the nation-state was falling into discredit, Canada could play a pioneer role by developing its regionalist tendencies and becoming a true confederation. In *Confederation Betrayed* I developed a denunciation of those who over the generations of Canada's existence had betrayed the confederationist ideals with which the country had entered the community of nations at roughly the same time as Germany and Italy. I believe that Canada's greatest contribution to the modern world might be by example, of a true working confederation, in its turn following the example of Switzerland, but on a continent-wide scale. I was invited to write *Confederation Betrayed* by Howard White, a small (though not in physique or character) publisher at Madeira Park on the British Columbia coast (Harbour Publishing), of the informal type I like; he started off with that splendid periodical anthology of coastal history and legend, *Raincoast Chronicles*. At that time Howie was interested in the movements towards secession that had punctuated the history of British Columbia's association with the central government in Ottawa. Might we not now, with our new orientation towards the Pacific Rim, be more capable of living as an independent polity? (Howie's ideas later changed somewhat when he ran, unsuccessfully, as an NDP candidate in the most recent provincial election.)

I also believed that British Columbia could be a viable country, provided its people regained control of its resources and if by some miracle we could start off without our share of the present national public debt. But my real concern was for all the provinces to regain their autonomy so that Canada might finally be reconstructed as a working confederation and an example of how to deal with the present disintegration of the nation-state. Much, of course, depends on one's reading of the original confederation document. I am one of those who, like the Québécois, hold it to be a document entered into by a number of virtually sovereign polities who petitioned Westminster to allow them to enter into this special form of unification. The British North America Act was the result.

From the beginning, with the arch-centralist John A. Macdonald, true confederation had its enemies, and they continued through Pierre Trudeau, who had all too deeply imbibed the doctrine of "the republic one and indivisible" initiated by the Jacobins of revolutionary France. As I discussed these matters, I pointed out that while some provincial leaders had resisted centralist pressures, and had gained important decisions favouring them from the Judicial Committee of the Privy Council in Westminster, others, in return for illusory favours, had played like white niggers into the hands of the centralizers. My final conclusion was that though the formation of a separate polity in British Columbia was possible, and might in the end be necessary, we should still direct our immediate efforts to developing Canada into a true confederation, both for the sake of our own collective well-being, but also as an experiment in the validity of other forms than the nation-state. My book had no immediate effect on Canadian political life, though it pleased many individual readers to whose frustrations as citizens it appealed. But books are like bombs with random timing.

In writing such books I was abandoning the absolutism of the old-fashioned anarchism I had once supported, and arguing implicitly that the essential ideas of anarchism, and notably mutual aid and the concept of a federalism that would generalize power and thus eventually destroy it, were also ideas by which societies not yet ready for a thorough-going pattern of nongovernmental cooperation might sustain their place in the world while changing radically within. I believe more and more strongly, as I began to feel when I left the organized and orthodox anarchist groups in the 1940s, that the truths of anarchism, of freedom and mutual aid, can be spread without necessarily labelling them, and that the present age when the very occupation of politician has become generally despised and all parties are becoming distrusted, is the time to bring forward ideas and methods that would generally put the control of their affairs back in the hands of the people. I would develop that idea further and a decade later in *Power to Us All*.

The publication of *Confederation Betrayed* with a small and very independent press like Harbour Publishing was perhaps another manifestation of my desire to see anarchist ideas working out, as Kropotkin suggested they might, in everyday life through small groups and local enterprises. Since my last English publication in 1978, I have not originated any books outside Canada, and within Canada I have avoided the larger metropolitan publishers, except for Oxford University Press, where I found William Toye such an admirable and constructive editor, and have turned either to small presses, like Quarry and ECW or — in my own country of British Columbia — like Harbour Publishing, Oolichan Press, and, above all, Douglas & McIntyre in Vancouver. One can in part live like an anarchist without needing a completely anarchist society.

Chapter 5

WRITING ON WRITING

My interests in literature remained extensive and broadly international until the 1970s, when they became more sharply focused. I continued to write critical essays on English writers, including a succession of introductions to English classics for Penguin Books. In 1957 I went to France on a Canadian Overseas Fellowship to gather material for a book on the French novel in the early twentieth century. Tendencies like the cult of existentialism in the 1940s and the *nouvelle vague* movement in later decades held my attention. I completed several essays to serve as eventual chapters for the book, on writers like Gide and Camus, like Cocteau, Radiquet and Alain-Fournier, and some of them were published by John Lehmann in his *London Magazine*. But the book, which would have involved a great deal of reading time, was held over indefinitely owing to the growing pressure of work with *Canadian Literature*.

But the idea of such a book was not abandoned, for I still feel that France is my second intellectual home, though I have done no serious work on it for almost a couple of decades. It is still there to be taken up again when the present book is completed, and I hope the delayed afterview on the writers I once studied with enthusiasm and urgency will make it all the better a book.

Meanwhile, my links with European literature have by no means entirely vanished. One of the discoveries I made during my readings — a discovery I shared with Vladimir Nabokov — was the inadequacy of Scott Moncrieff's translation of Proust's masterpiece, *In Search of Time Lost*. For years I intended to replace it with something better, and now I have begun. Moncrieff was much influenced by the more romantic kind of fiction being written in England during the 1920s, and even by the sentimental fascination at that time with Elizabethan and Jacobean models: hence its appallingly misleading title of *Remembrance of Things Past*. Moncrieff presents to us a softly emotional Proust; what characterized the real Proust was an almost scientifically precise observation of the mind and the emotions, often austere in its expression, and a pervading irony. These qualities are emerging day to day as I work on my new translation, for translation in the end becomes its own form of criticism. It will already have become evident how this involvement with Proust has actually affected the way in which, in this last autobiography, I approach my own life.

I am still the critic whom the New York magazine *New Leader* calls on when it has books to review on literature and the arts in France during La Belle Époque and after, and I have a permanent role as critic of books about Russian literature for the *Sewanee Review*, the senior American literary quarterly.

Still, I no longer "keep up" with new French writing as thoroughly as I did, or, for that matter, with new British writing, though over the years essays on European and English literature have formed a large enough proportion of my work to deserve a volume each, some day when I have a little more time on my hands. As for American writing, I have never been so attracted to it as I have been to French writing. Melville, James, Crane, Faulkner, Bellow, Thoreau, Edmund Wilson, with a few poets like Wallace Stevens, Kenneth Rexroth and, of course, the old masters Pound and Eliot, perhaps mark the limits of my interest. Recently American writing has been far too dominated by the pundits of Iowa and other writing schools, and in that I see a peculiar development of the kind of majoritarian democracy which so disturbed that urbane and intelligent observer among Americans, Alexis de Tocqueville.

The trend began — I think — with the idea, fostered by the old American land-grant universities, that everyone, regardless of the power to use it, had the right to an education terminating in a degree. I once taught at such a university, and was taken aside and told that the only reason to fail a student was some actual dereliction, like not presenting papers or attending an exam, or plagiarism. One did not fail a student for stupidity or for mere inability to write a sentence; it was an implicit rule I broke from the beginning, causing a minor sensation when I failed two of the football team thugs whom the coach had recommended to me for kind treatment. From the same source of misunderstood democracy came the creative writing schools with their assumption that every person might have it in her or him to write a good novel. The result has been a debasement of standards, a crippling banality that destroys even the writers who teach in such schools so that at times they seem to forget entirely the ideals of creating a new literature, vigorous as the New World, with which Melville and Whitman set out.

I started *Canadian Literature*, among other motives, with the conviction that for a literature to be mature it must develop a critical tradition, as happened among English writers in the Restoration-Augustan period, and in the United States during the early part of the present century. There were already some academic critics in Canada, notably Northrop Frye, and some rather inferior newspaper reviewers, while the CBC ran a Sunday programme of varying quality called *Critically Speaking*. But the kind of mediational man-of-letters critic, free of academic ties, like Edmund Wilson in the United States or Victor Pritchett in England, had not yet evolved in Canada. I had to find academics who were not pedantic (A.J.M. Smith was a notable example in the earlier years of *Canadian Literature*), and writers who would move outside poetry to write criticism, as Margaret Atwood, for example, did.

I had taken on *Canadian Literature* largely because I knew the art of editing, and my immediate knowledge of the field itself was, to say the least, incomplete, but obviously I could not continue in this state of enlightened ignorance. Fortunately I was beginning at the time when a distinctly colonial literature was taking on its local identity. I lived, as it were, among the classics, for A.J.M. Smith and Hugh MacLennan, P.K. Page and Ethel Wilson became my friends, and I knew Frank Scott and Louis Dudek and Irving Layton reasonably well, considering the physical distance that parted me from my Montreal contemporaries.

The 1950s was the real formative decade of a Canadian literature, and it was also, as I believe W.H. New first said, Hugh Maclennan's decade, dominated in fiction and even in poetry by a didactic nationalism and by a concern with theme rather than form, which was encouraged critically by that rather Victorian literary scholar, Northrop Frye, and pursued by some of the younger critics — notably, for a while, Margaret Atwood. By the 1960s, the decade during which *Canadian Literature* itself took shape after its foundation in 1959, the scene had changed; in its turn the 1960s has been called the decade of Margaret Laurence, when character and memory and language were considered as important as theme, and the study of local ways of life as important as nationalist politics. By the 1970s, with a national literature well established, the process of variegation, which is as much the sign of a literature's maturity as a critical tradition, began and nationalist sentiments retreated into their own political territory.

In *Canadian Literature* I was in the centre of this movement, though I did not invent it as some people have said. The journal flourished because of the growing number of new critics, and the growing volume of new books, quantitatively and eventually qualitatively rich. I began not merely to edit essays and reviews by others. I began to write my own criticism, partly to show my involvement, but partly because I enjoyed partaking in this remarkable naissance of a tradition.

Some of my own critical pieces I published in *Canadian Literature*, but I have always believed that an editor should not assume the proprietary view that his magazine is there to indicate the fullness of his own commitment. And thus, when I did prepare my first collection of studies of Canadian writers, *Odysseus Ever Returning*, for Malcolm Ross to publish in his New Canadian Library, only six of the seventeen pieces had appeared in *Canadian Literature*, though they included my major essays on Hugh MacLennan ("A Nation's Odyssey), on Morley Callaghan ("Lost Eurydice"), and on Irving Layton ("A Grab at Proteus") which were to become influential texts. The rest had appeared in other journals, both Canadian and American, or as introductions to books (a reprint of Birney's *Turvey*, for example), and one was a radio talk much revised.

As a continuing process, while I was editing I tried to keep up with the progress of Canadian writing, reading the books that were reviewed or otherwise discussed in *Canadian Literature*, and the result after seventeen years was that I had an extensive direct knowledge of Canadian writing and now had the time to write about it.

As a consequence, most of my more important studies of Canadian writers were in fact the product of the years after my editorship. They were collected into two volumes, *The World of Canadian Writing* (1980) and *Northern Spring* (1987), both published by Douglas & McIntyre in Vancouver. The basic stance uniting the essays in these books was what I called a geohistorical one: that the country's unique combination of terrains, its history and demography, have in fact imposed a cultural regionalism on Canada, which runs parallel to the unacknowledged social and political regionalism that lies at the base of the problems and prospects that have motivated so many fruitless constitutional debates over recent years. This theme I also developed in a shorter book, *The Meeting of Time and Space: Regionalism in Canadian Literature*, which George Melnyk published at NeWest in Edmonton in 1981.

Half-accidentally — for much depended on the invitations of editors

— these two volumes seemed to complete, with *Odysseus Ever Returning*, a study of the most important figures in the Canadian literary tradition up to the 1980s. They included especially studies of the women writers who have so strikingly assumed a commanding position in Canadian writing during recent decades, so commanding that it would seem possible from our present perspective to write a kind of matrilineal literary history, starting with Frances Brooke and Susanna Moodie, carrying through the marvellous but neglected Sara Jeannette Duncan and Ethel Wilson, and ending with that fine group of writers who have been our contemporaries, and on most of whom I wrote in one or other of my two volumes. Margaret Atwood's potentialities were evident to me early on, in her first published poetry and in *The Edible Woman*, and on her I wrote a long composite essay, combining two early pieces discussing her poetry and fiction respectively, and another on her later poetry. On Margaret Laurence I wrote two pieces, one on her as a novelist and another on her importance as a travel writer, a genre neglected by most Canadian critics. I still think she did more than any other novelist to make Western Canadians aware of their past as myth and history combined (as well as being a notable experimenter in the fields of memory and character). This theme I largely followed in a third essay in which I compared her and Rudy Wiebe as prairie writers, largely to Wiebe's detriment. Early in the 1980s I also compiled a volume of critical essays about her, *A Place to Stand On*, which NeWest in Edmonton published in 1983.

The World of Canadian Writing and *Northern Spring*, apart from a few general essays, contained pieces on other women writers — Marian Engel, Mavis Gallant, Ethel Wilson, Pat Lowther, Sara Jeannette Duncan, Alice Munro, Dorothy Livesay and Phyllis Webb. I also wrote pieces on Hugh MacLennan, John Metcalf, Timothy Findley, F.R. Scott, Patrick Lane, Hugh Hood, Matt Cohen, Roderick Haig-Brown, Malcolm Lowry, Earle Birney, David Watmough and Al Purdy, as well as those two strangers in the garden, whose ideas were so fascinating and yet so perilous to literature, Northrop Frye and Marshall McLuhan. These essays had appeared in a wide variety of journals and symposia. One of them, "Northern Spring," a survey of recent Canadian literary developments, was originally written for the Canadian Embassy in Washington to introduce Americans to Canadian writers.

Some of the men I have mentioned I regard as writers of first importance, but on reading my essays again I found there was a special intensity in my reaction to the women, and I am not sure how much this was due to a peculiar vibrancy in their work or to some aspect of my own sensibility. (If it has any relevance, I rely more on my women friends than on my men friends.) The fact is that, whatever the reason, I found Canadian writing immensely enriched by the contribution of women, to the extent that — with no intent of feminist propaganda which I regard as irrelevant to such issues — I believe we would not have had so notable a literary development over the past decades if we had not been so creatively invaded by women.

Now, years after their comparatively early deaths, both from cancer, I dwell especially, with affection as well as admiration, on Margaret Laurence and Marian Engel. Laurence perhaps was the larger figure, in nature, in imagination, in sheer verbal power, yet Marian Engel I believe was one of our great stylists, particularly in *Bear* and *The Glassy Sea*, and a woman of high courage. Apart from glorying in their work, I was happy to have them both as friends.

Margaret I had known since she came back from Africa in 1957 and settled in Vancouver to write her stories of the dark continent. When she moved to England we corresponded regularly, and after she came back to Canada and settled in Lakefield, we kept in touch by letter and telephone. There was a kind of uncertainty that stayed with Margaret to the end, in spite of her assuredness as a writer and her success as an artist. She needed her friendships.

She and I respected each other. She liked what I wrote and herself contributed a splendid essay to *Canadian Forum* on my *Gabriel Dumont* (and picked it for inclusion in her book of essays, *Heart of a Stranger*). (The Métis were an interest we shared — a moral as well as a historical issue for both of us.) She was always pleased when I wrote something about her work, and particularly when I uncovered an aspect of which she had been only half aware, as I did by suggesting how her novels fitted in with the ancient pattern of the four elements. On such occasions she would ring up excitedly. In fact, the calls from Lakefield came quite often, usually when Margaret had a moment of triumph or a mood of distress. The ring would come round about 11 p.m., which meant 2 a.m. Lakefield time, and Inge would pull up a chair for me at the telephone and pour me a Scotch a moment later so that I could keep company with Margaret. I and her other friends worried about the immensity of her phone bills, but she refused to make collect calls. After her death I missed for a long time that phone ringing in the middle of the night.

My relationship with Marian Engel was quite different, and founded on challenge. We encountered each other — rather than meeting — through a quarrel I had with the executive of the Writers Union of Canada for their attempts to impose a virtual censorship on Fraser Sutherland's magazine because he had published an article that offended Margaret Atwood. Marian was president of the WUC and I wrote furious letters, once accusing her of being a sultana, and she wrote back in the same vein until we became amused at the exercise and settled into a friendship-by-letters which lasted until her death. Only once, I believe, did we talk on the telephone; otherwise our relationship was entirely epistolary. Yet I valued it greatly as the long letters arrived every two or three months. She was wise and witty and I remember — who could forget? — the stoic humour with which she received the approach of death, jesting to the end. A luminosity seemed to go from one's life like the fading of a star when she died.

Chapter 6

TRIPS AND JOURNEYS

Our lives in the years of liberation were not so completely dominated by writing as the last two chapters may have suggested. Travel still seemed necessary to us, even if it was perhaps not of the same world-girdling scale as in the past, and we continued our journeys into known and unknown places until arthritis and other ills finally grounded me in 1988.

We yearly continued our visits to Bavaria until after Otto's death and Gertrud's some years later in 1987. Often our European journeys went beyond the Inn Valley, into the grey mountain wildernesses of Styria where the snow still lay until late in the spring and we could trace the floral frontier receding as the drifts retreated, with tiny ivory-coloured crocuses coming up on their dwindling edges and soldanella burning its luminous purple way through the snow itself, and on to the softer lake country of Carinthia, or the great marshes and lakes of the Burgenland, with their dense reedbeds populous with waterfowl and their Hungarian-style villages of low, heavily thatched white houses. Hungary lay beyond a high barbed wire fence, with watchtowers and steam trains still puffing on the other side of them.

Sometimes we would go westward into the eastern cantons of Switzerland, where a revolution in political forms took place several centuries before the French Revolution; it was in fact more truly revolutionary through its emphasis on local autonomy and direct democracy, and its opposition to the centralism that destroyed the French Revolution and the Russian Revolution in its turn. Appenzell, Schwyz, Uri, Glarus, are examples of local autonomy and direct lawmaking in which what we think of as Athenian democracy still works, with the people assembling once a year in the town square or a great meadow to vote the laws of the canton directly and appoint a group of delegates to administer and not go beyond them, all ratified by great and solemn oaths. I have always liked the medieval half-rural character of the minute capitals of these cantons, like Appenzell, where the citizens vote around a great old lime tree, the public buildings are still decorated with the emblems of ancient guilds, and at evening the stench of cow dung hangs in the streets as the herds are driven home to be milked for the making of pungent cheeses. Of course, Athenian democracy had its limitations, for the slaves could not vote, and so did the democracy of ancient cantons like Appenzell until very recent years; it is not long that women have been able to stand around Appenzell's lime tree and vote with their men.

Sometimes we lingered a day or two in Zurich or Basel. By now we had lost our taste for the great cities even of Europe. We found that the quality of city life had diminished and lost its individuality, while physically the cities have been made so generally unattractive by post-war rebuilding, that the pleasure one got from earlier visits to Paris, London, Rome, Athens, was no longer evoked, owing to their growing homogenization. All this is due to the spreading influence of American styles of living, but it is also the long-term effect of what happened during the war years, of the bombings that destroyed the physical fabrics of communities, of the occupations that corrupted civic values. But it is, as well, a matter of rival traditions, urban and metropolitan.

The metropolis, so far as the Western world is concerned, is a product of centralizing urges that are linked to the rise of the national state during the great monarchies of the seventeenth century. These were the cities that grew up as the centres of royal power as the kings managed to discipline the barons, and they provided an authoritarian alternative to the free cities set up in the Middle Ages by merchants, craftsmen and escaped serfs. The tendencies among such royal or quasi-royal cities towards the magniloquence implicit in kingly rule has been sustained and exaggerated in modern great cities by the steady erosion of the old local and distinctive ways of life in the *quartiers* that had once been villages and small towns in their own rights. It is in the smaller cities that remnants of the old free culture linger — and the accompanying individuality; that one still finds traces of local ways continuing in building styles as well as daily intercourse. I find this is so in Zurich and Bern (which has so marvellously survived being a capital city), in Austrian Graz, and in Rhineland cities like magical Colmar, to which we almost went often during this period.

It is not a question of crowds. Peasants can crowd as much as city people when there is a motive for swarming, and I always enjoyed the small Upper Austrian towns like Ried and Schärding and Braunau when they were packed for May Day celebrations, with the dancing and the guzzling and the bum-slapping and the vast consumption of *wurst*; or pilgrimage centres like Einsiedeln, where the faithful would gather in procession on feast days as the strains of Bach swept out through the high open cathedral windows towards the virgin mountain peaks, and the peasants moved across the great square, village after village, each in its own colourful and distinctive *Tracht*. Crowding is as natural to human beings as to bees. It is the terrible metropolitan homogeneity of the great city crowds that so appalls one, and the appalling sameness of metropolitan lives that it reflects.

The little baroque towns of Upper Austria, the prosperous villages of Bavaria, the rustic canton capitals of eastern Switzerland, have so far resisted or avoided the threat to their individuality, and the people who inhabit them recognize the individuality of others, and remember it, so that in the second season of visiting a place one will be recognized and greeted by the shopkeepers and the hosts of inns, and given the illusion that one may in some strange way be returning home. And indeed one is returning to a way of human relationship that in most societies has retreated to the little ghettoes of family and friendship.

One of our European trips in the mid-1980s reached eastward into Greece, where we had been before, and Turkey, which we knew only from a two-day visit to Istanbul, with the treasures of Top Kapi glittering in our memory. I had become impressed — almost obsessed — with what I called "The Marvellous Century," meaning the sixth century BC when simultaneously, in the hearts of great and mutually distant civilizations, the old gods moved into the shadows and the first Age of Reason, for better or for worse, began. It was the century of the great pre-Socratic thinkers (mostly in Ionia which is now part of Turkey), when Sappho wrote and Homer was committed to writing, the century of Buddha and Mahavira in the Ganges Valley, of Confucius and Lao Tzu in China, of Zoroaster in Iran. This extraordinary simultaneity struck me as mysterious and wonderful, probably the greatest example in history of what Jung called synchronicity, and I worked intermittently on a book, *The Marvellous Century: Archaic Man and the Awakening of Reason*, which was eventually published in 1989. Because of the special concentration of intellectual events there during the sixth century BC, I was attracted to Ionia, which is now mostly in Turkey and where I had never been. I knew that authentic Greek buildings of the sixth century BC were rare indeed, the Persians and the Hellenistic kings having carried out notable clearances, though I had seen some fortuitously preserved buildings of the time at Paestum and in Sicily. I knew that rivers had silted up ancient harbours and turned them into wheat fields and fig gardens, and that Poseidon as Lord of Earthquakes had laid his heavy hand on the land. But I felt that if we went there we would find something in the light and the shape of the land and the emanations of places that might help induce the mood of Ionian sunlight in which I hoped to write my book.

We went first from Munich to Athens. It was April, the beginning of the German holiday season, and the plane was crowded with German working women taking the cheap Neckerman Tours to the realms of antiquity. We were amused — rather sadly — when they rushed forward as soon as the plane was announced in a hustling, elbow-wielding horde until Inge shouted at them in loud clear German and they immediately calmed down at such a small voice of authority.

The Athens we knew before had been the city of Athena's clear light, when one could stand on the Acropolis and see a detailed landscape on the slopes of Hymettos, when at evening the mists would still form the clear violet crown of which the poets had talked above the dark outline of the city. Now it was one of the most polluted of towns, the fumes for a noisy multitude of cars and buses mingling with the dust of cement plants near Eleusis and the vapours of oil refineries at Daphne; half the statues of the Acropolis had been taken indoors to save them from rapid decay. Where new buildings had gone up, the ground around them had been left uncleared of building rubbish. It had become a dirty as well as an unbearably noisy city. We were glad for once to be at an outlying hotel overlooking the race-track where the air was still relatively clean and we could watch the horses exercising.

I had to visit the museums of Athens and go up to the Acropolis in search of sixth-century clues and relics; there I was especially impressed by the powerful innocence of the archaic statues of young men and women that had been dug from the rubble left by the Persian vandalization of Athens. Otherwise, we were so eager to escape from the city that we rashly enrolled in what purported to be a "first-class" tour of antiquities that would take us through the Peloponessus and as far as Olympia.

The first major stop was Mycenae. On our earlier visit there the site had been deserted except for two other people (it was February), and we were able to wander about the citadel on our own and people it in our minds with the angry ghosts of Clytemnestra and Agamemnon and

Orestes and the pathetic shade of Cassandra, who knew it all though nobody believed her. I remember standing alone on the Cyclopean wall and surveying the countryside until I saw the break in the hills to the south through which Agamemnon had ridden up from Argos on the day of his death.

But now there was a great bus park on the slope facing the old city, and when we arrived it was already filled with vehicles, while the site itself looked like a teeming anthill, so crammed it was with clambering tourists in their rainbow holiday clothes. In Corinth there was little left from the sixth century except the remnants of the Diolkhos, the primitive stone railroad over which ships were pulled across the isthmus to avoid the long sail around the Peloponessian peninsula. The theatre of Epidaurus was as splendid among its green woods and ruins as Henry Miller had described it, but even here there were American college boobies shouting their sporting cries to test the famous echoes. (Though perhaps Greek sportsmen in their day were just as rowdy at their games.) At the end of the day's journey we came to Navplion on its beautiful harbour, and found ourselves lodged in a third-rate hotel where the beds were hard pallets and the young louts of waiters were insulting as they served the dull set meal. Everyone in the party grumbled. We withdrew from it, moved to the one good hotel in town, and next morning took the bus by way of Argos to Athens, driving through famous cities that, apart from the ruins in their outskirts, had settled into sleepy Levantine country towns. I could never decide whether the organizers of the tour were fools or rogues; they honourably returned our money when we went to complain the next day.

Now we took the plane to Samos, on our way to Turkey, and immediately everything was changed. The tourists had not yet landed on the island and we found a new hotel near the airport that was almost empty. It was within walking distance of a small town called Pythagorean, which stood on the site of the ancient city of Samos and was now named after the great Samian philosopher who had fled the anger of his former patron, the tyrant Polycrates, and lived his life in exile, wandering in the Magna Graecia of southern Italy. Here there were quite a number of relics of the sixth century when Polycrates created an island fortress that made him one of the powers of the Levant and a friend of the Egyptian pharaoh whom the Greeks called Amasis. The stone blocks of the great breakwater he built to shelter his fleet of swift warships were visible at low tide, and behind the town we climbed the hillsides brilliant with anemones and other spring flowers to the tunnel which Eupalinos of Megara had driven at the same period through a mountain a mile thick to provide the water for the city; there was an entry tangled up with brambles and a dark hole beyond into which we did not venture. A few miles along the shore were the ruins of the colossal temple of Hera — one of the largest in antiquity — which Polycrates' great architect Theodorus had built on the swampy verge of a river, making his foundations of sheepskins and brushwood on which he eventually laid the great stone platform that still remains unsubmerged and on which we stood looking up at the tumbled drums of the gigantic Doric columns and watching the emerald green lizards that darted among them.

The modern town of Samos lay over a hill range dense with brightly flowering trees; it was built around a small trim harbour and was the nearest approach to a city on the island, with its museum filled with great relief carvings of the battle of the gods and giants from the Heraeum, and those little wooden statues of the gods to which the archaic Greeks attached so much importance. Also, along the harbour, there were taverns where we could eat good Greek food as opposed to the bad imitation French food that was served in our hotel.

From the old harbour of Polycrates at Pythagorean we eventually took the ferry — which looked like a converted World War II landing craft — to the nearest Turkish port of Kuşadasi, whence we intended to take a bus to Izmir, the former Greek city of Smyrna and the most important surviving city in what used to be Ionia. Though we had heard that martial law was in operation, we had no difficulty entering Turkey, and the little town of Kuşadasi, as we booked our bus tickets and wandered around the bazaar and looked at the vast old caravanserai facing the port that had been turned into a cheap hotel, seemed peaceful enough. We sat in a café and drank narrow glasses of sweet tea — for import policies had made Turkish coffee virtually obsolete in Turkey — and we observed how grave and quiet were the Turkish men who alone used the café in comparison with the noisy and excitable Athenians; they played checkers, a notably unpassionate game. We also observed the thoroughness and durability of Kemal Ataturk's revolutionary changes in Turkish life so many decades ago. Arabic lettering had vanished; everything written was in Roman letters. Men and women dressed dully and usually shabbily in Western-style garments. Islam may not have been dead, but it was barely visible. All these changes we had observed when we paid a brief visit to Istanbul years before, but we did not realize how countrywide they had been. Clearly the Turks were doing their best to detach themselves from Asia, but how far they had succeeded in joining Europe was problematical.

The bus took us northward, never far from the sea, and sometimes through the shabby modern parts of cities with classical pasts whose ruins — like those of Ephesus — lay mostly off the road. Izmir was a modern Levantine city with almost as many banks as Beirut in its heyday. The new hotel had been hastily built, so that the plaster walls were cracked with a semblance of spider webs. But it was clean and there were good restaurants in the streets around it. Izmir was a handsome town, with a centre rather like Haussmann's Paris in terms of architecture, and large bazaars, and stone quays along the waterfront on which one could walk for miles.

But here, in the city, the manifestations of martial law were heavy. At every crossing on the main street there would be an armed soldier on each corner, and most of them looked like raw recruits whose fingers would be nervous in their triggers. In the evening and presumably through the night, trucks full of soldiers would cruise quietly around the parks and public places. However, nobody interfered with us as we wandered in the city, and the Turks moved nonchalantly around the guards, with an air of being used to this sort of thing.

As soon as we settled in our hotel we went round to a government tourist agency we had seen in one of the streets, and there we encountered Alexander, as he insisted on calling himself as if he had no Turkish name. He was tall and skinny for a Turk, a student, and as we questioned the young woman at the counter he entered into the conversation in excellent English. He remarked that it was pointless for us to hire a guide (which in fact we never do, preferring to follow our own ignorant but sensitive noses), and offered to show us around the city for the sake of talking in English about the Western world. He seemed such a pleasant companion that we agreed, and he took us to historic sites or recommended museums, and at evening we would eat together in restaurants where Turkish people went, and wander about the night streets and along the quays, learning from him a great deal about Turkish life and politics, though almost nothing about his personal life; in such matters the Turks oddly resemble the English. I was surprised that as a young intellectual he was willing to accept without great resentment the ruthlessly authoritarian structure of the country, but, as he explained, this was no longer a city in Ionia, BC. The Turks had never known real democracy. That was something he knew he had to experience elsewhere. All this was said with an unemotional matter-of-factness that struck me as perhaps typical of the Turkish persona.

Alexander would accept dinners and drinks from us, but at the end of our week in Izmir he would take nothing as a keepsake but one of the jars of Nescafé we had been warned to take with us as presents. The most helpful thing he did was to find us a good driver for our trips into the hinterland to see the various sites that interested us. Since then I have often wondered, because of the place of our meeting and the way Alexander kept a kind of eye on us during our time in Izmir, whether he was not a plant set up by the security service to watch over foreigners who did not travel collectively. But if that was the case, we were the ones who gained most from the encounter.

I do not know how far the driver he found, Suleiman, was a typical working-class Turk, for he was the only one I knew and that slightly for three days. He was taciturn, more from nature I think than from the fact that he appeared to know no more English than to understand where we wanted to go; he also, like many Turks, knew a little German which helped in emergencies. He was a stocky, well-filled-out man clad in a reach-me-down suit in that kind of fustian cloth they make in countries like Turkey and Iran, and his fair yet hauntingly Mongol face was crowned by a flat cloth cap.

Suleiman had a great sense of his own dignity, and unlike the servile drivers we had employed in India, who were still obsessed with status though caste was supposed to have ended, he would take his place at the table whenever we stopped in some small place for lunch, but always picked a modestly priced meal, in which I would accompany him to sustain the democratic feeling he seemed to want to project. On a commercial level he clearly regarded his word as his bond. At the end of the trip he asked exactly the sum he had named at the beginning, though our changes of mind had incurred extra mileage, and he seemed to consider it excessive of us when we added to our modest tip a large pot of Nescafé. Above all, we appreciated his self-sufficient quietness. If we asked a question, he would answer as best he could in broken English-German, but he did not thrust irrelevant information on us.

Yet was he too good to be true? Thorny in my mind remains one incident, when we were pulled up at a police post on the way to Colophon. The guard gave Suleiman a friendly greeting and hardly looked at our passports. As we drove away, Suleiman turned round and said, with a barely perceptible smile: "I come this way often." But few tourists could have wanted to go to Colophon, since there was only a museum and no interesting remains. And in the end I wondered about Suleiman too. For if Alexander was a plant, why should he not introduce another plant. And if there were times when Suleiman's sturdy figure and his emotional self-sufficiency struck one as the characteristics of a traditional warrior, why should they not be the characteristics of a policeman?

Still, apart from Alexander and Suleiman, whose labour if they were spies must have seemed singularly unrewarding, I did notice that as a whole the people of Izmir were more restrained and dignified in their behaviour than the people of Athens. There was a natural democracy about them, perhaps extending from the warrior past, despite the authoritarian style of government that then existed. And insofar as one of the aims of Ataturk had been to eliminate the inequalities of gender in traditional Islamic societies, he seemed to have been successful. Everywhere, in offices, in banks, in shops, in restaurants, in our hotel, we encountered women who seemed very certain of themselves, but perhaps the most striking thing of all was the public appearance of family life in a land where purdah had once reigned. On the one weekend we stayed in Izmir we saw hundreds of family parties, father, mother and children in their bright cheap spring clothes, visiting the museums and playing and picnicking in the parks, a sight one was unlikely to see in even a modestly orthodox Islamic society, even less in some Christian Mediterranean societies, like those of Sicily, Calabria or rural Greece.

Our journey with Suleiman through the grain fields and the vast fig gardens of Ionia was impressive even if it did not lead us to much of a concrete nature related to the sixth century, except small relics in museums. Miletus, for example, the leading city of archaic Ionia and a cultural centre whose pre-Socratic philosophers permanently changed our ways of thinking, had been destroyed by the Persians in 494 BC in revenge for its leadership of the Ionian revolt the preceding year, and later elaborately redeveloped by Hippodamus as one of the first cities planned on a quadrilateral grid. This meant that it had many splendid post-archaic monuments, including perhaps the finest of all Greek theatres, but nothing of my period.

Even in Turkey, where the remains were generally in better shape than most in Greece, Miletos was typical; there were no sixth-century places that had preserved the pristine quality of the great Doric temples of Paestum south of Naples, whence human beings had been driven and kept away for centuries by the anopheles mosquito. Even the great shrine at Didyma, the Ionian equivalent of Delphi, was rebuilt in Hellenistic times after its destruction by the Persians at the same time as Miletos; only a few of its tall columns stood complete, though the great courtyards and staircases gave me a sense of the importance of the place in Ionian life, especially when I sat on the low wall of the sacred well where the local pythoness had made her forecasts, leaning over through the fumes of burning laurel to see her vision in the small mirror of water many feet down; I saw only the clear agnostic blue of the Ionian sky.

Perhaps the most impressive place of all was Ephesus, late and decadent though much of it was. One climbed one's way up the long street, its flags deeply cut by wagons and chariots over two millennia, through a procession of Graeco-Roman ruins, much lighter and elegant in form than those of Rome because Ionians built them; buildings like the fine Library of Celsus, and the temple of the imperial gay, Hadrian. Yet Ephesus did give one an image, however negative, from the sixth century. The great stone platform of the temple of the many-breasted Artemis (St. Paul's abhorred Diana of the Ephesians) still existed, but it was invisible, sunk under a rectangular pond several feet deep. Here was another marshy site where Theodorus's method of sheepskins and brushwood had been tried in the sixth century, but has not worked as well as on Samos, so that now one just looked at the sullen water in the centre of which the archaeologists had built a hybrid column out of miscellaneous drums that had not been taken away for building material.

Perhaps the most pristine place of all, though it lay quite outside my immediate area of interest, was Priene. Priene had been the centre of the Ionian League, the place where the Greek cities of Asia Minor sent their delegates to plot the great revolt against the Persians in 499 BC. The town had been the victim of the sea more than any other enemy. Even in the fourth century BC a new site had to be found because the harbour had silted up, and now, as we stood on the low hills of Priene, we again looked over fields of grain and blossoming orchards and the sea was a gleam miles out to the west. But if Poseidon had been mean with his harbours, he had been sparing with his earthquakes. Priene was remarkably well-preserved, and had not been built over, so that the clear Hellenistic outlines of the roofless city had been recovered by excavation; the very stone chairs where the city fathers had sat in the Boulesterion were still there, and the theatre was in good enough shape for a tragedy to be enacted there in the next few days.

Sardis, the capital of the unfortunate Croesus and his land of Lydia was much less visible, though his invention of money still plagues mankind. The great temple of Cybele had sunk under the rolling sward, with a few angles of stone in the hollows that must have been the corners of chambers. In one of them we found the only inhabitant, a large and handsome tortoise.

After Sardis we departed, leaving a heavily guarded airport at Izmir where the security arrangements were lengthy. We returned with mixed feelings to the freedom, pollution and noise of Athens.

Our trip to Turkey had brought us little concrete to touch on or feel or look at of the sixth century. Too many later cultures, too many revenges of nature, too many local masons picking up stone where they could find it, and the floating dust of two millennia and more had obliterated the image of ancient Ionia, except for the fragmentary works of poets and philosophers who helped shape our world and our minds. Yet it was no wasted journey, for, especially in Samos and at the Turkish sites, it gave us the sense of the land, its colours, its atmospherics, that had provided a setting to the great intellectual revolution of the sixth century, and I returned reinforced to write my book, *The Marvellous Century*.

Chapter 7

EREWHON REVISITED

Because we were going to Europe every year, our visit to Turkey seemed like an excursion to a near place rather than a real journey. But the far places still called us in those final years of the 1970s and almost through the whole of the 1980s. It was not that with retirement there was more time to travel. My restless appetite for work has always filled what time I had available, yet at the same time I always found time for the travels I wished to make. What began to urge me now was the sense that I should make a point of seeing some of the countries I had missed while the going was good and my health still held. It was a just premonition, since as the 1980s came to an end I would find my mobility seriously and exasperatingly curtailed.

But our first far journey at this period was actually a return one. We had been to New Zealand when we were involved in our great CBC film project in the South Pacific out of which I wrote *South Sea Journey*. We stayed there for a few days of rest between the arduous clearing up of work in Vancouver before a half-year's absence and the rigours we knew we would encounter when we flew to Fiji to start our wanderings and researches among the islands. For lack of time we had taken a bus tour of South Island in the company of a small mob of Australians who condescended in a big brother way to the New Zealanders, who in their turn detested them. I had always been surprised at the anger with which the normally placid New Zealanders who so often came to work in Vancouver as anthropologists reacted to being mistaken for their antipodean cousins. By the end of that first visit to New Zealand we knew. As for New Zealand the land, it still remained largely terra incognita to us, the distant home of Erewhon.

This time we meant to find our own ways of travel, and to begin we flew south to Los Angeles, where we spent half a day in that ugly and bewildering airport, and then at nightfall caught the Qantas flight to

Sydney, which stopped at Auckland. You travel most of the Pacific from Los Angeles in darkness. Dawn brightens over a glittering sea that continues for another thousand miles without rocks of islands: the vast empty sea over which Polynesians voyaged from Samoa in their great canoes six centuries ago to found the Maori settlements of New Zealand. They called it Aotearoa, the Long Bright Land.

Most of the passengers were Australians going on to Sydney. But the woman beside me was a New Zealander, and as we approached her country she began to talk about returning home. Twenty years ago she had gone into the world for a life New Zealand seemed too narrow to provide. She told me how she had worked in England, Hong Kong, Malta, Canada, and at times she spoke with zest and gratitude. Then the shadow came over her face, shutting out the youth, bringing on the middle age.

"Now I'm going back. The rest of the world is killing itself."

"Do you think home will be any better?"

She gave an odd, grim look, as if I had expressed her own doubt. "I don't think we've gone so far," she said slowly. "We're not so polluted. We don't hate each other so much. We're a minor backward country without a history. I never thought I'd thank God for that. But I do."

She stirred in my mind the old novelists' vision — Samuel Butler's and Aldous Huxley's — of New Zealand as the far corner of a ruined world where a germ of civilization might fecundate a second spring of humanity. A land with an undefined future; a land without a history. Nowhere; Erewhon.

The land slid into sight beneath us in a scatter of islands, their western shores white with surf. Descending over pastures bright as bowling greens, where the cattle fed in great black-and-white holstein herds undisturbed by the plane's noise, we landed at Auckland's airport, and as we did, saw the city's intricate geography spread beneath us.

Auckland is one of those cities, like Vancouver and Hong Kong — where land and sea combine to make splendid natural settings. Here the long upper arm of North Island is almost severed by deeply biting inlets on each side. The city's special feature is a score of small extinct volcanoes from whose summits one looks out over those glittering harbours. Manukau to the west was the old sailing-ship harbour; too shallow for modern ships, it is now inhabited by the forty thousand sailing dinghies and yachts (one for every twenty Aucklanders) that at weekends crowd the waters like flocks of floating butterflies. Waitemata is the modern port where cruise ships and freighters dock and to which the city is oriented.

The view from Auckland's little volcanoes also shows how sadly the setting has been misused. Except for a tight centre dominated by the Gothic hilltop towers of the university, Auckland is a vast anti-greenbelt to which at night the workers depart, leaving the real city to tourists, waiters and night watchmen. New Zealanders believe fanatically that every man's home is his castle, and their cities (Auckland was then the largest with 800,000 people, Wellington next with 350,000) are afflicted not with high-rise apartments shutting out the sun, but with sprawling red-tin-roofed bungalow suburbs through which one drives for miles of sameness to reach the pastoral countryside on which New Zealand depends for its life.

Even in Auckland's centre after we had settled into our shabby (but cheap) Edwardian hotel there was little impressive except for the great parks filled with enormous old trees that exist in all New Zealand cities. Victorian warehouses built with round grave arches and massive buttresses to withstand earthquakes have an impassive Roman kind of dignity; the old hotels were given adventitious charm by silver-painted traceries of fire escapes clambering with apparent caprice over their façades; glass-roofed Victorian arcades harboured boutiques and teashops frequented by old ladies of improbable ornateness and fragility. They reminded me of childhood in time-halted corners of England rather than evoking a characteristically New Zealand past to which one might give the name of history.

From the start, New Zealand's immigration policy made it more British than the other dominions. Here are no equivalents of the Québécois or the Afrikaners or even the Italians after World War II in Australia. The pattern was set by early migrations sponsored by philanthropists like Edward Gibbon Wakefield, whose colonists founded Wellington in 1840, or by religious bodies like the Free Church of Scotland, which founded granite Dunedin in 1848, or the Church of England whose followers founded Christchurch in 1850 and gave it a cathedral designed by the Gothic revivalist Giles Gilbert Scott. A tenth of New Zealanders are Polynesians — Maoris or migrants from Samoa and the Cook Islands. The rest are still almost wholly British by descent, and London is their cultural mecca; in New Zealand we saw mainly BBC television.

In some ways the influence was good. An imported Victorian radicalism led to pioneer innovations: votes for women in 1893, old-age pensions in 1898. Since then it has congealed into a rather stifling welfare paternalism, one of whose results we encountered by arriving on a Sunday; it was somewhat worse than the traditional English variety, for in New Zealand shops close from Friday night to Monday morning and most restaurants put up the shutters on Sunday. Not long ago, pubs closed at 6 p.m. and the habit of drinking against time has survived. If we entered an Auckland bar any time between five and eight we would be drawn into a fast-drinking circle of total strangers and treated to great glasses of strong beer with a good fellowship from which we had to escape quickly so as to escape upright.

Little history and a cultural colonialism more rampant than Margaret Atwood ever dreamed of; dull cities and dead weekends; New Zealand is no place for self-respecting culture vultures to alight. But that accentuates the good things that do await a patient traveller. After a few days one either seeks the next plane out or confronts the country and its people directly, with no myths intervening. Fortunately, people and country are both easily accessible and the hinterland has more to offer than the cities seem to promise. It is as a land, in a physical and literal sense, rather than as a nation, which it hardly is, that New Zealand is worth seeing.

Since New Zealand is not really a country of destinations, where you leap from one centre of life and culture to the next, it has to be experienced while you travel, and the most rewarding way is to travel by bus. The Road Services of the New Zealand Railways criss-cross most of the country; where they are absent there are regular private services. All these buses work on mail runs, which means that towns and settlements on the way are visited, with frequent stops at the ubiquitous New Zealand tearooms to eat scones, pikelets, sausage rolls, meat pies filled with strange brown glue, and a vast array of cakes and sandwiches; New Zealanders have an enviable ability to consume vast quantities of starchy foods and still remain reasonably trim. Often the coaches stop at ranches to pick up mail bags and at remote houses to toss out newspapers; one feels involved in the life of the country.

Our choice of travel from Auckland started by defying New Zealand recommendations, which always begin by suggesting a start at the Bay of Islands 180 miles or so north of the city. This is a predilection born of the beach summers of Auckland childhoods. In fact, the scenery of this complex of inlets and low islands, where we had been on our first visit to New Zealand, is insipid, and there is nothing to do except fish tunny and marlin and snooze in deck-chairs. Instead, it is best to start south at once, heading into the pastoral Waikato region and on to the Maori heartland of Rotorua.

On this road, passing through places with sonorous Maori names like Otahuhu and Papakiris, we got the first sight of what primeval New Zealand looked like to the explorers. Copses of bright green mangrove reached out on stilted roots over estuary mud-flats; among them strutted strange waders called pukekos like giant coots with blue breasts and red beaks. In the deep gullies wild bush survived, looking like old engravings of Amazonian jungle; tall, umbrella-shaped trees, covered with sword-leafed epiphytes, hung with lianas; an undergrowth of forty-foot-high tree ferns and ragged pandanuses. The rain forests of South Island show New Zealand jungle far more abundantly, but these North Island fragments suggest how wild and impenetrable the land must have seemed before the settlers felled and burned and made it one of the most grazed and cultivated countries, with a dairy industry that sustains three cows for every human New Zealander.

One lush pasture monotonously followed another, filled with fat cows, dotted with wooden farmhouses shaded by great magnolias, and offering here and there some mild surprise like an English hedgehog proceeding with a sense of invulnerable dignity over the road. The hedgehog's ancestors were imported by the first settlers, who wanted to recreate in detail England's green and pleasant land, and who also introduced the rabbit, which ate up the pastures. To deal with the rabbit, they introduced stoats, but the stoats killed off the native ground-nesting songbirds, and English blackbirds, bullfinches and greenfinches were brought in to replace them, and sing in all the parks and woodlands of the country. A classic example of how easily adaptable foreign species can destroy an ancient ecosystem. Today even the New Zealanders' totem bird, the shy nocturnal kiwi, may be nearing extinction.

Yet one curious native species was spectacularly present on the way to Rotorua. On the edge of North Island's central massif of limestone cliffs and volcanic crags, we went through the wooded gorges leading to the Waitamo caves. They were limestone caves with stalactites, narrow passages that stirred my claustrophobia, vaulted chambers that relieved it, dark underground rivers. What made them different were the so-called "glowworms," larvae of an ephemeral water fly, *Arachnocampo luminosa*. A gigantic Maori Charon took us on the underground river in a leaky scow which he propelled by pushing on spurs of rock that came perilously near to our heads as we drifted into the darkness of the inner caves. We were told to be silent, for noise makes the glowworms switch off, and the quietness, broken by the soft swishing of the river, intensified the onrush of pure wonder as we entered the chamber lit by dense galaxies of turquoise points of light, shining steadily against the dark night of the rock like an elfin miniature of heaven and reflected in the dark water beneath. It was a bizarre, haunting sight, a hidden sunless world of abstract beauty, and hard not to exclaim at with delight.

You descend from the hills into Rotorua through wastes of volcanic ash and rough maquis, until the wide grey lake appears, with the Victorian resort town beside it, and the hot springs fill the air with a stench like that of a badly run pulp mill. Maoris are numerous in Rotorua; they own much of the land and control much of the tourist trade.

Our night's entertainment was a show of Maori clowning and dancing, mostly to lilting tunes borrowed from hot gospel missionaries. Here we met a Maori woman with two children who was so acculturated that she had come to see her people's dances for the first time, and of course saw them unauthentically. She was delighted to hear we came from the great timberland of British Columbia, for she was working in the forests of North Island in an office of Fletcher Challenge (the only New Zealand-based multinational corporation), and she talked to us enthusiastically about how, when the kauri pine forests were almost all felled, they had imported Douglas fir from British Columbia and found that in the longer periods of warm weather on North Island it grew twice as quickly as in Canada. I told her of the concerns of our native peoples about felling first-growth forest, but living apart from her people had given her a curious lack of historic sense, and she merely said, "Why worry about big old trees when you can grow big new ones so quickly?"

On a headland steamy with vapours from the springs, we found a Maori village with a big, ornately carved and vermilion-painted meeting house which with its carved grotesque figures seemed like a red rococo version of a Kwakiutl longhouse, echoing over thousands of Pacific miles. An old man quietly whittled wooden images for sale, and little girls in front of a lava-rock statue of Queen Victoria offered in precise mission English to sing a Maori song; they screeched a hymn. Another clan of Maoris lived by organizing tours through the weird Whakarewarewa Valley. On the scrubby hillsides, where a chill trout stream ran between farting pools of boiling mud and geysers steamed fifty feet into the air, they had built some creditable reconstructions of traditional forts, and we felt nearer to a real past here than anywhere else in New Zealand, in spite of the chic Western clothes worn by the highly educated Maori ladies who lectured us.

We went from Rotorua through the mountains to Lake Taupo, and then by way of the river gorges to the west coast at New Plymouth, a fretwork Victorian town settled by Devon men and women in 1841, and overshadowed by the isolated 2500-metre cone of Mount Egmont, looking so much like Fujiyama that it draws a regular traffic of Japanese tourists. At New Plymouth we experienced an act of hospitality that typified the goodwill we encountered everywhere among ordinary New Zealanders. The lady who ran the tourist bureau and her husband spent the whole of their Sunday driving us up the mountain and around the surrounding countryside; they did not even accept lunch for they had thoughtfully brought it.

From New Plymouth we followed the coast south to the capital, windy Wellington, where the gusts blow at more than thirty knots for more than half the days of the year. The National Museum had a fine collection of Cook-period Maori artifacts, we found a good exhibition of New Zealand's only great artist, Frances Hopkins, and we were oddly amused by the new parliament building, designed by Basil Spence and looking like a gigantic egg with the bottom cut off (New Zealanders call it The Beehive). Though the presence of our Canadian friends Bill and Peggy New (he had succeeded me as editor of *Canadian Literature*) enlivened our time there, we found little else to justify braving Wellington gusts and gales, and we soon crossed Cook Strait by ferry, sailing through rugged-shored Marlborough Inlet to Picton, where we took the bus down the east-coast road, with its broad empty beaches and bold headlands, to Christchurch, which became our South Island base, with Mount Cook, the country's tallest mountain, as our first destination. We went southwest over the Canterbury wheatlands and up the gorge of the Waitaki River into the dry grasslands, whose tussocked pastures support most of the seventy million New Zealand sheep. The sheep were scattered over a vast area of hill country with meagre grazing; only when we saw hillsides white with flocks rounded up for shearing did we have a physical sense of what such numbers mean.

Mount Cook dominates the Southern Alps that fence off the sheep country to the west; it rises twelve thousand feet sheer from a low valley at the head of Lake Pukaki. I have seen much higher mountains in the Andes, the Rockies, the Himalayas, but have never felt so close to natural vastness, and the grand pyramid of Cook stays in my memory as the most satisfying mountain I know to stare at, lounging in a meadow and eating wild gooseberries at its foot, willing to contemplate, never — with my heart problems — hoping to conquer.

The other natural sights not to be missed on South Island were the deep fjords on the southwestern coast and the glaciers to the north. The grandest fjord is Milford Sound. We reached it by a devious journey through the old Otago gold-fields and then over the passes, where snow flurried in the air and into the west-coast rain forest, whose dense evergreen cover, flowing down to dip its branches in salt water, gives the tight trench of Milford Sound a special quality of menacing luxuriance. Even as a Vancouverite remembering Howe Sound, I was impressed, particularly as we had struck one of the sound's few fine days; the rainfall averages something over three hundred inches a year.

Another coil of looping roads, another pass descending into the rain forests, brought us to the Fox and Franz Josef glaciers, which dip wondrously near to the sea. In these regions a kind of poor white society had come into existence. The farms were as decrepit as those of northern British Columbia had been in the 1950s, and when we reached a bus-stop eating house all the cretin who served could offer us were lettuce sandwiches. People and lifestyles alike seemed to have degenerated, as they often do in old half-forgotten settled areas.

We found our way south to Invercargill, the extreme end of New Zealand where even in January, summer's height, the breezes from Antarctica blew bitterly cold, and one day there were veils of snow drifting over the rush-grown ground. It was a Sunday, with no cafés open, and we shivered in our summer garb into doorways to protect us from the south wind until the bus arrived.

We ended our time in New Zealand at Nelson, a neat place facing out on Tasman Bay on the north side of South Island. It was well planned, as if some British surveyor general with a hint of classical knowledge had laid it out, and it was dominated by a cathedral on the crest of a hilltop park whose loud bells would awaken us in the enormous hotel room we rented at a remarkably low price. Down in the town there was an excellent restaurant run by Austrian immigrants, and the presence of a kind of intellectual life for those who had elected to spend their days in this comparative isolation was shown by an excellent bookstore (there are many of them in New Zealand, where they are a positively civilizing element) and many crafts establishments, offering sturdy pottery, durable earthy weaving, little hint of elegance.

But it was not the society or even its fragile history that occupied us in Nelson. We explored the fine coastline of Tasman Bay, but the incident that remains most strongly in both our minds was at the same time absurd and grand. One day, to while away an afternoon, we took a tour in a minibus. Among the attractions we were offered was "The Eel Feeding." We were herded down a steep path beside a small river to a low stage built out over the water, and an old woman with a bucket came scrambling down beside us. She gave a high-pitched call, and all at once the water before the stage was alive with the heads of scores of large eels which fed like chickens from the old woman's hands. I never found out what was the species of these antipodean eels, but I remembered the stories I had heard years before in the South Sea islands about various forms of "calling": calling sharks and dolphins, calling fish and even prawns. This was our last experience before we flew back to Auckland and took the plane home.

What one sees in New Zealand, more than in most other countries, is the land itself. As for New Zealand society, let me confess at the end a haunting sense of *déjà vu*. What I remembered was the anglophone society of the Canadian west coast that I found surviving in Victoria when I got there forty years ago. I could not help thinking, as I looked at New Zealand with that memory in mind, how narrowly Canada had escaped a continuing colonialism. "There," I thought, "but for the grace of Québec, go we."

Chapter 8

CAUGHT UP IN CAUSES

Ever since the 1940s I have been living a kind of double life whose rationale I have not yet been able entirely to construct. On one side I have been the writer, dominated by a code of enlightened individual and artistic self-sufficiency derived largely from the kind of aestheticism — also modified by humanitarian impulses — that my early master Oscar Wilde had projected. Though at times I committed myself to collective ideas, notably that of anarchism, beginning in the 1940s and continuing lifelong, I have never been able to accept that they can overbear the independent intelligence, the sovereign creativity of the artist, and this view I have followed in my writing. And perhaps this need to defend at least the central keep of my individuality has selected and modified and perhaps even justified the kinds of activity into which the sense of engagement I share with so many of my contemporaries has led me. I have never allowed the Cause to take over, though I was perilously near it in the 1940s when my friendship with Marie Louise Berneri meant that the psychic power and general attractiveness of an exceptional woman anarchist were added to the collective pressure of a dedicated group of associates.

Later occasions were somewhat, though not entirely, different. I abandoned close political involvement, even in anarchism, because it seemed to me that any form of propaganda in fact compromises one's integrity as a writer, and in the end compromises the cause itself, which is never well served by a chorus of servile gramophones. Later I took up a variety of unpolitical means of helping living beings, under the influence of another powerful woman, my wife Inge, as well as of my own conscience which might not alone have been sufficient, though probably the cluster of extraordinary circumstances through which I met the Dalai Lama for the first time in 1961 and witnessed the extraordinary distress of the Tibetan people who had followed him into exile in 1959 would have stirred me in any case out of my defensive laziness.

I had looked with mistrust in my politically active days on anything that seemed to be charity, the condescending help given by righteous and superior people to the unfortunate, which seemed to me an enhancement of the arrogance of the givers and a diminishment of the dignity of the receivers. Yet when I encountered the Tibetans I found it impossible not to help, and by a not entirely semantic shift of thought I realized the difference between pity, which is an aristocratic notion, and compassion — or feeling with — which is an egalitarian notion. Translated into terms that accorded with my anarchist views, this meant in practice — as Gandhi understood it — providing the means and the advice (if asked for) to people who want them and can use them effectively. The danger, as I had seen with Spanish refugee anarchists in France after the civil war, was turning them into permanent pensioners, but if one helps groups rather than individuals that risk is diminished.

Soon, on our return to Canada from India in 1962, we founded the Tibetan Refugee Aid Society, our first funds being raised by a student stunt at UBC, selling votes to elect the ugliest man on campus. I became executive vice-chairman, doing most of the administrative work, and Inge did most of the fund-raising work. All this I have told in *Beyond the Blue Mountains*, where I also described our successful cooperation with foreign voluntary agencies and the Tibetans themselves in settling large numbers of Tibetans in South India. I have also told of my eventual abandonment of my "office" through sheer exhaustion. During the mid-1970s, when it seemed to us that the refugees were well established in India, we withdrew from active roles in the Tibetan Refugee Aid Society.

Yet we were drawn back before the end of the same decade when the plight of other victims of Communist tyranny was forced on our attention through the news of the boat people fleeing from Vietnam and Laos and Cambodia. By 1979 the Canadian government had committed itself to receiving boat people from the Malayan and Thai and Hong Kong refugee camps who were sponsored by groups and individuals. We turned back to the Tibetan Refugee Aid Society and offered to raise money if they would provide the organizational umbrella. They agreed, and we set up a money-raising campaign which, through our good friends Peggy and Lam Lai, involved us quite deeply with the local Chinese community, who were raising their own funds for the boat people, as well as with the Mennonites.

Local racial prejudices were still, not much more than a decade ago, strong enough to impede our efforts in various ways. With a singularly sympathetic immigration official we had worked out a plan with the help of the local Seventh Day Adventists by which a camp of theirs near Hope could be used as a half-way place where boat people could stay until their ultimate destinations were determined. It seemed after all that a comfortable camp in Canada was better than what they had endured. Everything was worked out, the federal government agreed, the Seventh Day Adventists were happy their camp would be put to good use, the municipality of Hope was pleased with its role of host, and we, with the Chinese committee and the Fraser Valley Mennonites, had been gathering funds and sponsorship guarantees for the boat people. All at once, W.A.C. Bennett, then still premier of British Columbia, declared, though his words may have been more politely couched — that he did not want his province to be invaded by poverty-stricken Asians. The federal government — conscious of Trudeau's declining popularity in the West — agreed demeaningly. I could hardly blame tough and wily old Wacky Bennett too greatly, when a local doctor whom I knew well chose to break our friendship by refusing to give to our fund on the racist grounds that in his view the influx of Chinese into the local medical profession had lowered its standards and he did not want to see that kind of degeneration occurring generally among us, as it would if we received too many Asians. He was not alone. The notorious Doug Collins was once my friend, whom I valued for his now long-lost freedom of mind.

In the end we raised more than enough money to bring about seventy boat people, a small number in comparison with the whole of the boat people, but it was the Gandhian one step we were able to make at that time with our resources in the community. Largely with the help of our Chinese friends, we found them places to live in Chinatown, that sponge-like community that is perpetually being emptied as the young Chinese become prosperous and move to other areas, and perpetually filled as new waves of needy Asians arrive. Unemployment for newcomers was no problem in Chinatown. There were plenty of jobs at minimum wages, and we found that the boat people were adaptable and resourceful and rarely stayed at the bottom of the pile. Most of them quickly learnt sufficient English, and often they were competent craftsmen who could help when we had to recondition apartments for them. Most were ethnic Chinese, which was why we got such help from the Vancouver Chinese. They were independent people, glad to be out of their predicament, but anxious to establish new lives of their own, which did not mean they were unappreciative of what we did. We never expected demonstrations of gratitude, but a number of them kept up personal contact, and would occasionally come to see us with little presents, particularly at Chinese New Year; now that their lives have blossomed, we see less of them, which seems to us appropriate.

One of the observations I made when we were working with these people was the ecclesiastical mutability of the Chinese abroad, as if sect were determined by some utility or other. Doubtless those who came to us had been Buddhists or already Catholic converts in Indo-China, but almost immediately they flocked to a new church for Chinese which the Mennonites, who were helping them, set up in Chinatown. It was strange to see Mennonite pietism united to Chinese pragmatism. Later, in my Chinatown wanderings, I was to encounter Chinese Lutheran, Presbyterian, Anglican, Baptist and Adventist churches, and I am sure that all our sects have received their recruits, though I often wonder how far the latter find their way back to the fair number of Buddhist temples we also have. Taoism alone seems to have been too fragile and perhaps too unorganized to travel well into the Western world.

Perhaps it was the fashions of the times, though I think it was more likely our long connection with Buddhists and their emphasis on compassion for all living beings that led us to take part during the 1980s in causes aimed at the diminution of cruelty towards animals and the enhancement of their lives. We put on art shows and mixed reading and performance shows to publicize and to raise money for the protests against the seal hunt, and I believe that two of my own initiatives helped to bring an end to the slaughter of the young whitecoats. In a lengthy article entitled "Bloody Lies" I showed in *Saturday Night* how truth as well as the seals were becoming a casualty of the hunt as government agencies resorted to shameless falsehoods in the attempt to defend the indefensible annual massacre. I realized that my efforts were hitting home when I later drafted a letter of protest against the continued killing that was signed by a leading group of Canadian writers, painters, actors and publishers. When our letter appeared in the *Globe and Mail*, the nonentity who was then Trudeau's Minister of Fisheries came out publicly squealing with his own letter of self-justification. Not long afterwards the seal hunt ended and the Minister of Fisheries departed.

I became involved, too, in the campaigns to put an end to that antiquated barbarism, the fur trade. Already a great deal of indignation had been aroused in Europe by revelations of the cruel trapping methods used in the Canadian industry. The counter-argument on which the Canadian government relied most was that if the fur trade were made impossible, then thousands of native people would be deprived not merely of a living but also of a traditional way of life. I wrote an essay which was circulated among members of the European parliament and aroused great interest in Brussels, pointing out the fallacy and dishonesty of this official Canadian argument. The trapping industry, as I showed, was not part of traditional Indian living, but instead was a feature of the dependency that the fur traders imposed on native people, and in the past it had been often detrimental because the Indians neglected hunting of food and quickly depopulated areas of fur-bearing mammals.

On occasions like these I had the satisfaction that what I was doing had some effect on the course of events. I never got very far when I tried to do something about the cruelties of modern mass production farming, and in the end I withdrew because of my problems with the militants in the animal rights movement. I found them self-righteous and egotistical in the extreme, as if this had become a last frontier for fanatics no longer acceptable elsewhere. They were jealous of their small efforts, so that the movement was split into many tiny groups, each with its own dogmatic guru, and I must admit that my own ego was strained when I offered to write for one group only to discover that the jargon-spewing leader was more interested in his own image than in the help of a professional writer.

In all ways, what with the "brutality" of those who imposed cruelty on animals and the petty fanaticism of the animal rights advocates, I felt my last remnants of humanistic idealism falling away, in the sense of seeing man as the crown of the beanstalk of being. I now saw him down in the mire with the rest, different only because of a special kind of intelligence he used to dominate the earth. I was reminded of my old friend and fellow poet Roy Fuller, long ago, answering with a devastating "All" an item in a questionnaire which ran: "What animals do you prefer to man?" I have no doubt by now that man is the cruellest of the animals, towards his own kind as well as other species, his gratuitous cruelty a far more complete dereliction of morality than the ferocity of a carnivore single-mindedly killing for food. And I think that man is morally the most despicable of the animals for the perversion of thought with which he justifies his atrocities against living beings, both animals and plants. Even our language is perverted by our hypocrisy. In our common phraseology we blame the "brutes" or animals for our own atrocities and elevate a nonexistent concept when we talk of "inhumane," as if "humane" with its derivation and its faults offered any better hope. To equate mankind with a superior state of being is eminently false. Perhaps womankind one day will show us something different. Yet I do grant that there may be a spark of the angelic in humanity, though I have spent a lifetime trying to evoke it without much success except in the narrow bounds of the one great human achievement, friendship.

It was friendship that aroused and has since in many ways supported us in what has been the main cause, outside literature, of our recent years, the small organization, unpolitical and unliterary, known as Canada India Village Aid. It all began in the early summer of 1981 when Patwant Singh emerged from our past. Patwant is an Indian writer and the editor of *Design*, his country's best magazine of architecture and planning. His father was one of the Sikh contractors who, under the direction of Sir Edwin Lutyens, built the dramatic complex of rose-coloured buildings in the centre of New Delhi that was designed to enshrine the authority of the British Raj as successor to all the alien rulers of India, and is now the node of power in independent India. Through a mutual friend's letter of introduction, we met Patwant Singh an hour after landing in Bombay on our first Indian journey; like many Sikhs, he was a tall man; his mobile, intelligent face was framed between a black turban and a black, carefully tended beard which I later learnt he kept in a net when he slept.

Within a week he and my old London friend Mulk Raj Anand, now in Bombay, had introduced us to all the local writers, artists and filmmakers. A couple of weeks later, in Delhi, Patwant performed the same service all over again with almost Mogul lavishness, introducing me to most of the people we wanted to meet (though Nehru would not bite) and giving enormous parties to which everyone came because nobody wanted to be left out. There we encountered not only great Indian writers like the superb novelist and tale-teller R.K. Narayan, but also great foreign writers like Octavio Paz, who was then Mexico's ambassador to India.

Patwant's social adeptness, his extravagant self-projection, and his love of pleasure made one think of him in those days that extended over almost the first two decades of our friendship as the intelligent playboy, capable of writing a good book on Indian politics, which he did, of editing an elegant magazine for sophisticates, and of wearing his highly starched black turban in just as elegant a combination with his Gucci shoes as he skittered over the tragic aspects of Asian existence. He mocked gently our efforts to help Tibetan refugees; he refused to admit, out of nationalist pride, that *poverty* was a word to be applied in India; and it was I, not he, who noticed that his night watchman had no shoes and was wearing the most wretched of worn-down open sandals in the bitter cold nights of a Delhi December.

About 1980, all this seemed to change dramatically, as life does so often among Indian men who approach the darker verges of middle age, and all at once become aware of the power of karma and the relation between present and future lives. Patwant suffered a heart attack. Recovering from it, he found himself considering what would have happened if he had been a peasant farmer from one of the poverty-stricken villages near his country house of Ghamroj in Haryana, sixty miles or so from Delhi. Almost certainly he would have died, for there was no hospital near enough to save him. The thought nagged, as thoughts do on sleepless hospital nights, and when he recovered Patwant went out to look at the areas near his leisure farm with a new uneasy eye. He found the villages poorer than he had assumed, the land arid, or salinated from bad irrigation; eye diseases caused largely by diet deficiency were so prevalent that any child who survived infancy had a ten-to-one chance of eventually contracting cataract or glaucoma; survival beyond infancy was itself reduced as a possibility by the high rate of gastroenteritis; tuberculosis was on the upspring among cattle and hence among human beings. The women were still in semi-purdah, living withdrawn and repressed lives inaccessible to family planning instruction, for though these people were Jats of Hindu faith, the area had been for centuries under Moslem domination.

The decisive incident came one night when Patwant was driving back to Delhi, and came upon a group of peasants at the roadside and among them a woman in agonized labour; she needed help urgently. Patwant got the peasants to load her into his car and drove to the military hospital in Delhi where he had connections; the woman's life and her child's were saved. He decided immediately to found a small hospital so that such a situation might never again occur among what he rather patriarchically regarded as his peasants.

He got to work immediately, calling in the debts of years of lavish hospitality. He badgered the state government of Haryana into giving a piece of land he specified must be barren. He persuaded architect friends to design an open campus of small pavilions to be built cheaply of local materials. He talked manufacturers into giving him beds and sheets and cement. He recruited retired army doctors to staff his hospital and charmed Delhi specialists into offering services at nominal fees. He persuaded a couple of English nurses travelling in India to stay on and help start up the hospital. And he turned to the vast circle of friendships he had built during his years of globe-trotting. His old self clearly enjoyed the drama of it all.

At this point Inge and I became involved. As old friends we were astonished at his apparent transformation, but rejoiced in it. We got together some other Old India Hands, like John and Marta Friesen, some doctors like Shirley Rushton and Douglas Forbes, a few other friends like Doris Shadbolt and Tony Phillips, a psychologist who became our first chairman, like the accountant Hari Varshney who became our treasurer, like Sarah MacAlpine and Judy Brown who had attended my lectures long ago at UBC and had worked with us for the Tibetans. We called the little organization we founded Canada India Village Aid. Here we had our first small difference with Patwant, who wanted us to call it Friends of Kabliji, which we pointed out would be meaningless to Canadians. In any case we had been attracted to Patwant's suggestion that his experiment was replicable and we joined to that a basic philosophy drawn from Gandhi's argument that village regeneration was the real foundation of India's regeneration, an idea long and fatally neglected by Indian politicians. We hoped the opportunities would come — and they quickly did — for us to extend our help beyond Patwant Singh's experiment. In fact Canada India Village Aid became such a factor in our lives that I shall inevitably be returning to it. But these developments were still in the future when we decided to go back to India in 1982.

Chapter 9

A RETURN TO INDIA

Among the people who joined Canada India Village Aid was the painter Toni Onley, whom I had known desultorily for a long time. Having watched us working at banquets and book sales to bring in money at a time when all charities were complaining of declining donations, Toni remarked: "It looks to me as if you're piddling away your time to earn a few dollars, George. Why don't you and I go to India together? I'll paint, you can write, we'll put a book together, and sell the paintings for CIVA into the bargain."

Inge and I agreed immediately, and Toni's wife Yukiko was game for the trip. We got out our maps and planned a trip with destinations that emphasized the great contrasts of India, that continent masquerading as a country. Starting from Delhi, our general base, we would proceed to the desert realms of Rajasthan, and then swing back to Agra and Fatehpur Sikri, the Mogul heartland. Tony Phillips and his friend Margo Palmer would accompany us thus far. The rest of us would fly southward via Bombay to Kerala, where I had once stayed long enough to write a book, and stand on the tip of India at Kanniyakumari. From Trivandrum we would then go northward over the Deccan to Orissa with its multitude of ancient temples in Bhubaneswar, Puri and Konarak. Continuing north through Calcutta, we would climb to Darjeeling with its Himalayan vistas and mountain way of life, and thence return to Delhi and so, via Burma, home. It was an itinerary that seemed to encompass the variety of India, its contrasts of terrain and climate, its contrasts also of culture that divided it like the walls of its ancient buildings, and would give the title to the book I would write at the end of it all, *Walls of India*. But first we would visit Kabliji, which had given us the reason for our trip.

★ ★ ★

87

Much of the trip was into areas new to Inge and me, despite our several previous Indian trips, but Delhi was familiar territory, and the moment we arrived we were immediately involved in that interplay of arrogant officiousness and private bluffing that so often entangles one in India. I was waiting near the luggage chute when Toni came hurrying over. Yukiko was travelling on a Japanese passport, not realizing she did not share the privilege of entering India without a visa that Canadians then had. As I went over to the immigration desk I realized that high-risk bluff was necessary, so I addressed the officer in a loud sahib voice and told him that we were the guests of Mr. Patwant Singh who was very well acquainted with Mrs. Indira Gandhi, and that if they did put Mrs. Onley on a departing plane some embarrassing questions might be asked. Did he want to be involved? I was banking on the fear of offending "high-ups" that I knew permeated the Indian public service even more than in the days of the Raj. The officer looked troubled and went to consult his boss. The boss came out and also looked troubled when I arrogantly repeated my message; he finally agreed to issue a two-day visa. We would have to negotiate any extension in his head office in Delhi. I am sure he thought he was calling my bluff while fending off the possibility of harm to himself. Fortunately Patwant did have the government contacts on which I had gambled and the matter was settled the next morning.

A welcoming party around the great central fireplace of Patwant's apartment, another in the Canadian High Commission, and we were on our journey, travelling by Ghamrog, where the Kabliji Hospital had been built, on a secondary way to Jaipur.

It was the kind of hopeless countryside Inge and I already knew from having wandered there in 1961 with Gandhian volunteers, and, like most things in India, it had got worse. The dusty soil, exhausted by three millennia of cultivation since the Aryans moved down from the mountains now grew stunted maize and sugar cane four feet high. The peasants' adobe houses were so near to literal mud huts that often we would be aware of a village only when we were about to enter it. When we reached the hospital, in its patch of salty, scrubby land, it had the same low-squatting look, the walls of its hexagonal buildings clad in fieldstone outside and whitewash within and roofed with lichened tiles from old British bungalows. Sitting on the beds in the wards, huddled under their grey-white cotton cloaks, the sick peasants were able to look out at eye level on fields like their own, where teams of oxen limped to and fro, dragging wooden plows like those used by Roman farmers two thousand years ago.

We stayed our first night on the road at Patwant's luxuriantly spartan grange and realized that the presence of the hospital had begun to transform the life of the countryside, at least in the villages from which the patients came. The squalor one sees normally in villages near the Jumna was partially mitigated. Open, fly-encrusted drains had been covered over, ancient infected wells had been relined. An energetic Sikh lady, Mehtab Singh, had lured women out of their purdah, and in a couple of big old granges deserted by absentee landlords, we heard the clatter of handmade looms and the lighter chatter of knitting machines. We halted in doorways decorated with ancient patterns of moulded plaster, and lifted our joined hands in *namaskar*, as we waited for the women in their bright red and yellow best saris to garland us with sacred marigolds and dot our brows with auspicious red powder, and offer us sweet chunks of *burfi*. Then they would invite us in to see the work that had changed their lives.

In the open courtyards hung with the bright dhurries woven there, we found women of all ages at work: teenage girls at the knitting machines, mature women at the looms, old women preparing yarn for dying and weaving. Within a few months of the looms appearing, the last vestiges of purdah had vanished in a quiet village revolution, and the women had begun to assume active roles in local life. The age of marriage had risen steadily, from fourteen or fifteen to nineteen or twenty, as young girls realized they now had earning powers. This meant an immediate dramatic fall in the local birthrate. Even the status of widows, traditional pariahs in Indian villages, had improved since the hospital began to employ them as aides and had given them a status in the community.

As we drove out of the compound at Kabliji, a cart drawn by white oxen with blue-painted horns was coming in: a man lay wrapped almost to his eyes in a dirt-grey cotton cloth, so that we could not tell his age, but the woman who squatted beside him on the jolting floor of the cart held the fold of her faded green sari over her face, leaving only her eyes visible; she was one of the old school. Whatever was wrong with the man — and the boy driving the cart shrugged when our driver asked him — he had a hope that would not have existed before Kabliji was built. Yet I took away a sense of unease. The hospital was run well and there was need for it. But I found something disturbingly patriarchal about its arrangements. The hierarchical style of a Western hospital, here accentuated by the presence of military doctors, did not accord with my Gandhian visions of popular involvement. I had not been reassured when I asked Patwant whether he was training paramedics, and he replied flippantly, "I don't want any of those fellows flapping their dirty dhoties around my place!" The possessiveness, the éliteness, disturbed me, and would influence my views when later on I encountered more popular and democratic models of medical activity in rural India.

We drove across the broad monotonous plain towards Jaipur, the capital of Rajasthan, in a couple of hired cars located by the driver of one of our friends in Delhi. They belonged to a stocky, sly Sikh named Surgit Singh, who had served in the army and knew some English. The cars were Ambassadors, a utilitarian but never comfortable Indian make. Surgit claimed they were new; we soon discovered they were not. Surgit himself drove one of the cars, and a tall silent Sikh called Ranjit drove the other; he spoke no English, and we communicated with signs and the odd bits of Hindi Inge and I had picked up on our travels. We solved the problem of three couples in two cars by alternating, so that in each car there would always be a couple and an odd person, couples riding together two times out of three.

In December the plain was almost colourless, the dun brown of a soil worked over by generations of cultivators, splashed here and there with the vivid squares of blossoming mustard. The trees were flowerless, sleeping their winter sleep; only the bougainvillaeas played at summer with their papery false blossoms, orange through crimson to purple.

The land off the road seemed traditional India; mud-walled villages and peasants plodding with oxen, little granaries of cane with conical roofs. But the road itself seemed to proclaim another culture, as top-heavy trucks painted gaudily with the emblems of Hindu gods pushed their great hulks through the diesel-permeated air to the sound of never-silent horns. The traffic had overwhelmed the quiet roadside villages we remembered on this road twenty years before. On the edge of each of them an agglomeration of makeshift shacks had grown up; traders' booths of worn and stained planks that looked like packing cases on stilts and were not much bigger; rough cane shelters posing as restaurants and surrounded by dozens of rope beds where truck drivers sat cross-legged, drinking tea and eating curry, or lay napping beside the noisy road; little repair shops surrounded by the debris of cannibalized cars and trucks, for India still has a make-use economy.

Gently, each side of the clamorous river of traffic, the country changed. There was no abrupt entry into Rajasthan; more than anything else, a steady drying of the land. Camels began to replace oxen, drawing painted carts, dragging ploughs, craning long necks to nibble twigs from the neem trees that sometimes turned the road into a shady avenue. Dormant rivers slashed the landscape with their arid trenches of shingle and sand. At some unnamed spot a small fort rose from a knoll, its structure as solid and expert-looking as any castle on the Rhine or Danube. We were at last in the abode of kings and warriors.

The land began to rise into ridges of low hills, as if it had been whipped into waves by some cosmic tempest. They were densely furred by a dwarf forest of small-leaved scrub. Probing their defiles, the road reached the real frontier of Rajput country at the little town of Āmer, where ruined walls clambered hundreds of feet up to steep infringing slopes. Beyond the conical towers of Āmer's temples a great yellow stone palace clung on the hillside and above it, topping the high ridge, a stark dark fortress looked back towards the plain we had crossed.

We went through Āmer and up the hill-ringed valley to Jaipur. Tiger Fort's dark and massive walls glowered over the city it was built to defend; on the next hill the castle-like Sun Temple, tutelary shrine of the ruling Kachhawa clan, sent its white spire glistening against the blue sky; its high yellow wall was painted with a great white swastika, symbol of the Sun cult of the Rajputs.

On the outskirts of red-walled Jaipur we found high-ceilinged rooms in the Rambagh Palace Hotel, which Inge and I had known twenty years before as the residence of the maharaja, a charming sporty man (he actually died of a heart attack during a polo game) who had entertained Inge and me to drinks on the lawn. It was an Edwardian rendering of traditional Rajput architecture — domes and airy pavilions, draughty corridors and park-like formal gardens. The traditional liveries of its servants reminded us of the old palace, and also a certain nonchalance due to the fact that the Rajputs are not servile by nature: their attitude may vary in manifestation from easy courtesy to an irritating casualness in meeting one's requests. At the Rambagh Palace the local celebrant, perhaps rightly, always seemed to have precedence over the alien visitor. It took me half an hour to get tea on the terrace when a group of Rajput women, as brilliant as parrots in their vivid skirts and shawls, occupied the waiter with endless requests. And on the night of a wedding party a drink was not to be had for two hours and we were forced to fall back on our own supplies as we stood on the lawn, in the light of flaming braziers, watching the queue of men in polyester suits climbing to the platform where the bride sat in her gold and scarlet mantle and the groom in his cloth-of-gold turban with diamond aigrette and received discreet envelopes of money. Patience and a due sense of the irrelevance of time were useful attributes for the traveller in Rajasthan, as they are in most of India.

In Jaipur Toni and I took our first passes at the prose and painting that would eventually appear in *Walls of India*. Downed the day after our arrival by troubled intestines, Toni staggered out in the sun's setting brilliance — astonishing me, not for the last time, by the toughness of his devotion to painting — to sketch in the palace gardens an atmospheric transmutation of the building's walls and domes and pinnacles, set in the lush greenery of a well-tended Indian garden. About the same time I began to note my recollections of our days in India in one of those fat, square books of ruled paper that one could still buy for a few rupees in the bazaar. These were mere beginnings — the tunings of the instruments — and it was in Amber the next day that our work really began, which was appropriate, for there we were touching the roots of tradition and history among the Rajputs.

By now the Jaipur we had known as a hardly transformed princely city had changed greatly, infected by the general Indian sickness of homogenization. There had been much unplanned building, and the streets were packed with cars, lumbering trucks, overcrowded buses. Sometimes a camel tried to maintain a disdainful contempt as he drew his cart through the traffic; sometimes, in a quieter street, a string of polo ponies trotted by, on exercise; sometimes, gigantic and formidable even among the modern traffic, a work elephant padded along through the faintly blue diesel haze, small eyes flicking from side to side with a look of incipient paranoia.

But camels, elephants, polo ponies, are vestiges of an almost vanished past. Only within the grounds of the City Palace does more than a flavour of the past remain, in the great rambling museum filled with limpidly coloured Rajput miniatures and elaborately damascened armour and all the Victorian junk that nineteenth-century Rajput rulers collected, and in striking structures like the Hawa Mahal and the Jantar Mantar. The Hawa Mahal — House of the Winds — was a tall structure of improbable narrowness, probably the most impressive false front in the world, built by Maharaja Sawai Jai Singh in 1799 because the ladies of his zenana complained of being excluded from all sight of the outside world. It was in fact a great honeycomb of latticed balconies with nothing behind them but the access stairs, the lattices all looking out on the main street of the bazaar. What from the street appeared a large rococo palace was no more than an airy façade blown through by the winds that gave its name.

The Hawa Mahal may seem like Indian Versailles; the Jantar Mantar is Indian Enlightenment, one of the five great observatories built in various parts of India by the astronomer prince Sawai Jai Singh in the 1720s. It has no relation to the traditions of Moslem or Hindu architecture, but consists of projections in gigantic masonry of scientific calculations about the nature of the heavens. Though they obviously make great use of Hindu mathematics (a noble, largely unrecognized tradition), they remind one less of modern European astronomical equipment than of the great stone instruments for observing the movements of the sun and planets that were constructed by the European megalith builders in distant prehistoric times. The biggest is a sundial whose gnomon is a masonry triangle ninety-eight feet high, creating a shadow that moves thirteen feet an hour. There are great ramps and stone circles and marble bowls chased with signs and symbols, each with its specific function in measuring the position of the stars, calculating eclipses, and so on. They are still used by Brahmin astrologers, but the impact of the Jantar Mantar on strangers seeing it for the first time is powerfully aesthetic; the assembly of massive geometric shapes looks like nothing so much as a Chirico painting put into three dimensions. Only the black-faced monkeys leaping the steps of the gnomon and the tall-crested hoopoes probing with long peaks into the lawns around the glistening bowls seemed to relate its frozen abstractions to the world of the living. For a Rajput prince, even the abstractions of the heavenly science came to be expressed in majestic and strangely shaped walls.

On the way from Jaipur, which Sawai Jai Singh built to replace the old capital of Āmer, not only were the hills capped by forts and temples, but the valley was dotted by little temples, pavilions, even small palaces in the light and elegant high Rajput style.

At Gaitor, in walled gardens among mango trees whose first modest but splendidly scented blossoms were beginning to open, stood the cenotaphs of the Jaipur princes. These were not tombs. The bodies had been burned and the ashes scattered in the Ganges, but something must remain to commemorate departed splendour, and so the Rajputs had traditionally built these elegant memorial pavilions. Sawai Jai Singh was remembered in a structure of white marble: delicately carved fences enclosing a rococo chhatri, a dome suspended on air and four slender pillars.

For relaxation in the hot months during the great task of building

Jaipur, Sawai Jah Singh built just south of Gaitor a Jal Mahal or Water Palace. Visiting it in 1961, it had struck a romantic chord in me, and I wrote in *Faces of India* that "among the reedbeds beside a lake like a flat disc of turquoise rose a deserted structure as frail as a vanishing fairy structure of Tennysonian legend. . . ." Now, in 1982, I saw the Jal Mahal again, but the turquoise water that had once reflected it was no longer visible. The palace seemed to stand up — and looked solid rather than frail because it had no reflection — out of a vast field of coarse green foliage. Only when I saw the heads of buffalo surfacing between the leaves did I realize that the lake had been choked in twenty years by a fast-growing plague of water hyacinth.

But the magic of art is strange and devious. We left Toni with his painting kit beside a small and still unchoked pool inhabited by white and stilt-legged spoonbills. That evening he showed me the painting he had done there. At this time he had not read *Faces of India*, but by some intuition he had recognized the origin and function of the structure he was painting, had ignored the vegetation, and had produced the image I had seen long ago, "a deserted structure as frail and romantic as a vanishing fairy castle of Tennysonian legend. . . ."

Coming to Āmer, as we saw the great golden structure of the palace reflected in its lake, Toni settled down under the shoreline tamarinds to paint. He had a wooden box of his own design that served in combination as paintbox, container for paper and finished paintings, palette and knee-held easel; a glass of clear water was all he needed to set up in the desert or anywhere else. The rest of us went up the zigzag road to the palace. The first time Inge and I visited Āmer, the way up was by foot or lurching on elephant back. Now the road was open to cars, but not many used it, and the elephants were still there, wearing elaborate silver brow ornaments, their cannonball turds steaming from under their tufty tails. "Elephant ride," noted the local guidebook I had bought in a Jaipur bazaar, "is a Royal experience and a good enjoyment."

When we reached the square before the palace and climbed the broad, familiar stairs from terrace to terrace, wandering under latticed gateways into the empty halls, I found myself making comparisons with our previous visit in terms of decaying splendour. The miniatures on the walls were more faded, the mirror work more blurred than I remembered it; down by the sinister old gate where, long ago, the princesses went out to burn on their husbands' pyres, the pathetic marks of their hennaed hands, still visible when we first came to Āmer, had been painted out by

94

someone who did not want the world to be reminded of the more savage aspects of the Rajput past.

I looked through the windowed turrets. There was an elegant little water palace beside the lake, with star-shaped flower beds now choked with grass and moss instead of being filled by the pinks and roses that the Rajputs loved. Out across the lake I could see Toni painting with concentration in a circle of curious cows, and from another turret I looked down on the narrow, muddy lanes of Āmer, the spires of the temples, the minarets of the mosque Akbar had built there in his effort to bring all religions into that simple unity of which he believed each was an aspect. The walls ran in every direction up the hills. The forts and watchtowers glowered, even in the noon sunlight. For all his alliance with Akbar, Man Singh of Āmer was not a man to take chances. Like all the Rajput princes he saw his security and independence in terms of walls, the higher and thicker the better.

The princes and princesses, courtiers and commanders had long gone, and the palace's most notable inhabitants were now a tribe of large, grey langur monkeys, playing over the roofs and from the walls critically watching the visitors, many of whom were simple village people. Some of the women made their way to the little silver-doored temple of the goddess Kali that stands in a corner of the main courtyard. Like other malign deities, Kali has power over childbirth, and the women queued to ring the bell before the sanctuary and put money in the silver chest that stood beside it. A priest, his brow painted with the trident sign of Siva, gave each a garland of marigolds and a *prasad*, a blessed gift consisting of a little cardboard box tied with ribbons and containing consecrated sweetmeats. The monkeys, themselves sacred, lurked outside the temple, cadging food from the people who came out and watching for anything they could snatch. One young women, large-eyed and innocent, they marked as their prey; three of them attacked her at once, seizing in their strong hands her purse, her wreath, her holy sweets. The purse was torn open and its pathetic contents thrown over the pavement; the floral wreath and the sweets immediately eaten. The woman wept. She had paid ten rupees for her holy gift, and the fact that the sacred monkeys stole it must have appeared a dreadful omen; the child she had hoped for would not be born. But nobody attempted to chastise or chase away the monkeys, for they, after all, were the people of Hanuman, the monkey king who in the far and legendary past had led his simian legions to the assistance of Rama, the forefather of the Rajputs.

Chapter 10

CITIES OF THE DESERT

The harsh clamour of another sacred creature, the peacock, calling in the gardens of the Rambagh Palace, woke me on the morning we left Jaipur for the cities of the desert. The Thar Desert encompasses northwestern Rajasthan, and the journey to Bikaner, our first destination, was a progression into barrenness. Surgit Singh put his hands together before his little medallion of Guru Nanak and silently prayed before he started the car and we drove out of the hotel grounds. He had made loud Sikh boasts about having driven the whole of north India, but it was soon evident that he had never been beyond Jaipur, and to him the Thar Desert was *terra incognita*, a place of marvels and monsters.

Twenty miles beyond Jaipur the phrase "crowded India" already seemed an insupportable cliché. In the two hundred miles between Jaipur and Bikaner we passed only two modest communities, Sikar and Ratangarh, and the country was so little peopled that where roadwork was going on, the men and women who chipped the stones and placed them by hand lived in improvised encampments of ragged canvas tents and shelters made of reed mats. These people were far on the far side of the poverty wall, earning at most a dollar a day.

Around Jaipur there was still enough scrubby vegetation to give habitat to a surprising number of brilliant birds — parakeets and barbets and rollers. But soon the only trees were a kind of tamarind whose gnarled and angular branches resembled those of olives. The camels browsed their twigs, and in the hamlets of mud houses the dust patches that passed for fields were fenced by long piles of thorny boughs.

This was the real camel country; loads were carried on the animals' backs rather than in carts, and red-turbanned men rode them at a sharp trot. The camels' presence had its own subtle effect on one's perception of the landscape, for as the country became more arid and open, their tracks going off towards the horizon, where sky and sand seemed to blend in a turquoise haze, gave a haunting sense of unbounded distance.

When it finally surrounded us without a tree in sight, the desert became a pale tan colour, suffused by the dull green, almost grey, of the low broom and dwarf thorn bushes and milkweed, whose stems Surgit warned us against picking, since their sticky juice could blind us if it touched the eye. It was a hostile landscape, yet it supported life. Once, in the most desolate part, we encountered three boy shepherds, with a dozen black and white goats, a hundred sheep or so and a pack donkey to carry their provender on the great circuits they made to find the green shoots to feed their flock. They rambled for many miles, but always in circles that narrowed down to their village. They were wandering shepherds, not true nomads.

Bikaner was not one of those grandly spectacular Rajput places standing at lordly height above the desert plain. We slid almost surreptitiously into the city between great army camps, with Russian cannon and tanks hidden beneath camouflage nets among the dunes.

In Rajasthan one travels from princely home to princely home, and in Bikaner we stayed in the Lalgarh Palace, built by the Maharaja Sir Gangar Singh who organized the famous Camel Corps which he led to fight beside the British in the Boxer Rebellion and against the Mad Mullah in Somaliland. The classic Rajput style of the eighteenth century had been followed by craftsmen who still worked in the tradition. Wherever one wandered, there were beautifully intricate stone lattices, elegant turrets at the turning of walls, gay little chhatris over the gateways. Not that one could wander unimpeded; when Inge and I went beyond an invisible line on a dried-up lawn, a figure in a ragged khaki greatcoat leapt up from a charpoy to wave an ancient firearm and point to a sign which read *Voie Privée*. Beyond this notice, with its suggestions of nostalgia for lost days of princely frivolity in Europe, the present maharaja lived, theoretically deprived of his princely role but holding his place in the hearts of good Rajputs, those martial men with jutting moustaches and the names of lions who regard the present rulers of India with resentment and largely deserved contempt.

In the Rambagh Palace we had encountered a valiant attempt to reconcile Hilton-style hotelmanship with the ambience of the Arabian Nights. In the chambers of the Lalgarh Palace there were no such pretensions; instead we endured the slow death of the Edwardian Raj. Our rooms were scattered along dim and lofty corridors through which bats flew twittering after nightfall. Immense padlocks had to be removed from the doors before we could enter them. Within were marble floors and great mahogany fireplaces, brass-steaded beds, rickety walnut furniture, and pale Victorian watercolours hanging on the damp-mottled paper where geckos clung and talked in clicks. Inge and I complained because we had no wardrobe in our room, and so the rustic boy who acted as a bearer brought a second stag-horn coat stand. But we had two bathrooms, equally useless, for in one the antique tangle of pipes and taps, like a bizarre bird's nest, had long ceased to work and rust had eaten in great wounds through the enamel on the bath, while in the other the new wash basin and toilet had been installed by some desert plumber so enamoured of the drip of water that he had neglected to seal the joints and we padded around in a perpetual shallow pool.

It all belonged to a far shabbier and less creative age than the bloodier times when Bikaner, whose rulers also became generals for the Moguls, flourished under Rai Singh and his successors. This became evident when we compared the apology for a museum in the Lalgarh Palace with the splendour — diminished as it was — of the vast old Junagarh Fort in the heart of the city. The later maharajas showed themselves true sons of the camera age, for the Lalgarh Palace museum was little more than a vast family album hung on the stone pages of the walls. The princes, past and present, placed booted feet on the heads of Bengal tigers, stood on the mounded backs of downed elephants, posed beside hills of slaughtered sand grouse, usually with friends of the ruling race: Curzon or a lesser viceroy, or that perpetual jaded boy, Edward, Prince of Wales. Morally there isn't much difference between basing one's prestige on the slaughter of many men and basing it on the slaughter of many animals. Nevertheless, these scenes of bloody vanity had a peculiar shoddiness that made one realize how far the Pax Britannica had diminished the fierce warrior rulers. I was so depressed by these photographs of aristocratic holocausts of beasts and birds that I could not bring myself to use the letter of introduction that would have taken us along the Voie Privée to the former ruler's part of the palace. That was perhaps unfortunate, for Bikaner had the repute of being a capable and cultured man.

The real heart of Bikaner's history is the Junagarh Fort which still stands in the middle of the city, its red walls blackened with the lichen of centuries. Rai Singh built the thousand-metre circuit of its walls in the later seventeenth century, and it served as the heart of resistance from which the horsemen and camel men of Karn Singh rode out in the next century to attack and defeat, among the dunes and bitter wells of the desert, the army which the fanatical Mogul emperor Aurangzeb had sent in a futile attempt to change the relationship of the Hindu princes from the kind of partnership Akbar developed to a subordination aimed at the total victory of Islam in India.

Some of its original rocky grimness still clings to Junagarh. As we circled the walls and entered the Sun Gate, we saw there on the side wall the signs of the *sati* victims, made clear and permanent, as they had not been in Amber, by the stone being cut away around the vermilion handmarks to throw them into cruel relief; no one in this desert city off the tourist circuit had tried to paint or plaster them over. Through that archway of death, one entered the ghost of a garden, the lawns gone to dust, and in the orchards only stubborn figs surviving. The last reigning maharaja had turned over Junagarh to the people of Bikaner so that it would not fall into the imperial hands of those who ruled in Delhi. A wisdom that had developed between the prince and people determined that the gardens, which differed very little in style or form from those of other Rajput princes or of the Mogul overlords themselves, might be left to time and nature, while the ingenuities of human craft, which some- times ascended into art, should be preserved.

For within the dark ramparts of Junagarh there were not only barracks and gardens, but also a whole succession of palaces, built and embellished by ruler after ruler, from founder Rai Singh down to that nineteenth-century successor who ordered that murals be painted to celebrate the arrival of modern inventions in his desert remoteness. On one high wall in the heart of the fort, a naïvely painted locomotive drawing wagons filled with turbanned court dignitaries, top-hatted white men and bon-neted memsahibs commemorates the arrival of the railway in Bikaner.

The linked series of airily balconied, turreted, domed structures within the formidable enclosure of Junagarh Fort — Moon Palace and Flower Palace and Glass Palace — celebrated the erotic element in the love-and-death complex of emotion and imagery which the Rajputs, reaching tangentially into the great curve of Indo-European culture, shared with hero-obsessed Homer and with the medieval European troubadours trapped in their dreams of knights without fear or reproach serving their ineffable *princesses lointaines*.

Everywhere in the palaces within the grim fort of desert Bikaner one sensed this union of Eros and Thanatos; women who would go, from a sense of religious and amorous devotion, to the funeral pyres; men who would don the saffron robe of renunciation and eat copiously of opium when pride and the needs of battle led them towards virtual suicide: together in these elegant chambers, contriving and proclaiming on their coloured walls the life of erotic gaiety, of emotional intensity, that is embodied in the legends of the Lord Krishna and his many loves which so delighted the Rajput princes and their painters — the Lord Krishna whose jewelled swing swayed in replica in the topmost room of Junagarh Fort, the room to which the rulers and their consorts would retire for their lofty consummations.

★ ★ ★

The desert shifts from sand to stone and back to sand, windswept dunes with a haze in the air from the blown dust. The vegetation becomes a tussocky herbage, rather like sagebrush, that barely holds the sand, and the edges of the road are blurred by drifting dunes. The colour of the dunes shades off from yellow to mauve and rose and back to yellow. We are now almost three hundred miles beyond Bikaner. At the end of a long, slow day of driving, our eyes are sore from the sun, our tongues grated by the dust. The Ambassador, its age beginning to show, bucks and rattles on the narrow road military convoys have chewed up, and with difficulty I scatter words on my pad, a mad shorthand I hope I shall interpret for my journal at the end of the day. Toni, sitting beside me, is unable to sketch and soaks in the colour and light with his eyes so that he can trap it all in paint once the endless fidgeting motion stops.

The desert continues, sand and stone and sand, broken by small sights that in the monotony take on the shining self-sufficiency of surrealist images. The picked-over skeleton of a bullock by the roadside, white kites prizing off the last morsels. A gazelle buck staring at the car from fifteen feet away, then doing a leaping turn to bound away over the desert. A herd of camels — perhaps a hundred — guarded by two small boys as they crop the wretched scrub. A frieze-like procession of women, red clay pots balanced on their heads, walking over the sand to a village whose round storage huts look like Basuto kraals and whose little cubical houses with smoothed mud walls could have been lifted from anywhere in the Sahara. The women's shawls and wide skirts are bright red, orange, and yellow — the colours of survival in the desert; they wear heavy silver anklets above their bare feet and tiers of ivory bracelets on their upper arms. Around the village, bits of roughly tilled ground, too ragged for fields, are being watered laboriously by men in immense red turbans from wells where oxen draw up great leather buckets; they seem to grow nothing but millet, the crop of a rainless land. No rain has fallen, a shepherd told us along the road, for four years.

It all seems as if it will never end. There are moments of doubt when the road shimmers into watery mirage and a man on a riding camel grows into a wandering giant and we wonder whether we are on the right road. But there is only one road across the Thar Desert, and eventually we top a small rise, and suddenly, perhaps four miles away in the midst of the flatness, see the great flat-topped outcrop on which the city of Jaisalmer grows like some vast mollusc of golden stone moulded impregnably to the rock, the spires of its nine Jain temples gleaming against the hard enamel blue of the sky.

We let out a thirsty cry, just as the camel men must have done during the long centuries when the great caravans trod their way from Persia through Baluchistan and Sind and eastward to the Great Mogul's cities of Delhi and Agra. Surgit pulls his Sikh beard, gives a thankful salaam to Guru Nanak, and puts his foot on the gas to speed down the long hill and land us at the spartan little guest house under the city walls, where we wet our whistles with tall bottles of Golden Eagle beer before entering the city.

★   ★   ★

Jaisalmer is India's ultima Thule, the last city of the northwest, about sixty miles from where the dunes merge without a break into Pakistan. Its remoteness has kept it less thronged than most Indian cities in the 1980s, and its lack of water has meant that there are few new buildings, and almost all of those outside the great city wall around which the traffic circulates without entering. The streets inside the gates are mostly too narrow, and on the upper parts of the rock too steep, to be more than walkways; in Jaisalmer, as in Venice, the sound of footsteps is always in one's ears because it has no rivals.

It was Arthur Erickson who first urged me to go to Jaisalmer; he had never before been in a city, he said, more magically "all of a piece." All of a piece it certainly was, for the whole city had been built of the same golden stone as the walls. On the outside it formed the massive blocks of the ninety-nine towers, in whose crenellations were poised global boulders of the same stone, to be tipped down on the heads of besiegers.

On the inside, the stone was carved into the geometries that covered the floating balconies of the havelis with screens which looked like rigid lace. In every street the stone-carvers had been at work, making the kind of airy, shady houses needed for the heat of the desert, and at the same time creating whole streets of architectural gems that were not deserted monuments but places where the Rajput people still lived.

The princes, as elsewhere, had gone. But the feel of the princely past was still strong; in the temples filled with hundreds of rigid Jain images where priests in orange robes appeared out of the incense-smelling shadows to direct one to the nearest money-chest of brassbound teak; in the bazaars of little smoky shops where spices and dyes were laid out in bright pyramids, and silversmiths sat weighing the heavy peasant jewelry which they sold by the gram, by weight rather than artistry, which was taken for granted; most of all, in the square high up in the citadel, the façade of the palace — covered with balconies like rococo swallows' nests — on one side and on the other a kind of Greek theatre of tiered stone benches from which the maharawal held durbars sitting on the marble throne that remained at top level. The evening we discovered the square, an old man sat on the throne drawing elfin music from a strange thin-toned rectangular fiddle, and on the lower benches other men played a kind of primitive chess, while little girls ran screaming in front of the palace dragging into the sky square kites decorated with bold patterns like Kandinsky paintings.

As in most of India, it was the women in Jaisalmer who seemed to sustain their traditions most faithfully. A girl in a doorway of filigreed stone, in her brilliant mirror-inset skirt, with a gold-edged mantle drawn partly over her head, looked exactly like a princess waiting for her lover in one of the exquisite miniatures that used to be painted in the courts of Rajput cities like Jaisalmer. Some of the old men also kept to past ways; one walked beside me in a gold brocade coat and white jodhpurs, and told me his son was a professor of agriculture in an Ontario college. But most of them — especially the men we bargained with in upper rooms over silver jewels and camel-bone bracelets called ivory — compromised shabbily between past and present, wearing old suit coats with muslin dhoties and white Gandhi caps instead of big, bright Rajput turbans.

Only the children in Jaisalmer had slipped entirely into the modern age. They clustered excitedly around us, anxious to touch, to hold our hands, not begging for money, but shouting, "One pen! One bonbon!"

They were being prepared for the future when the planned airport would be open and the big new hotel would be built on the site already marked for it. A boy greeted me in German. *"Guten Morgen, mein Herr!"* A girl excitedly whispered a warning in French to Inge to have nothing to do with the two boys who spoke such smooth English. These boys told us that in high school they were being taught tourism as a subject, and offered themselves as guides for the sake of practice. We accepted; they were informed and resourceful and refused payment beyond a treat of Qwality ice cream and a couple of Bic pens.

While the rest of us explored the narrow lanes, clambered on to the high walls and bargained in little holes of shops, Toni was busily painting within and outside the walls. It was fascinating to see at this stage of our journey his experiencing self struggling with his remembering self — the painter of newly discovered Indian life emerging from the painter of cold northern lights and shadows. It was obviously not an easy transition, and at one point towards the end of our days in Jaisalmer, he could endure no longer the relentless azure of those vast and empty desert skies. So he painted in a broad swatch of heavy gunmetal cloud hanging like a doom over the yellow towers of the city. The next morning, in that town where it had not rained for years, we woke to the smell of dampened dust as a shower licked over and vanished into the desert. Driving south from Jaisalmer that morning, into the quickly breaking sunlight, we wondered aloud at this startling vindication of Oscar Wilde's dictum that nature imitates art.

Bikaner and Jaisalmer represent one extreme of Rajasthan, the arid heart of the Thar Desert. East and south lie the chains of the Aravalli Mountains, and beyond them the lake-dotted foothills of Mewar, the realm of the Sisodias, whose maharana is the highest ranked of all the Rajputs.

It is about four hundred miles from Jaisalmer to Udaipur, the capital of Mewar, which would take a day driving comfortably on Canadian highways. In Rajasthan it took us two exhausting days, the first by desert roads to Jodhpur, and the second by a tortuous route through the defiles of the Aravallis from Jodhpur to Udaipur.

My Rajasthan guidebook described the road to Jodhpur as "a miracle of modern engineering." In fact it was a deteriorated track which gangs of women dressed in broad crimson skirts were repairing. It was steadily shaking to pieces Surgit Singh's two old Ambassadors, and at one point, in the car where Inge and I were travelling with Tony Phillips, we heard a terrible clanking up front of the steering wheel. The radiator had broken away and the fan was beating against it. "No problem!" said Ranjit, using his one English phrase as he tore the tail off his shirt and tried to tie the radiator back in place. In half an hour it broke adrift again; this time Tony and Ranjit searched around, found a flat stone and a bit of old blown tire lying by the road, and managed to wedge the radiator upright. Stopping every now and then to adjust this precarious contrivance, we limped our way through stretches of cactus desert, areas of outcropping rock where everything — from houses to fences — was made of red stone, and plateaus of parched grassland grazed by immense flocks of sheep. Finally, we breasted a last hill and looked down from its crest on the green and tree-shaded oasis where the town of Jodhpur lies, white and rather Moorish, dotted with sugar-loaf pinnacles like those of Le Puy but crowned with white temples instead of churches, and dominated by Mehrenangahr Fort, the tallest, darkest and grimmest castle in all Rajasthan, standing on its own bare rock above the lower town, lofty and more compact than Jaisalmer, and in awkward isolation from the life surrounding it.

Even the rulers of Jodhpur eventually became depressed by the grim gloom of their fort, and created the most extraordinary of recent Rajput follies, the Umaid Bhavan Palace which Maharaja Umaid Singh built on a hillside that looks across a deep valley towards the old fort. It was started in 1928, and Umaid Singh did not rely on local craftsmen, working in their traditional forms. Instead, he hired Sir H.C. Lawrence, then president of the Royal Institute of British Architects, who designed him a grandiose structure of local marble and red sandstone; the few Rajput motifs were dwarfed by the immense neoclassical dome which a German visitor remarked to me should be called St.-Peter-and-St. Paul, in allusion to the great cathedral domes of Rome and London, and also, ironically, to the great prison-fortress of St. Petersburg. The palace was completed in 1943, and survived the débâcle of the extravagant world of Indian princedom by becoming yet another in the circuit of literally palatial Rajasthan hotels.

Shortly after our arrival, a young man came tapping at our door. He was one of the secretaries of the maharaja, who still occupied a wing of his palace. He had heard of our coming, and invited us to take cocktails with him and the maharani. We gathered at the appropriate time under the echoing dome with the other guest, a braying Oxford don, and were shepherded into the princely apartment, making our way through corridors of playing children to the parlour where Jodhpur awaited us. A tall man, dressed at casual expense in the Western way, he had the kind of handsomeness one associates with popular Indian film stars and the prominent dark eyes I had already noticed in portraits of his ancestors on the walls of our room. A little later the maharani flitted in; with her manner of ethereal distress, and her traditional garb of mirrored skirt with a mantle of fine lilac and gold-threaded lace over her head, she looked as if she had stepped out of an early eighteenth-century miniature, so conservative is women's dress in Rajasthan.

The Scotch was excellent, the curried snacks piquant, and the conversation alert and interesting. Toni was encouraged to fetch his paintings, which our hosts discussed perceptively. They were pleased of course to recognize their own fortress, but they also talked of colour and light in a way that befitted the descendants of those who employed the great Rajput miniaturists, and the maharani called her children so that Toni could talk about his craft.

The maharaja recalled his days at Oxford for the benefit of the visiting don, and then, when we told him of the hospital at Kabliji, he began to talk in a way which showed how strangely the unofficial viewpoints had come together in modern India. He talked of his concern for the villagers of his former principality. Inevitably, the former princes are local in their sympathies, attached to their former subjects by personal loyalties and by the sense of noble obligation that in the last decades of the native states made many of their rulers turn into benevolent despots. He had established a trust to keep as much of his wealth as possible out of the hands of the central government, and now he was planning to use it for his villagers, the people who were once his subjects, and who have been ignored by distant governments, whether in Delhi or even Jaipur.

Talking of the villages led us to talking of Gandhi, and I was surprised to hear this former prince denounce the hypocrisy with which the Congress leaders paid nominal homage to Gandhi's fame but in fact pursued policies that in every way contradicted his teachings. Jodhpur seemed to admire Gandhi as a kind of hero, even though he did not fight with the swords and arrows the Rajputs themselves had used, and at the same time he found nothing heroic about the contemporary Congress wallah with his cap and his corruption. But he also recognized that Gandhi's most important message for independent India was that it would never flourish unless it began to regenerate its villages. He promised to get in touch with us and tell us about his schemes; he never did.

Jodhpur was the end of the real desert in Rajasthan. To reach Udaipur
we travelled south on backroads through a rustic countryside still
uncorrupted by the great trunk roads and full of strange and interesting
places that up to now had largely evaded the homogenization and
industrialization that passes for progress in modern India.

In the small town of Pali, hundreds of potters were making enormous
earthenware vessels with beautiful geometric slip patterns; they built
them up coil by coil and beat them smooth and thin with a little wooden
paddle. Despite their elegance, these were entirely utilitarian vessels used
for storage, and we saw many of them standing outside huts in the villages.
Here we saw the first running river since the Jumna at Delhi, a feeble
stream between great gravel banks coloured bright crimson and azure
and emerald by the cloths which the dyers had spread to dry, and which
would be made up into the vivid skirts the Rajput women wore. At Rani
a large deserted fortress, an outpost of the lords of Jodhpur, enclosed the
top of the hill. One tiny town whose name I never learnt was a religious
centre with no fewer than five temples and several hostels for pilgrims,
yet here the road degenerated into a muddy lane that would be impossible in the monsoon when the river we had to ford became a torrent.

A little farther on, we entered a haunting landscape, shimmering under
the noon sun, of small hills whose bare rockfaces had been smoothly
worn as if glaciers had ground them down. They reminded one of giant
reclining elephants, for the rock had a grey pachydermatous look. In a
village hidden among them a large and elaborate temple had recently
been whitewashed into a Brobdingnagian wedding cake. In another
village we stopped at a dak bungalow, thinking we might get a pot of tea
brewed. But only an ancient man in dhoti and shawl, grey with dirt,
shambled from a shack inside the gate as we walked through the
dried-out garden, and opened creaking doors onto the decrepitude
within; ragged rat-chewed mats on the dust-grey floor, worn-out rope
beds with shreds of rotting mosquito nets hanging above them, chairs so
obviously tottering apart that one hesitated to touch, let alone sit upon
them. Whether it was ever used now, and by whom, we could not
imagine. The old man looked at us as if we were ghosts, dream figures
from some vanished past of itinerant collectors and district magistrates,
but hurried to receive his baksheesh for carrying buckets of water to
flush the hole-in-the-ground latrines.

Eventually, the first slopes of the Aravallis rose up, hog-backed and
covered with low, thin, bosky forest. The narrow, twisted road clung on

the valley sides above the riverbeds where no water ran in this season, but enough moisture remained to feed the tiny polygonal fields of paddy and dry rice. Out of these tortuous defiles, where the road rarely ran straight for more than a hundred yards and the sun was visible intermittently because of the shading cliffs, we ran eventually into a foothill region; here, after the wintry fields, we rejoiced in small farms brilliant with spring grain; the women working there were tall and handsome and covered their arms with wide silver bracelets. We descended into an area of lakes populated by herons and cormorants, surrounded by walled green gardens and hilltops outlined by forts and watchtowers. We were entering the old realm of Mewar and crested a final low hill where a fortified gate guarded the pass with a notice announcing its elevation at 776 metres. A landscape of misty valleys surrounded by pointed lyrical hills out of Chinese paintings lay before us, and through it we drove into Udaipur.

Compared with Jaipur or even Jodhpur, Udaipur is a sedate city with many gardens, gentle traffic, aristocratic buildings turned to democratic uses as part of a decentralized university. In Indian terms, it is a recent city, founded only in the sixteenth century, when Maharana Udai Singh retreated to the hills after the capture of his great fortress of Chitor, the original capital of Mewar, by Akbar's forces. Beside the lake of Pichola, which the tribal peoples of the hill country had already created by building a great earthen dam, Udai Singh began in 1568 to build the city that bears his name.

Despite its newness, the city of Udaipur has an irregularity of planning quite unlike the quadrilateral arrangements of Sawai Jai Singh's Jaipur, and we found our way by devious and difficult routes to the great City Palace on the lakeshore, through whose gardens we reached the Bhansi Ghat, where we boarded the launch for the Lake Palace, the last of our series of princely Rajput hotels.

Among its many processes, travel involves the constant revision of images, and especially of the images emerging from that other process of illusory verisimilitude, photography. The Lake Palace Hotel is one of the most familiar images of India outside that country; it appears in newspapers, in advertisement brochures, in the windows of travel agencies; the vision of a white and sparkling fairy palace set in the heart of a blue romantic lake. But the water through which we chugged in the old wooden launch from Bhansi Ghat towards the island palace was no more blue than the Danube, though it was green rather than brown, the green of a murky pea soup in which floating turds took the place of croutons. It stank, with the malignant sourness of the worst canal ends in Venice. I was not surprised when, later on, a waiter pointedly assured me that the freshwater fish he was serving were from another lake. As for the palace, it had grown grey from the weathering monsoons, and the stone steps onto which we leapt, with Proustian memories of Venetian palazzi communicating from our footsoles to our brains, had the cracked, worn feel of outlived splendour, like the great state barge of the maharanas that was moored beside the palace quay, a freshwater galleon whose gilded carvings were slowly rotting with neglect.

There still remained the advantages Persian culture had transmitted through the Moguls to the Rajput princes who built in the seventeenth and eighteenth centuries. The courtyards were shady and airy, arranged for cross-draughts; we walked on winding paths through a charming water garden; our rooms, thanks to our travel agent being a Rajput princeling, had the best views of the lake.

We arrived the day before Christmas; the hotel was crowded, but not with the foreigners who would have been dominant a few years earlier. Most of the guests were members of India's *très nouveau riche*, the people who in recent years have emerged as a modern middle class, less bound by traditional inhibitions than the earlier moneyed class of hereditary merchants and money-lenders, and anxious to assume, by imitating Western ways, the role which Mulk Raj Anand once defined to me as that of "the brown sahibs." Most of them were Hindus, gathering without any sense of anomaly to celebrate a Christian festival which had been the great holiday of the Raj, the men in polyester suits with no hint of native garb, and the women in gaudy saris and so laden with gems that I was often reminded of Oscar Wilde's marvellous title for an uncompleted play, "The Woman Covered with Jewels." They revelled, as we did, in the ropes of lights that had been woven through the vines in the courtyards, so that everyone sat in the water garden drinking execrable Indian gin with even worse tonic water, yet enjoying the magical combination of the flickering turquoise and roseate light, the musky smell on the air that hovered between jasmine and frangipani, and the intricate aural patterns of a sitar played in a room off the courtyard.

The buildings of Udaipur had little interesting except their bulk; the City Palace stretched for nearly half a mile along the lake with a brutality of mass and outline that seemed to express the warlike history of Mewar. Yet the atmospherics were extraordinary, and the Lake Palace, set in the water between the City Palace on the eastern shore and the bosky pointed hills receding to the hazy Aravallis to the west, was the best place to observe them, so that Toni hardly moved off the island and did more painting here than in any other spot in India. All of us were happy to be back in a setting of mountains and woodlands and water of the kind in which we usually live, and though our surroundings of Udaipur looked a great deal different from those of Vancouver, they had all the elements we missed in the desert, and most of all the magical light filtering through the moist air above the lake. The nightfalls and dawns were especially splendid. At evening a peach-coloured glow would irradiate the whole sky, turn the ochre-coloured walls of the City Palace into a golden orange, and magnify the mountains as they darkened and turned flat against the sunset. At dawn the palace would appear as a splendidly malevolent black silhouette, all its imperfections darkened out, against a light-filled roseate eastern sky in which Homer's goddess seemed to have dabbled her fingers. The lake fascinated us and held us and even when we took the launch to the shore it was usually to wander along the gardens on its banks and watch the women washing their clothes and the fishermen casting their nets in the murky polluted water which provided such evocative mists and such extraordinary Venetian reflections. Turner would have thrived in Udaipur.

We left the city on Boxing Day, driving north towards Agra and Delhi, on one of those cool, limpid winter mornings when India, for all its worn antiquity, shines in the low early sunlight like the most pristine country on earth. The hillsides were wide and open and scantily peopled. The lantana bushes bloomed in rich orange for miles by the roadside. The sugar cane was thin and ragged in the fields, and the cormorants stretched their wings in mimic crucifixion beside the shallow lakes. The men were muffled to the eyes in thick shawls; the women, striding erect under their water-pots, wore heavy silver anklets between the hems of their mirrored skirts and their calloused bare feet. An old gentleman walked out on his morning business with a carved stick in one hand and a brass lotah for ablution in the other. Pack camels padded the road with great bundles of straw or reeds jutting on each side of them.

An hour or so out of Udaipur, near the village of Kankroli, we began to see women in bright orange mantles, glittering with stars of silver or gold thread, hurrying along the road. In a little while we were held up by white-clad marshals with red flags and whistles; a procession was about to start off. There was no band, no singers; the marchers walked silently and with pride under their banners: first the schoolchildren, all neatly dressed European-style in shirts and shorts, blouses and skirts; then the women in their bright garb, some carrying babies; finally, the men and the older boys.

"Jaini peoples," commented Surgit Singh, who could read the banners, and indeed, immediately we had passed this procession of lay people, we encountered the real Jain pilgrims, the renunciates clad entirely in spotless white, with white face-masks covering their mouths and nostrils to prevent destroying minute organisms by breathing them in, and bundles wrapped in white cloths balanced on their heads. "So many ladies, some old men," said Surgit with his soft giggle that implied superiority to all people who were not Sikhs. There were, indeed, only three or four old men, but they were the most devout pilgrims of all; they carried little besoms and gently swept the road before their feet so that they would not step on any worms or insects.

We thought it strange that in leaving Rajasthan, the land of warrior kings, the last people we see should be these men and women of peace and — more than ordinary peace — of the total unharmfulness of living that was preached by Mahavira, the great contemporary and rival of Buddha, the founder of the Jain religion and one of Gandhi's most important philosophic ancestors. The dry land through which they were walking glistened with mica as if it had been strewn with diamonds.

Chapter 11

THE TEMPLES OF ORISSA

In this book I am dealing with new experience: the later years of my life. Much of the trip to India was the past revisited in which I was really acting as Toni's Virgil. I had often visited Delhi, seen Agra in a better moonlight than now, and Kerala had been the subject of a long descriptive and historical book, *Kerala*, which I wrote after a visit in the 1960s. Even Bangalore, that charming refuge of the spirit of the Raj, we had visited while organizing settlements for Tibetan refugees in the jungles of Karnataka. It was only when we set off for Bhubaneswar, the capital of Orissa, staying a dark night in Hyderabad, that Inge and I were again on unexperienced territory.

There is only one incident that seems worth recording in the Kerala phase of our journey, because it dipped briefly into the unfamiliar. When I wrote my book on Kerala I was so absorbed in the life of that fascinating state, that I neglected to go the few miles through Tamil Nadu to Cape Comorin, Kanniyakumari, the sacred southern tip of India. Now we did go, the difference between the two southern cultures, Tamil and Malayali, was immediately evident. Keralan people are remarkable in India for the neatness and cleanliness they maintain, often in extreme poverty. Tamil communities are different, and the town of Kanniyakumari seemed like a monstrously noisy and filthy Lourdes as we walked down the main street to the temple between stalls selling gaudy votive items and blaring Indian film music, and garbage lying thick in the gutters. "Very dirty place!" our driver remarked with a disgusted look; he was a Syrian Christian.

We made our way through the clamour and the ugliness to the temple and the steps beyond it that led down to the beach. A heaving turquoise sea beat into white foam on the rocks that probed out to form a natural breakwater between the Arabian Sea and the Bay of Bengal and ended in an islet on which a pretentious shrine had been erected to Vivekananda. Even this twentieth-century sage had become an object of pilgrimage;

a big, heavily laden old launch with a sagging awning lurched through the waves to moor at the rock and discharge its cargo of devotees.

There was nothing much to do at Kanniyakumari unless one were a pilgrim. I sat among the rocks making my notes. We looked in the rock pools which had a surprisingly dull fauna compared with those of northern seas. Toni found himself a rock to paint from and went to work with his usual stoical disregard for the less pleasant aspects of his setting. Eventually I went out to join him. The tide was coming in, but there was a stretch of rock that was obviously submerged only at spring tides, and I walked along this; I had to pick my way with care, so thickly were human turds deposited here, on one of the holy spots of India. It was somewhat like seeing the close of Canterbury Cathedral turned into a public latrine, and I could understand the driver's disgust. But Toni had found an excellent spot for viewing the Vivekananda Rocks, and had produced a couple of paintings that satisfied him; the heavy whiff of human ordure seemed to perturb him not at all. As we delicately stepped away, all he said — in a tone of quasi-scientific speculation — was "How strange that such small people produce such enormous droppings!" "It's the vegetarian diet," was all I could answer. "Just think of the elephants!"

★   ★   ★

Bhubaneswar immediately attracted us. It lies down over the Eastern Ghats in the green alluvial plain beside the Bay of Bengal. Until India became independent, Bhubaneswar was mainly a religious centre, and the core of the old town still clusters around the great Lingaraja — or Kingly Penis — Temple, one of the holiest shrines of all India, dedicated to the Lord Siva in his phallic manifestation. But in 1948 Bhubaneswar replaced Cuttack, the old British provincial capital, as the administrative centre of Orissa, and a new-built residential quarter came into being, of low modern structures in gardens bright with a bewildering variety of tropical flowers. One of the miracles of India is that, with so many people, there always seems to be enough room to create — working with instinct as much as with deliberation — towns that are well-spaced and do not run up to shut out the sun.

We stayed in the new town in a congenially run government hotel, but it was to the old town that we constantly gravitated, for here, in a profusion to be rivalled only a few weeks later in the great Buddhist centre of Pagan in Burma, we found the relics of a golden age of devotion and creation that had lasted a millennium, from the Hindu revival that displaced a dominant Buddhism in the seventh century AD down to the Mogul conquest of Orissa in the sixteenth century.

Once there must have been a vast city here — one of those South Asian cities like Angkor Thom in Cambodia or Pagan in Burma, where in the early centuries the buildings in which men, kings among them, lived and worked were made of perishable wood and bamboo, and stone was reserved for the sacred edifices. In the tempests of history the houses and even the palaces vanished, and the temples remained. Around the Lingaraja, where pilgrims had been numerous for a thousand years, such a continuity had produced a closely inhabited quarter of narrow streets lined by big hostels or dharamsalas for the pilgrims. The old houses of this area were built of rust-red pumice stone and often thatched with reeds, but some of them had extraordinary façades of coloured cast iron, depicting ancient myths with a brilliant naïveté that resembled the folk art — the gaudy pottery and papier-mâché figures — to be found everywhere in Orissa, on wayside stalls as well as the stuffy handicrafts emporia which the state government operates.

Religion in India, as in medieval Europe, never wholly dissociated itself from commerce; the money-changers — by some door or another — have always managed to enter the temple. When we circled the Lingaraja, passing the Lion Gate and the Elephant Gate and the Tiger Gate and the Horse Gate, each with its freshly painted animal guardian, there were always, facing the high walls of the temple compound and clustering under them, the stalls and shops of which a few sold religious items, but most carried the kind of things one could buy in any bazaar, from fruit and rice and spices to brilliant machine-made clothes and gaudy plastic ware, which in India as in France is usually of excellent quality, made for long use rather than discarding. One of the stalls, however, had the chunky little animal figures of bell-metal made by nomadic braziers in the Orissa villages, and we all bought some of them: sturdy caparisoned elephants with gods riding on their backs, as solidly satisfying and heavy in the hand as early Inuit stone carvings.

In Orissa the major temples are closed to non-Hindus. But at the Lingaraja, Lord Curzon had ordered the building of a platform from which infidels could look into the great courtyard, if not into the sanctuary. We climbed up there with a little boy called Krishnarama who spoke English. Krishnarama pointed out the various buildings that culminated in the *deul* or sanctuary with its immense tower that housed the image of Siva. We saw the dancing hall and the hall of offering, but little else. We could hear, over a public address system, the ringing of bells and the chanting of mantras, so that we assumed a ceremony to the great lingam which represents Siva was going on. We saw people, mainly women, hurrying into the hall of offering with bamboo trays loaded with fruit. And we watched a young long-haired sanyasin in an orange dhoti who had seated himself on the flagstones of the courtyard and carried on his own puja, with flowers, rice and coconuts. It was the only worship we were allowed to see in Orissa, one of the great heartlands of Indian piety. Still, we were impressed when Krishnarama, having been so helpful, observed the spirit of Lord Curzon's gift by refusing any kind of payment, particularly as we had no sooner descended than we were mobbed by other boys asking for pens and "country coins," by which they meant the coins of our own country.

Near the Lingaraja lay the Ocean Drop tank where we could wander beside the murky depths that were said to contain water from every sacred river in India. The Ocean Drop had not only a fine water pavilion where the god is taken from his sanctuary for a bath every year, but also many small shrines around its perimeter. At one spot stood a group of eight such shrines, each consisting of a miniature tower about twenty feet high and an entrance porch tall enough for a short man to step into; all of them were covered with carvings depicting sacred legends, and in some, when we peered in, we could see ashes and smell the scent of flowers. An image of Nandi the sacred bull stood among the shrines, its head blackened by the hands that had touched it over the centuries — among them those of a covey of young women who swept past us to dip in the tiny tank that belonged to this precinct, and to emerge, wet garments skin-tight over nubile bodies and run giggling away.

What made Bhubaneswar unlike any other Indian sacred centre I had seen was not the great Lingaraja Temple, but the multitude of small shrines scattered in the fields and lanes where the present town shreds into its rural outskirts. Most of them were built a millennium ago, between the seventh and twelfth centuries, when Orissa was ruled by the Kesari dynasty, devout Siva worshippers. Legend has it there were originally seven thousand of them, and that most were destroyed by fanatical Moslems when the Hindu dynasties ended in the sixteenth century. The remains of at least five hundred survive, beside the rustic lanes and often in fields and gardens. One day when Toni was painting a roadside shrine, a boy asked him, "Would you like to see my family's temple?" and took him into a courtyard where he was welcomed by an old farmer and his wife and taken to a fine little shrine, lush with carving and faced by its own little Nandi figure.

The small temples around Bhubaneswar each consisted of a sanctuary, with a tower between thirty and forty feet high and a porch ten or fifteen feet high, within a paved and sometimes walled compound. There were no plain surfaces; every inch of the outer walls was covered with intricate carvings of virtually anything that could be regarded as celebrating the fullness of existence, from lovers caressing and coupling to processions of elephants and horses, from birds and animals and flowers to the extraordinary series of Naga queens, with their cobra hoods and human faces and long serpentine tails that decorated the Raj Rani temple. The towers were not pointed like Gothic spires, but stubby topped, their corbelled shoulders supporting big capstones rather like the tops of gigantic mushrooms. The mood of the carving varied perhaps according to period, from an austere baroque kind of grandeur to — in some of the smaller shrines — rococo fantasies of miniature figures.

A few of Bhubaneswar's more neglected temples were greatly eroded, and tufted with vegetation like Piranesi ruins, and one at least had been gripped as if by an octopus in the roots of a young peepul tree that was prizing its stones apart. But some of the oldest temples were in extraordinary preservation, their carvings almost as crisp and clear as when the sculptor laid down his chisel. The best of them were in a small cluster of about twenty temples at a place called the Grove of Perfect Beings, where they stood like strange stone fungi among the ancient peepuls that overshadowed them. The most exquisitely carved of all, the Parsurameswar Temple, is said to be the oldest, built around 650 AD, yet its carvings were astonishingly sharp-edged, and the many animal figures were vigorous and alive. "Every stone had its antic value," my local guidebook remarked, and its unconscious ambiguity was strangely expressive of the gaiety of feeling this ancient shrine projected.

In recent years many young Brahmins have attached themselves to the smaller temples around Bhubaneswar, perhaps because the old priests have established an irrevocable control over the larger temples. Usually these self-appointed guardians of the shrines have had an education beyond mere Hindu dogma and mythology, like the bespectacled man in yellow sanyasin's robe who approached us at Parsurameswar and was unusually fluent in English. He flourished a donation book showing substantial gifts from foreigners and asked me for ten rupees. I offered him two, which he accepted with good grace and lit a candle so that he could take us, respectfully barefooted, into the sanctuary. It contained nothing but the most simple and expressive symbol of the union of the god and his shakti — the combined lingam and yoni carved from a single stone, the tip of the lingam crowned with betel leaves and the shaft hung with jasmine garlands. Bats rustled and chirped in the heavy cone of darkness above our heads, and the floor was spattered with their droppings, from which a sharp smell impregnated the air. Standing there, I wondered what in the past had gone on in so many small temples, and it struck me that the young Brahmins we encountered here and there were probably reenacting an original pattern, that of hermit priest, each tending his little shrine and receiving a few devotees who brought to altars as simple as we had seen the same kind of gentle offerings. I felt a little mean about my own offering and gave the priest another five rupees, and then we went to the tank down the road to wash the bat dung off our feet.

The three great temples of Orissa form an isosceles triangle, with Lingaraja at the apex and the base points on the coast at the Sun Temple of Konarak (the Black Pagoda of English mariners on their way to Calcutta) and the temple of Jagganath at Puri (the White Pagoda), the first a vast archaeological relic and the second a major centre of religious activity even today.

The Orissa countryside through which we drove down to Konarak by a little-used road had a look of pastoral peace and plenty. Most of it was paddy, where the men worked with ox ploughs and backhoes, wearing loincloths and roughly twisted turbans and looking remarkably like the figures of peasants in the Bhubaneswar temple sculptures. Some were irrigating fields with a scoop attached to ropes, which they would dip into a pond or stream and then heave and tip into the irrigation channels. Market gardens were planted around the villages, growing potatoes, cauliflowers and other vegetables for the Calcutta market, only a night away by train, and here scarecrows had been erected with demon faces painted on their calico heads. Every now and then there would be a high, tightly woven cane fence surrounding a rectangular plot where betel vines grew, a valuable crop that needed protection against thieves.

The villages were tiny places of thatched mud or pumice-stone houses, with bright yellow stacks of rice straw standing among them, shaped exactly like the temple towers, even to the extent of having a kind of woven thatch roof like the capstones of the towers. Every village had its large tank surrounded by greenery, and bearing on its surface red lotuses and drifts of white flowers like water crowfoot. We were out early and the villagers were performing their ablution; in one tank I saw a man enthusiastically gargling water he had lifted with his hands, while no more than four feet away another man was squatting down and vigorously scrubbing his behind with the same water. We wondered at a version of "cleanliness is next to godliness" that made a fetish of washing the body but took no notice of the filthy water in which it was washed. Was there a metaphor here, I speculated, for India's present political condition where corruption is ignored so long as the pious patriotic forms continue to be observed?

As we drew nearer Konarak the villages became fewer, the land less cultivated. Large marshes harboured flocks of egrets and many paddy birds and cormorants, and from the trees hung pendulous nests of weaver birds. Then the dunes began, piling inland several miles from the coast, and it was here that we came to the Black Pagoda — not on a sea beach as I had imagined, but among the sandhills from whose grip it had been rescued early in this century by the archaeologists.

The temple of Konarak was an extraordinary, original and unimitated concept in Indian religious architecture. The sun god Surya, like the Greek god Helios, is said to travel in his chariot on the daily journey across the heavens from sunrise to sunset. The temple was to be a grand architectural and sculptural representation of his chariot which at the same time would embrace the essential elements of an Orissa temple — towered sanctuary, entrance porch, and dancing hall. Twenty-four enormous stone wheels were lined along the base of the structure; seven gigantic stone horses strained as they hauled the mighty vehicle, of which no surface was left uncarved.

Records of Konarak are extraordinarily slight. We do not even know for certain which king built it. Desecrated by the Moslems, it appears to have been deserted by the early seventeenth century. Sand began to drift in, covering the wheels and the straining horses, and the massive capstone collapsed, removing the key that held the corbelled walls of the sanctuary tower. The lower buildings were largely protected by the encroaching sand until in the early twentieth century the Archaeological Survey — one of the finest services of the British Raj — undertook the uncovering of the great chariot and the shoring up of what remained of the tower, so that one can once again climb up to the first platform and see the three majestic chlorite figures of Surya, facing with their ineffably sweet smiles the sun at its rising, its zenith and its setting.

Splendid as the great temple-chariot must have appeared when the sanctuary stood in its full height of more than 260 feet, the effect was almost completely destroyed by the tower's collapse, which left a building quite out of traditional proportion, a stump of a tower beside its porch and dancing hall. But in detail the Sun Temple remained fascinating. The spirit of the original concept may have left the broken and marred structure, but it remained in the component parts; the intricately deco-rated wheels with lively vignettes of human activities on every spoke; the horse and elephant and lion figures so massive and stone-solid and yet so full of life; the serenely beautiful female musicians in the high galleries of the porch, and the celebrated erotic groups which, irrever-ently perhaps, I saw as representations less of the ecstasy of sex than of the comedy of man's preoccupation with it, for many of them are best seen as small pieces of Rabelaisian fun. There is much in Tantrism — like much in Zen — that, considered less seriously than most Western scholars take it, can be interpreted as Wise Men's laughter at the human conditions.

There were no real pilgrims at Konarak, and the only hint of religion was a long-haired young man in yellow robe who came with a sweet, disarming smile and hibiscus flowers in his hand; he told us a few facts we already knew, demanded the customary ten rupees, and accepted two; this time my conscience did not go into operation. But even without pilgrims, the temple precinct was crowded with visitors, and apart from a small contingent of Japanese and four or five Europeans, they were all Indians, again reinforcing my impression that the people of the country are at last beginning to gain the kind of historical sense that found no place in traditional Hinduism. They spread around in families, photo-graphing each other in front of the images of Surya, chaffering with the peddlers who were selling postcards and fresh coconuts and necklaces of red coral from the beach, and looking at the erotic carvings with the giggling embarrassment that betokens the puritanism of most modern Indians.

There was not a touch of religious devotion in their response; they showed as little emotion as American tourists traipsing through West-minster Abbey, and watching them I wondered what this great temple must have been, in the days of its glory before it was desecrated and deserted and finally ruined. Was it a grandiose dynastic chapel built only for the glory of the kings who identified themselves with the ancient Aryan warriors, worshippers of Surya, a Vedic god already out of fashion by the time the Black Pagoda was built? Or was it devoted entirely to pilgrims, for not a relic of a town associated with it has been found.

That possibility grew in my mind as we drove along the new coast road to Puri, through one of those virtually uninhabited stretches of country that seem to dispute the image of overcrowded India: mostly sand dunes covered with casuarina trees and a kind of scrawny pine, at times very much like the sandy woodland of Gascony.

Not far from Konarak was a long open beach of pale, almost white sand. Some wandering Frenchmen were plunging naked in the surf, but otherwise it was deserted except for a little booth covered with palm leaves where an old man was selling shells and fresh coconut. Off to one side, with no houses near it, stood a little shore temple. According to the old storekeeper, this shrine too was dedicated to the sun god, and once a year there was a festival lasting several days to which thousands of people came, living and sleeping on the beach and then departing. Might not this have happened to Konarak, which in the days of its glory, before the dunes had drifted upward, must have been right on the seashore, as the old mariners' reports also state? And was it not likely that, as the sea receded and the Sun Temple became deserted, this little shore temple took its place and received its pilgrims?

There was virtually no cultivation in the thirty or so kilometres between Konarak and Puri, and no habitations except for the reed huts of the fishermen and some rough shacks inhabited by woodcutters from which the smell of burning pine would sometimes drift across the road. We entered Puri from the south, by way of Gundicha Ghat where the images of Jagannath and his brother and sister were brought every year to recover from some human illness. When they were cured the three great ceremonial carts of the gods (which we call juggernauts after Jagannath) took them back to their real temple. Jagannath's cart stands nearly fifty feet high, is thirty feet square, and moved on twenty-four great wheels; once devotees would throw themselves into its path to be crushed to a holy death, but in the present faithless age, it is many years since this happened.

The Sri Jagannath, with its two-hundred-foot tower, dominates the skyline of Puri as the great medieval cathedrals dominate some of the towns of France, but as a living corporation its influence over the city is greater, since there are no fewer than seven thousand Brahmins and temple servants engaged in the multitude of minute and varied tasks required to serve these extraordinary deities whose bodies are wooden cylinders, whose faces are grotesque masks, and those truncated arms look like those of the victims of thalidomide poisoning.

The temple occupies a ten-acre enclosure in the centre of the town, surrounded by a wall twenty feet high. We were forbidden entry, even though this is a Vaishnavite temple that has always welcomed Hindu untouchables. When we arrived, the building from which one gets the best view into the courtyards was closed and we drove around the great enclosure, past the gates guarded by gigantic animal figures, and eventually found a man who would take us up through an old house — a tenement swarming with poor people in squalid rooms who resented the passage of strangers — to the roof where we could look over the temple wall. But the Sri Jagannath also has an inner wall so that we could only get a better view of the roofs but none of the courtyard. As we came down there was a long wrangle between our driver Krishnan and the owner of the building over the value of the view. The owner wanted twenty rupees, but after much shouting in Oriya, he came down by stages to five, which we paid.

Sri Jagannath is the local manifestation of the great god Vishnu, whose cult is in many ways the nobler cult than that of Siva; even Buddha has his place as one of the avatars or incarnations of Vishnu. But this great preserver deity, who has been the subject of so much elevated metaphysical and ethical speculation, seems very far from the glorified fetishes who preside at Puri, and it must be a far more elemental devotion that responds to these tribal godlings elevated into the Hindu pantheon. I have a papier-mâché model of the high altar at Puri which I bought from an old woman in the bazaar there; I open the little painted doors to the shrine, and see the gaudy miniatures of the gods staring at me with enormous ghostly eyes, and it is Africa and Melanesia, the great reservoirs of primitive tribal cultures, that come to my mind sooner than India.

We felt no urge to linger in Puri. Apart from the temple, freshly whitewashed and painted, it was a decrepit and neglected town, its buildings stained by monsoons, its narrow streets full of dusty booths where the flies flourished extravagantly, and its seedy, cheap hotels lined along the waterfront, where the surf-swept yellow sand and the blue water of the Bay of Bengal seemed the only clean things in sight. The combination of devotion and dirt, cynical commercialism and deep poverty seemed to be characteristic of Indian religious centres, and in this Bhubaneswar was the exception and a place we were glad to return to through the gentle, vividly green Orissa countryside.

On the way back we crossed a wide river, sluggish and dry-season shallow. Legend — physically represented by our driver Krishnan —

associated it with one of the more dramatic events of Indian history. In the third century BC, Orissa was the kingdom of Kalinga, against which Aśoka, king of the great northern realm of Magadha, had marched to fulfil his destiny as Chakravartin, the traditional Indian King of the Wheel who, like the Persian King of Kings, claimed to rule over other rulers. In the eighth year of his realm, somewhere about 260 BC, Aśoka defeated the king of Kalinga, but his victory turned to dust in his mind when he stood beside the river and saw it jammed with corpses seeping blood that stained the water red. With this dark epiphany, the Buddhist teaching of which he had heard came home to him with the force of revelation. He was converted to the faith and renounced for ever the use of warfare, choosing a new way of conquest by dharma, which for him meant the practice of the social and moral virtues of compassion and nonviolence and in general caring for the welfare of all living beings, including men.

The following day we drove into the Dhauli Hills to search for the relics of Aśoka that survive there to this day. Once, before the British antiquaries set to work, Aśoka was merely a Buddhist legend, but in the 1820s and 1830s James Prinsep, assay master of the mints in Benares and later Calcutta, not only identified the Bactrian Greek kings of the Punjab by their coins, but also deciphered the rock inscriptions in ancient Prakrit which established Aśoka as a monarch in history. These inscriptions were the edicts by which Aśoka instructed his officials and his subjects in the new order of dharma he sought to establish.

Up at the top of the Dhauli Hills, we came to the smooth-cut face of rock outcrop into which the first of the edicts had been carved in Prakrit, an alphabet derived remotely from the Phoenician and therefore related to our own. They were very clearly cut, though the thick wire screens protecting them made it hard to read them distinctly; however, translations into Oriya and English had been painted on boards beside them. The edicts lamented the great killing at Kalinga, exhorted the people to peace, honesty and hard work, warned the king's officials against injustice, abjured hunting and the sacrifice of animals, ordered the digging of wells and the planting of trees by the roadside for the benefit of travellers, and the growing of medicinal plants, and enjoined "great love of righteousness, great self-examination, great circumspection, great effort." Reading them, one felt a mingling of joy that a king so long ago should have framed such an enlightened plan for existence, and sadness that two thousand years later, his injunctions had been neither bettered nor sustained as a practical way of living, even in his own country. In one

way or another the inhumanity of our practices has persisted as stub-
bornly as the ideal of a better life has lingered in men's minds, periodically
revived by teachers like Gandhi and the Fourteenth Dalai Lama, but
never completely triumphing.

Still, standing on that fresh, clear morning under the trees with not a
person in sight and reading those fine injunctions from the dawn of
history, we could not fail to be moved by the persistence of that longing
for a better life which had at least made the world a better place than it
would have been without the Aśoka and the Gandhis. The goat-cropped
grass in front of the inscription was so thickly starred with minute
blossoms of a bright cerulean that it offered a kind of benison, so narrowly
did it seem to mirror "heaven in a wild flower."

Beside the inscribed rock was another outcrop, out of which had been
carved, at the same time as the edict, one of the oldest stone sculptures
in India. It was the foreparts — head, shoulders, forelegs — of an elephant,
quite naturalistically carved, so that he seemed to be emerging from the
grey rock; I realized with delight that two thousand years ago, a sculptor
must have had my vision of the big rock outcrops so common in India,
as sleeping elephants, ready to emerge at any moment from the impris-
oning stone. This sculptor had caught the vision on its way out and, with
fine artistry, had refrained from completing the figure; the sense of the
great beast emerging was far more potent.

Long before the kings of the Kesari dynasty began to build their
multitude of temples at Bhubaneswar in the seventh century, the Dhauli
Hills were already the haunt of holy men, and in the second century, a
hundred years or so after Aśoka, Jain monks patronized by a local king
called Kharavala created a kind of Thebaid of hundreds of caves and cells
honeycombing the two hills known as Khandagiri and Undaigiri, which
lie not far from the Aśoka monuments. Nothing was built; everything
— according to early Jain and Buddhist practice — was cut out of the
rock, not only the rough-hewn little chambers where the monks lived
and meditated, but also the relief carvings of the twenty-four Thirtan-
karas or legendary Jain teachers, which were chipped out of the living
rock and in style closely resembled the roughly contemporary figures at
the Buddhist stupas of Sanchi and Bharhut; at a distance the long open
galleries cut into the rockfaces were reminiscent of the later and much
more famous central Indian caves of Ajanta and Ellora. While Toni
painted, Inge and I sat in the caves, looking out at the woodland that
climbed up the hill and inhaling the dense fragrance of a mass of wild

mangoes in full bloom. Once we had got rid of a persistent man offering himself as a guide we were able to absorb the extraordinary serenity of the place, which was so intense that we felt our mental feet dipping into the shallows of some vast reservoir of stored-up spirituality.

After a time, we noticed movement in the trees below us, and when we went to look found that it was caused by a troop of monkeys led by a big old grizzled male, and including a number of females and young of various ages, from the hairless infants that clung all the time to their mothers' fur, to the older children playing incessantly in the branches, leaping from one to the other, and staging mock fights. They were completely undisturbed by our presence, and went on playing as if nobody were there. But all this changed when I fetched a bag of peanuts from a stall by the roadside. Then they gathered around us, taking the nuts gently from our hands, but leaping up to try and grab the bag when they thought my attention could be distracted. Apart from liking the nuts, they seemed to enjoy human company for its own sake, and when the bag was empty, one of them settled down at Inge's feet, silently looking into her face and holding her legs with its small black hands. There seemed such an accord between animal and woman as to indicate that in a small way the spirit of Aśoka's edicts and of the teaching of the Jain monks who followed him had survived among these holy rocks with the monkeys, the descendants of many generations that had been able to live there without fear of predatorial man, since monkeys in India are everywhere sacred. It shifted one's barometer just a shade in the direction of hope.

★ ★ ★

In the Dhauli Hills, with the sacred monkeys and Aśoka's emergent elephant, we came to the end of the exploratory stage of our trip to India. Orissa had offered us a new aspect of the subcontinent. Now we ended our journey by travelling through familiar territory with some difficulty and with a growing feeling of how much the best in India had deteriorated since our earlier visits. We had felt this already in Jaipur and Agra and even in Trivandrum, places where in the twenty years since we first saw them, tourism had played its corroding role.

We flew from Bhubaneswar to Calcutta, and missed our connection to Bagdogra, so that we had to stay the night in the airport hotel and, as we disliked the city from past experiences, we spent the rest of the day hanging around there and bargaining with a jeweller for a silver bracelet with a large lemon topaz which Inge eventually got at her own price.

The next day the plane was so late leaving that we did not reach Bagdogra until it was dusk, and by the time we had gone through the army checkpoint there it was dark; as we drove by taxi up to Darjeeling we missed all the spectacular hill scenery. At Darjeeling the old Windamere Hotel, with its view of Kanchenjunga, which we had enjoyed so much in the past, was now shabby and dirty and almost without heating in a Darjeeling January with the night temperatures well below zero. We quickly found a warm room in a new Oberoi Hotel where we were the only guests and the charming manager would come at breakfast to know our wishes for dinner, and provide what we asked — pheasant, trout and so forth. Inge and I wandered in Darjeeling and lamented the deterioration of the town through the change in fuel, the denuding of the hills having ended the traditional supplies of charcoal, which was replaced by a bituminous coal from the Bihar mines that had transformed this once glittering city into a murky semblance of the old Black Country towns. We also walked along the hill paths to visit our old friend Mrs. Thondup, wife of the Dalai Lama's elder brother, in the craft centre she had set up on one of the hillsides and in which she employed many Tibetan refugees. But Toni went on his own and showed here an endurance in the cause of art that I found astonishing and impossible to imitate.

Each morning, while I took my first look at Kanchenjunga in the full morning sunlight before we went down to warm ourselves with the chef's excellent porridge, Toni would already have got picked up by a Nepali in a jeep and was driving up the rough roads to Tiger Hill, which lay a thousand feet above the pass at Ghoom. Rime would lie thick on the ground, and as Toni prepared his materials, the driver would forage over the hillside, picking up scraps of wood to build a bonfire behind his back that would give him a little warmth while he painted. When a watercolour was finished, Toni would light sheets of newspaper and wave them over it, so that the paint dried quickly and he could stow it away and move on to another equally exposed spot with a view over the mountain pastures, and the cairnlike structures of the Tibetan chötens, or shrines, clustered under their flapping lines of prayer flags.

Travel difficulties attended us out of Darjeeling, for we were delayed a whole twenty-four hours getting away from Bagdogra, and, after a virtual passenger revolt, stayed the night at the airline's expense in a meagre new hotel in the trading town of Siliguri. At last, a special plane arrived that took us via Patna to Delhi, and there we prepared for our next country, which was Burma.

Chapter 12

SEVEN BURMESE DAYS

Inge and I first attempted to enter Burma (since renamed Myanmar) in 1965, and got as far as Chittagong, just over the border in Bangladesh, when we found that our visa was useless since the government had suddenly put an end to all visits to the country; it was expelling its resident Indian population and wanted no witnesses. We flew back from Chittagong to Calcutta, met the refugees there, trailing off a Thai plane with their wretched bundles of belongings. We saw Burma only from the air and in the gathering darkness, a mass of dark forest with pale rivers running through it and the occasional fiery circles of the peasants burning off their paddies. The ban on travel remained in force for many years, but by 1983 it was relaxed so that one could go in, for no more than seven days, and we decided to take advantage of the situation, and got our visas — the four of us — without difficulty in Delhi.

We found that the only way to enter the country was to fly via Bangkok into Rangoon, for the land frontiers were all closed to travellers. The simple reason for this was that the Burmese government controlled hardly any of the country's borderlands, which were in the hands of various disaffected resistance groups, ethnically based in the case of the Karen and Shan rebels, and politically based in the case of some of the communist-inclining bands in the northern part of the country.

One of the reasons for my eagerness to go to Burma at this time was that Inge and I had a good contact there, for our Tibetan friend Samphe Lhalungpa was working at the Unesco mission in Rangoon. Samphe was there waiting for us at the airport — tall and Tibetanly broad-faced — when we had emerged from the alarmingly elaborate but remarkably inefficient immigration, customs and currency procedures. Remembering past experience, we had put a couple of ten-dollar bills at appropriate places in our luggage, and after they quietly disappeared we noticed how the customs officer's initial scowl changed to a smile and all was passed through without difficulty.

Samphe took us to our massive, ugly, Russian-built hotel, where the plumbing never worked, in a park on the edge of Rangoon, and then invited us to his home and afterwards helped us to explore this shabby, melancholy city where everything seems from the outside in a state of lamentable deterioration. Plaster and paint were peeling off the façades of buildings, fences were falling down, the edges of properties were choked with tangles of weeds and untrimmed bushes. It was not from poverty, we soon gathered, but from precaution. The sight of well-kept houses and gardens might arouse the envy of some general or colonel driving by in his Mercedes, and soon an appropriation order might come, which would mean appropriation by the officer concerned.

So, inside the shabby-looking buildings we sometimes entered elegant apartments, and I remember particularly well the house of a hospitable doctor, reached through a tangled shrubbery, which contained a notable collection of Burmese antiquities; there the host arranged for a dancer and a harpist to entertain us with the sinuous *pwe* dance which Orwell described so vividly in *Burmese Days*, a more lyrical version of the formalized dances of Southeast Asia. I remember our host warmly, but hesitate to record his name.

Protective modesty was not merely a matter of private houses. The best restaurant in Rangoon was then a place which I cautiously call Daisy's, where foreign diplomats and local intellectuals sat in shabby booths at tables covered with oilcloth to eat superb seafood dishes and the elaborately delectable soufflés which were the specialty of the house.

Samphe took us around Rangoon, and together with him and his wife Ellen we climbed the long flight of steps, lined with antique shops and stalls selling paper votive offerings and fruit and flowers for sacrifice, that led us up to the great Swe Dagon Pagoda, still covered, after all the wars and crises, with its coating of solid gold, for religion was the one area of Burmese life military rulers were still chary about attacking. On the paving at the bottom of the pagoda families had set themselves up to make offerings and the smell of tropical flowers was heavy. There was a slightly higher terrace to which entrance was restricted, and it was full of men praying — no women. There is a sense of male superiority in Burmese Buddhism; we observed that the nuns around the pagoda looked much poorer than the monks, and far less arrogant, perhaps because many of the young men, but none of the young women, were temporary monks putting in — according to Burmese tradition — their three months' novitiate, rather like a military training, before going back into the material world. We did not contribute to any of the religious functions, but spent a few dollars gaining merit by releasing a cageful of sparrows. The birds immediately, in the presence of their captors, began to hop around picking up the grain other benefactors had scattered, and we caused great amusement by hollering and gesticulating violently to induce them to fly to relative safety.

If the Swe Dagon Pagoda showed us that religion, at least in 1983, was still relatively unmolested in Burma, Scott Market offered some interesting glimpses into the economic situation at that time. Burma at first gave the impression of a monolithic totalitarian state, run by a single party, the Burmese Socialist Programme Party, which was the front for army rule in fact if not yet in name. There was a political police trained by the West German Stasi, which was zealous if not very subtle. One of its agents haunted the hotel coffee shop, and would always sit at a table close to us and lean his chair so far trying to listen to us that he seemed in peril of sprawling on his back. At such moments we would loudly declare our praise of all things Burmese until he moved off.

But if in political terms Burma had the look of a totalitarian regime, despite its differences with Russia and China, in economic and social terms it resembled more than anything else a colander, rigid in shape but full of holes. And this was partly the result of the actual political weakness of the central government and its failure to control its own frontier areas. Vast amounts of goods found their way from Thailand through the Karen territories where the local insurrectionaries levied a flat tax of 5 percent and provided a base from which the great black markets in the towns were fed. The difference between the official market and the black market was made evident to us one morning when we visited a large government department store and then walked on to the Scott Market, two streets away. The government store was a spacious concrete building, bleak and unfriendly, almost completely empty of customers and lacking the goods to tempt them in. For example, there were plenty of shoes for small feet or for great size-twelve Orwell feet, but none for people with ordinary feet. There was lots of oil this week, but rice was being doled out in small quantities. Inge bought the only attractive and inexpensive item, a great length of geometrically patterned cotton print from which she has been making house skirts ever since. The attendants were as dead as the place, defeated by the store's limitations.

The Scott Market was a great covered structure extending over several acres, and arranged bazaar-like in groups of related stalls, all the tailors for example together, and all the makers of paper offerings for ceremonies and funerals. Compared with Indians or Chinese, the Burmese are not a noisy people, but the market was alive with the voices of people offering and bargaining. And everything I could summon by my imagination was there. Under the eaves as one went in were hill women selling strawberries and apples, and fishermen had laid out their catches. Within the market, aisle after aisle of stalls succeeded each other, selling everything from meat and poultry to plumbing fixtures and furniture. Great areas were devoted to fruit and flowers and vegetables, the bases of a Buddhist life, but any level of materialism or sophistication seemed also to be catered to; one could buy single malt Scotch whiskeys and French brandies and liqueurs, American cosmetics, Rhine wine, Swiss and Belgian chocolate, and cheeses from almost every country of Europe, as well as a Hong Kong–like range of electronic products, and most of it at prices no higher than those charged in North American cities. The place was crowded with customers, and there were no police to be seen. The market seemed to be a self-regulating entity within the monolithic state. The underground had seized the trade of the city and enabled it to survive.

We moved around Rangoon freely and without interference, except for the occasional listening spy, whose attentions the local people also endured. It was when we went outside the city that we found our movements hampered. To begin, visitors were excluded from most of the country except the Irrawaddy corridor from Rangoon to Mandalay and a few enclaves like Moulmein and Maymyo. The seven-day limit on visas was another hampering factor, for it meant virtually that one had to travel under the aegis of Tourism Burma, the local equivalent of Intourist. Theoretically, one could arrange one's own travels, but it was hard to buy an airline ticket, and one took the risk, if the plane were full, that one might easily get bumped off by an officer or bureaucrat who wanted one's seat.

Tourism Burma chartered its own planes, only for the use of its customers, so that one could be sure of travel arrangements even if the planes never arrived on time. One had also to accept guides in the Intourist manner, but they turned out to be students who never gave the impression of being trained spies. Their English was poor, like that of all young Burmese, for there were no teachers whose first language was English and students were rarely allowed abroad. Our guides were easy and accommodating, so that we would let them show us where to find things in the mornings, and at noon give them a couple of packets of Camels and tell them to get lost till next morning, which they gladly did, since they got bored waiting for Toni to finish his paintings.

Mandalay was a disappointing place, a rundown Anglo-Indian provincial capital endowed with many pagodas, some ancient monasteries, and the rambling remnants of the last palace of the kings of Burma enclosed within the crumbling walls and moats of the British Fort Dufferin. Mandalay is probably the most active centre of Burmese Buddhism, and there were many monks in their yellow robes, most of them young and callow and as unsaintly as one might imagine. There was also the immense Zenyo Market, where there was a great deal more in the way of local craftsmanship, such as handwoven local silk, than in Rangoon, and also more in the way of exotica, for it was nearer to the permeable border regions than Rangoon.

Mandalay was not a place to expect comfort. The hotel was even more spartan than that in Rangoon. It was in fact a kind of bleak barracks where old Japanese men were being packed four or five in a room, so that they relived their service along the Irrawaddy during World War II, when the Mandalay that Kipling sang of was almost destroyed. The food was coarse and bad, consisting mainly of stewed pork in a pungent sauce, which apparently is a favoured dish among the Burmans, despite their Buddhism. The feature of the city that lodges most sharply in my memory is the rotting stench among the riverside huts where a special fish paste for which the city is renowned in Burma was being cured. I took some for dinner, and it tasted as repulsive as it smelt — even more repulsive than Bombay Duck.

We flew south to Pagan above the broad grey flow of the Irrawaddy, the ground below checkered with rice paddies, some green, some winter-dull, and dry hills rising on each bank of the river, small villages built of split bamboo and palm leaf, fishing boats and barges occasionally on the river.

For a time in the Middle Ages Pagan had been the capital of Burma, and the centre of such religious fervour from its founding in the ninth century onwards that even today, seven centuries after the Mongols rode in to sack the place in the thirteenth century, there are at least the remains of nearly five thousand Buddhist buildings, from small pagodas to majestic temples. In a way I knew of the look of Pagan in its glory, for once fifteen years before I had been in a near-death dream — or vision if you choose. Lying heavily drugged with morphine on the night of a heart attack, I had seen myself riding by train along the bank of a great Asian river. The train stopped at a little platform, below which was a wharf with a white ferry steamer standing there. I stepped quickly from the train but as my feet touched the planks of the platform, the steamer hooted once and then swung out into the stream and headed towards the splendid city of glittering pagodas and temples, all white and golden, that stretched on the other shore: the other shore, that Buddhist expression for death, which I was not destined then to reach. I stood there in my dream, feeling a mingling of relief and regret.

Now I was seeing Pagan again and recognizing it, not in its flower but in its decadence as we approached it out of the hills, from the airport side. There were pagodas everywhere, filling the landscape on both sides of the road by the hundreds, most of them small and now drab, many in various stages of ruin, down to heaps of bricks; only a few of the temples and pagodas still kept their pristine whiteness. The arid soil, the virtual absence of people, the strange shapes of the buildings reminded me of those haunting landscapes of deserts of the mind that Yves Tanguy used to paint. The few people, apart from the occasional goatherds, were throwing up heaps of earth as they sought, not for antiquities, but for treasure, of which local legend said there was much secreted at Pagan. Before the Mongols swept in, it is said, there were even more pagodas and temples at Pagan than those whose relics now survive. Then it was a city of great population, the capital of Burma. But the ancient houses have gone long ago, and all that remained when we arrived was a village of split bamboo houses near the river with a couple of cafés and a few shops, or rather stalls, selling fruit and vegetables and also the lacquered bowls that are a favourite in the Burmese tourist market.

Most of the people were very poor; the per capita income in Burma at this time was less than $150 a year, and there were many areas where cash circulated hardly at all and the people lived reasonably well by barter because of the cooperativeness encouraged by Buddhist teachings. In Pagan the actual wages of people working for cash were minimal. Some of the men spent their days splitting bamboo with long heavy knives into strips for house building that were exported up and down the valley. And others carried out the intricate stages of lacquering, earning anything from 7 to 10 kyat a day, which at the official exchange rate meant from $1.00 to $1.50 and on the black market from 40 to 50 cents. At the government-run hotel where we stayed in stuffy cabins made of aromatic wood, the room boys were getting 10 kyat a day and hoping for tips which were officially forbidden. We split our tips, giving some beforehand to save us from immediate neglect.

Outside the village one rarely encountered anyone directly, except the monks at two or three of the large and better preserved temples, and the furtive men who would sometimes appear at the older ruins, telling one legends in broken English and offering images they claimed to have found. They rarely showed us anything of interest. In general, indeed, Bhubaneswar in India had spoilt us for Pagan, whose bland Theravada Buddhism had nothing to offer compared with the zestful sculptures of life and nature in the little temples of Orissa.

One night we heard there was a Burmese concert in the village hall. Toni hired a local jeep without consulting our bargaining expert, Inge, and so we paid an unreasonable price; in fact the first price asked. The hall was a vast ramshackle structure of bamboo; the villagers were sitting on the ground, but there were some chairs at the back to which we were directed and where we sat maitreya-like, with our legs right down to the ground. The music was emphatically Burmese, with many gongs, cymbals and drums, metallic bangs and crashes, and it was amplified to such a level that with our unaccustomed ears we could stay for no more than half an hour, which was enough, since the dances were imitations of Hollywood revues with lots of girls in long white flowing dresses swaying around to exemplify the truths of Buddhism and of Burmese nationalism.

One day there was a great dust storm blowing down the Irrawaddy, with extraordinary light effects, and while the rest of us huddled in our cabins watching the sand seeping in under the doors and around the window frames, Toni disappeared, until we began to be worried for his safety. But it was the cause of art again, and finally, when the storm had blown out, he appeared. Fascinated by the strange light effects which the storm created, he found a sheltered corner and remained there painting. It was one of the best paintings he did on our trip to Asia, and he gave it to me as an immensely cherished souvenir of our joint journey.

Though I found its political ambiguities interesting and in some ways alarming, I did not find a great deal of Burmese life surprising since I had read Orwell on the subject and talked to him often about his life in that very conservative country. The surprises I remember most were largely gastronomic, like Daisy's in Rangoon, and the last of them ornamented our departure from the country. We had said goodbye to Samphe Lhalungpa at the Rangoon airport, had passed with surprising ease through the departure formalities about which many people had warned us, and had time enough for a lunch in the airport restaurant. And there we ate the most delectable *omelettes aux fines herbes* we had ever tasted outside the boundaries of France, cooked by an old Chinese who knew a little French and must have learnt his art in Indo-China.

Chapter 13

PREPARING FOR 1984

When we came back from Burma in 1983, I faced a year of hard work. There was, to begin with, *The Walls of India* to be written, and, just as important, a publisher to be assured, for it would be an expensive book to produce with the reproductions of Toni's paintings, and most of my early approaches resulted in dark talk about the need for a subsidy when in fact we were seeking to earn money for Canada India Village Aid. It was not until late in the year that I began to see light at the end of this particular tunnel. However, I carried on with the writing, publishing essays that span off the book in various periodicals, including the lamented *Quest*, where Michael Enright was much more congenial as an editor than he later became as a radio personality.

Then, barely had 1983 begun than I became involved in the coming celebrations of 1984, the year of George Orwell's best-known novel, *Nineteen Eighty-Four*, which still held the public imagination and stimulated speculation regarding the future.

I had suggested to the CBC some kind of reminiscent programme on Orwell, and I found the corporation had already had in mind producing an elaborate radio biography on him. The producer Steve Wadhams was already gathering material from Orwell's surviving friends and acquaintances, and he came out to Vancouver for a long talk with me and some sample recordings of my own recollections, after which he decided that, as Orwell's friend and the author of *The Crystal Spirit*, I would be the best person to act as host, linking the other recollections and providing a unifying thread of my own memories.

At the same time Howard White of Harbour Publishing suggested that I write the book of reassessment that eventually appeared as *Orwell's Message: 1984 and the Present*, an idea I accepted because it fitted in with what looked like being a massive radio assignment, and also because it seemed important to reassess the relevance of Orwell's teachings in the actual year 1984. Clearly the book had not yet worked out as a prophecy, but then he never intended as such, but rather as a warning of totalitarian tendencies and possibilities in our society, and it was from this viewpoint that I wished to present Orwell. I do not believe in historical prophecy, and I do not think Orwell did, but he saw the circumstances that might produce even in the so-called democratic countries a kind of tyranny resembling that he portrayed in *Nineteen Eighty-Four*. To me he was more an analyst of political directions and trends, and a recorder of the degeneration of language that had become part of the political process, and he was as much concerned about defending the clarity of prose so as to save us from the vagueness or pretentiousness in which politicians concealed their intents, or lack of intents, as he was with the physical aspects of dictatorship. I was trying in fact, in both my book and the radio programme, to save Orwell from the false concepts of his teaching that had allowed so many unsavoury right-wing groups and individuals to seize upon his insights and distort them. There was a certain irony in all this, since I have never considered *Nineteen Eighty-Four* Orwell's most interesting book. *Coming up for Air* is a better novel, and *Animal Farm* a better and more contained satire. But I was given an opportunity to write and talk about Orwell in general that would not otherwise be offered and so I accepted it.

I finished *Orwell's Message* in the fall, in the hope that it would appear on the Christmas list for 1983, just prior to the beginning of 1984, when the interest in Orwell would be greatest. However, the printers delayed and it did not appear until the spring of 1984 when interest in the subject was already falling away, since the real 1984 was obviously not shaping up to resemble the fictional one. In compensation I found there was a renewed interest in my original book on Orwell, *The Crystal Spirit*, with its balanced interest in the whole body of Orwell's work. A new paperback edition was published in England, and the first translation into German appeared in Switzerland.

The year was dotted with other literary enterprises. *My Collected Poems* appeared in 1983 with Sono Nis Press under the aegis of Robin Skelton. The book did little good, if nothing bad, to my status as a poet in Canada where I have always been seen — except for a few perceptive people like A.J.M. Smith and Margaret Atwood, who both included me in their historic anthologies of Canadian poetry, and like P.K. Page and Al Purdy, whose response may be suspect because they are such good and old

friends — as a man of letters who happens to write poems. Even among
critics there are very few who have suggested, as W.J. Keith has done, that
my poetry has been too much neglected. Yet I consider it my most
perceptive, my most originative, my most personal work. But now,
obviously nearing the end of my life, I have perhaps to accept that this
will not change and that I have written my poems for the love of the
craft and not the glory. Yet I still grasp the stub of my ticket in Stendhal's
lottery, to be read in a hundred years' time.

Some of the other literary enterprises at that time were really works
of pious but justified tribute. I edited a group of writings by and on
Margaret Laurence and her work (*A Place to Stand On: Essays on Margaret
Laurence*), which was published by a small cooperative Edmonton house,
NeWest, founded by my friend George Melnyk and devoted to the
literature of regionalism. I was moved by Margaret's delight when she
rang me up, half-seas-over, at midnight from Lakefield. She was such a
humble woman, as well as a remarkable novelist, that praise she knew
was sincere touched her deeply, for like so many of the best writers she
was in perpetual unsureness about her achievement, though while she
was writing she knew her way as accurately as a bat at evening.

Round about the same time Dimitri Roussopoulos, the spokesman of
the collective that operates the quasi-anarchist publishing house Black
Rose Books, asked for my cooperation in a collected edition of the works
of Peter Kropotkin which he planned to publish. Most of the books
would be reprinted unchanged, with introductions by me establishing
their historical backgrounds and relating them to contemporary times.
Here and there, especially in the case of *Fields, Factories and Workshops*, I
would have to abridge and provide epilogues to each section relating
them to changed and current situations. In the case of *Paroles d'un révolté*
I would have to translate a book never rendered into English before,
which did not trouble me, for I was already successfully engaged in my
translation of Marcel Giraud's *The Métis in the Canadian West*. And we
also planned a volume of *Fugitive Writings*, consisting of the major
pamphlets, like *The State, Anarchist Morality, Anarchist Communism*, that
did not form part of the substance of *Paroles d'un révolté* or *The Conquest
of Bread*, and should therefore be collected.

I accepted, because I knew Kropotkin's life and work well, having
written, with Ivan Avakumovic, the first biography of him in English,
The Anarchist Prince. True, I would be involved in a good deal of hard
work — researching and writing — lasting over a decade. The task is

only now, at the beginning of 1994, due to come to an end with the creation of a new Kropotkin title out of an incomplete series of essays on evolution, considered from a quasi-Lamarckian point of view which he published in *The Nineteenth Century and After* just before the Great War and which I rediscovered a year or so ago. And it has been, in financial terms, unprofitable work. Neither Dimitri nor I upheld the notion I had encountered long ago at Freedom Press, that an anarchist must expect nothing when he writes for the cause. A comrade must live, and if the only way for him to earn was by writing he must be paid, however modestly. And the pay, with my consent, was modest. Dimitri and other members of the collective took a minimal wage for their work, and I agreed to similar rates. As a kind of bonus, I persuaded Dimitri to reprint in facsimile some of my more important out-of-print books, so that my early studies of William Godwin, Aphra Behn and Oscar Wilde became available again, as well as *The Anarchist Prince* and my book of essays, *The Writer and Politics*.

And I did get a great satisfaction out of the task, for Kropotkin was one of the earlier anarchists who most influenced my ways of thinking. Not merely did I learn from him the principles of traditional anarchist communism, but also — in much the same way as other recent anarchist thinkers, like Paul Goodman and Colin Ward — I had been influenced greatly by his demonstration in *Mutual Aid* of the extent to which even the most authoritarian society is permeated and in fact sustained by mutual aid institutions. I knew from practice, having helped in the creation of two small relief agencies (TRAS and CIVA) on Kropotkinesque principles, that what he talked of was possible, and I believed that the conquest of bread, and other things more interesting, by peaceable means was the ideal way to anarchism. What I had learnt from Herbert Read and *Education through Art* fitted in happily with this philosophy, and in my more recent polemical writings, like *Power to Us All*, I have talked not of overthrowing the state but of bypassing it with changes involving the greater direct participation of the citizenry.

At almost the same time in 1983 as I came to my agreement with Dimitri over the Kropotkin series, I undertook another task that also occupied me for the next ten years. Jack David of ECW PRESS approached me with the invitation to write unifying introductions to twenty volumes which they would call *Canadian Writers and Their Works*. I imagine that Jack and Robert Lecker, his fellow editor, chose me because of my experience as editor of *Canadian Literature*, but also, perhaps, because of my standing as a critic outside academia — the nearest thing — as had been said — to a Canadian Edmund Wilson.

I accepted immediately, intending to make my introductions into something that could be taken as a continuing commentary on what makes a Canadian literature and holds it together over its few generations. And, indeed, this is what would happen in the decade that it took Jack and Robert to assemble their essays on individual writers and me to do the introductions. I always felt that it was a waste of time for my pieces to be published in this fragmented way without their ever cohering as a book, and soon we all agreed that I was offering the substance of two books, one on Canadian fiction and one on Canadian poetry, and when I had finished my work, and the last volumes of CWTW had been published in 1993 ECW PRESS appropriately published them, under the titles of *George Woodcock on Canadian Fiction* and *George Woodcock on Canadian Poetry*. They seem to be a fitting culmination of my work on Canadian writers, though I am still writing about them and shall probably put together another book of essays on them before I leave the scene.

As the year passed I became increasingly involved with George Orwell, keeping touch with Steve Wadhams as he told me of his success in gathering statements and comments from people who had known Orwell at every stage from childhood. It was to be an elephantine production, so far as radio was concerned, five hours long on New Year's Day, 1984, and by far the biggest venture of its kind in which I have been involved. Steve began to plot the general outlines of the programme, and I made notes for a uniting narrative but we resolved to keep the plotting to a minimum and to rely on the to-and-fro of studio contact. We arranged to get together in Toronto in October for a week of recording.

It was a good season to be in Toronto, for the air had an autumnal bite, there was no rain, and it was excellent walking weather. In the past I had never really liked the city, and had not been there for several years, but now I found it changed and greatly improved by the emergence of ethnically dominated districts and the general spread over the city of European and Chinese restaurants. I stayed in a hotel a short walk from the old girls' school building — brick neo-Gothic — that CBC radio still occupied on Jarvis Street, and Steve and I worked out a schedule that would give me a great deal of time during the day, for we would not meet until everyone else was leaving and the broadcast building was almost empty; then we would work with an assistant producer and a technician far into the night, the kind of time pattern to which I was accustomed at home. We did, I remember, do one daytime session in an old Toronto cemetery to get the sounds of birds and wind whistling in the trees, but why we did that I have no recollection.

During the day, at breakfast and at lunch, I would see my Toronto friends, Matt Cohen and Doug Fetherling, George Robertson and Robert Weaver. I spent an afternoon drinking beer with Elizabeth Smart and remembering Soho places and people, and almost a day with Phyllis Grosskurth, whom I have always admired as a fine biographer, and with her I lunched with Mavis Gallant, then teaching at Massey College. I liked immensely her bittersweet wit, which resembled that of her stories, and her evident contempt for all things academic. I also called on Louise Dennys in her publishing office near the Dundas Street Chinatown. Louise and I had been in communication for many years since she first came to Canada and made a tentative try at publishing in partnership with an antiquarian bookseller. Then we talked about doing a book of my essays, but I never put the right collection together for her.

Now she was part of the firm Lester & Orpen Dennys, with its interest in European books and its special connection, through Louise who is his niece, with Graham Greene. I thought of Louise as a possible publisher for *Walls of India*, which was now almost completed, so I rang up her office and she invited me to go in for a cup of tea. I had never met Louise in person, despite our past correspondence, but her height was legendary in the literary world. "Six foot eight," said some and others ventured "seven feet"; Matt Cohen flippantly suggested "eight feet." I found indeed a very tall young woman and a beautiful one, with great greenish eyes and auburn curls, and we immediately took to each other as people talking the same tongue, the same literary dialect. After some initial hesitations, she and Malcolm Lester agreed to commission *Walls of India*, which would eventually appear in 1985.

I had been given a room of my own in one of the CBC buildings where I could work at any time, and I would usually go there about five o'clock and type up my notes for the coming evening's section. Steve and I and the assistant producer would meet about 6:30 for a quick dinner, and then go down into the murky cellar studio, I gripping a mickey of gin to reinforce the water provided. They were amazing sessions, for I would find myself responding spontaneously to the clues provided by Steve's occasional questions and the clues provided by other people's memories, and we hardly used the rough scripts both of us had prepared as safety nets. It was to me a quite new oral form of creation, and I enjoyed it greatly, though I was obviously suffering from great tension, for urination became difficult and I suffered a temporary attack of bleeding piles. Still, I regretted when it was all over the comradeship and the spontaneous creativity of the little group of two producers, one technician and one writer working in the deep cellars far into the night. When it was all over in the early hours of the morning, they would all escort me back to the hotel in case there were muggers around; Toronto had a bad name in Vancouver in those days.

Soon Steve put the tapes together for the big programme, and I received copies of them. The production was a great success. It was taken by American Public Broadcasting, and aired throughout the United States as well as Canada. Eventually I would be awarded an Emmy, the clumsy bronze dancer which is the award of ACTRA, the broadcaster's professional association. But I did not hear the broadcast on New Year's Day, for we had flown to Australia on Christmas Eve.

Chapter 14

DOWN UNDER WITH THE DIGGERS

Though we had paid two visits to the South Seas, and on both of them had gone to New Zealand, we had on each occasion felt that we did not have enough time in our schedules to do justice to the mini-continent of Australia. We had encountered Australians on our trips through the Oceanic islands, and some of them were fine people, like the Dominican missionary Father Mees in the Solomons and the hotel-keeper Peter Barker in the Gilberts. Others had been singularly unpleasant, like the Australians who gravitated to a yet unliberated New Guinea and whom we would encounter in the pubs of Port Moresby, where their racial prejudices were expressed freely in the presence of the native barmen and waiters. Even the schools were racially segregated in Australian New Guinea; at Mount Hagen there was a native school and a separate white school to which the Chinese were admitted as a favour.

We had run into Australians also on our guided tour during our first hasty visit to New Zealand in the early 1970s. Some were impenetrably hostile, evidently regarding my pommy speech and manners with resentment. Others were easily companionable, as we supped big cans of Foster's Ale together. One thing that struck me was a collective dislike of history. "We don't need history, mate. We've got more than enough geography," one of them quipped to me, and I sensed they must have had a kind of *horror vacui* as they looked back towards a past that really began with the convict ships. Better, it seemed, to see themselves as a new country, a new people with its ancestry forgotten.

So it was not the idea of a series of strange traditional societies that interested me in Australia, as it had among the South Sea Islands, but the idea of the land, a land of vast monotonies like Canada, but monotonies of a different kind. I expected boredom; one can experience that in the most exotic of societies. But I expected enough of the new and unusual to keep my interest alive.

So far as interest went, the journey started off with an absurd adventure well before we reached Australia. We were flying to Sydney on a Qantas plane, and planned to stay overnight in Hawaii so as to break the journey. At Hawaii, we joined the passport queue, expecting to pass through easily as transit passengers. A smiling young immigration officer, wearing a lei of orchids and ginger flowers greeted us affably, and then opened a great black book like a thick encyclopedia. She looked, and then her manner froze, and she directed us to sit aside until her supervisor arrived.

I realized that my past was absurdly catching up with me. Almost three decades before, in 1955, on the dying verge of the McCarthy era, I had been refused an American visa to take up a professorship at the University of Washington, on account of my past of anarchist opinions and associations. As the years went by I began to ignore the prohibition, and whenever we wished we would slip over the border and take brief holidays in the American Northwest, down into Oregon and as far east as Montana, and nobody in the little frontier posts thought of looking in a big black book and holding me up. I had been through Los Angeles twice as a transit passenger, and once even through Hawaii without interception.

All this I told the immigration inspector when he called me into his office, but he banged on the black book. "I'm not responsible for what happens in little places in the country of Washington State. This is how we do it in Hawaii. You are inadmissible to the United States of America!" And, turning to my wife, he declared, "There is nothing against you, ma'am." "Of course," he added, turning back to me, "you're entitled to a hearing, but since this is a holiday we cannot hold one for another three days."

I was about to ask him what would happen to me in those three days — would I be stuck in an immigration department cell? — when I was aware of a big Polynesian Hawaiian standing beside me. "I'm from Qantas," he said, "and you're in luck. I've another plane leaving in an hour for Sydney. And it's almost empty. Let's go get your bags." And as we walked away he said disdainfully, "You don't have to take any of that shit. Those guys aren't real Hawaiians. They parachute them in from the mainland. A Hawaiian would have found a way to let you in for one night."

The plane indeed was almost empty. We had whole rows of seats on which we could lie down and have a good sleep, and whenever we were awake the crew plied us with champagne, so that we were wide awake and slightly tipsy when the plane curved over Sydney's great blue harbour and the summer bright December trees and we saw — an immediately recognizable emblem — the great segmented monolith of the Opera House.

We were so impressed, after our official reception in Hawaii, by the genial side of the Australian national character, as exemplified in an easygoing, sunburnt, golden-haired and polite immigration officer, that we listened with impatience to the gloomy-looking Polish taxi-driver who took us to our hotel. "Australia," he said with a kind of indurated wretchedness, "is all right for Aussies and kangaroos. I've been here twenty years, and still I'm treated as an outsider." I pushed his remark aside in my mind as perhaps due to irritation at having to work on Christmas Day while we drove past the rows of neat little terrace houses with the elegant cast iron railings on their balconies and the bright summer gardens. I was later to remember him.

Our agent had booked us a hotel up on top of the hill at King's Cross, the Montparnasse of Sydney. It was one of the casual atrocities of modern architecture, a hexagonal building with triangular rooms like slices of pie. True, it had a fine view of Sydney Harbour and out west to the haze of the Blue Mountains, but it aroused my claustrophobia because it made me think of the model prisons that Jeremy Bentham's disciples planned in the early nineteenth century. We moved next day to the Menzies, an older downtown hotel where we had a good room looking out on to an alley of public gardens.

In some ways the physical aspects of Sydney made me feel at home, for in a great deal it resembled Vancouver, without the grandeur. There were the surrounding and interpenetrating waters of Sydney Harbour, with its quays and docks, its numerous coves and bays. There was the vast span of the Harbour Bridge, even more astonishing than the Lion's Gate Bridge; there were large parks, and though there were no mountains the city was perched on a set of hills, where one often felt the sea breezes, which were a great boon in that muggy high summer. The landscape was not without its romantic qualities. On the outskirts there were rocky tree-covered crags at whose base the sea beat, and on their slopes houses were perched as in parts of West Vancouver.

What strikes one immediately about Sydney is that it is a working-class town in a way Canadian cities are not, just as Australia as a whole is a more working-class country than Canada. Edgy bonhomie turning easily to paranoiac hostility, patriarchalism (no wonder Germaine Greer emerged as an emblem of feminine reaction) and the macho ways of the pub and the working man's club are dominant in Digger society in the same way as they were in the working-class area of England described by George Orwell in *The Road to Wigan Pier*. One of the manifestations of this working-class predominance is the shabbiness of appearance of the downtown parts of Sydney and the shabby — not ragged or destitute — look of people in the Sydney streets. It did not seem as if they could not afford good clothes; it seemed that they did not care and had — even the women — almost no sense or style of elegance. But Digger society, as we soon discovered, did not include all Australians.

Still, unlike our earlier Australian acquaintances in New Zealand, the people of Sydney seemed to have rediscovered their past in a kind of rush like that which happened in Canada round about the centennial year in 1967. Bookshops where they did not know — or pretended not to know — of the dubiously macho Patrick White (a great world novelist if not entirely an acceptable Australian one), would have little corners devoted to Australian history and literature, though the proportion of Australian books available was still much smaller than that of Canadian-published books in Canada. And up on the Rock, where settlement began at Sydney, a great deal had been done to renovate the barracks and warehouses designed by middle-class forgers transported to Botany Bay. On Boxing Day people crowded round there, buying at the little craft stores that had been carved out of the often handsome old brick buildings and treating their kids to ice cream and pop in little open-air eating places. It was strangely reminiscent of English bank holiday crowds, and it made me think of the strange ambivalence of Anglo-Australian relations. In custom, in everyday life, Australia and New Zealand also are far closer to England a generation ago than any part of Canada, and the flattened out Cockney of their speech is a symptom of this, as is the love for beer in a country growing excellent wine. I often felt that my English accent was grating on Australian ears, but I concluded this was a matter of class antagonism rather than xenophobia. My accent had been resented as much at times in London's East End as ever it was in Sydney, which of course fits in with the notion of Australia as a working man's country. Australians cling to England because in some deep ancestral way they are English, and they hate standard English accents because they are working-class people. Interestingly, I never found the same love-hate relationship between English and New Zealanders. The New Zealanders were too much occupied in resenting the Australians.

In the evenings we would go back to King's Cross. It was the liveliest part of Sydney after sunset, and if we were not particularly interested in the nightclubs and the girly shows and the nancy shows, or in the tarts and gays who tended to swarm there, we did find it the best quarter for good food, and ate often at an Austrian restaurant that combined such Teutonic dishes as excellent wiener schnitzel and bratwurst with local seafood, the big langoustes which the Australians call lobster, and the curious crayfish they call Moreton Bay Bugs.

Because there is so little on the grand scale to trap one's attention, travel in Australia tended to be episodic; what one remembered were the brief encounters and incidents that opened the casements of the imagination a little. Into that Austrian restaurant came one evening a tall bulky bearded man of about fifty, with a tittering and obviously tipsy girl of about sixteen. She was the first aborigine I had ever seen out of a photograph, and perhaps she was a mixed breed, for her skin was pale, a kind of smoked ivory. She had smeared a great clown's mouth for herself with lipstick and wore a short dress more like a child's frock than a miniskirt. She stared and giggled at the tawdry ornateness of the restaurant with its stags' heads and candelabra. "What a wonderful place," she squealed. "I have never been in such a wonderful place." The fat man sat there murmuring phrases, and looked like a great purring cat intensely watching his prey. The name of Svidrigailof immediately came into my mind. They ate something quickly; the girl drank more and her speech began to slur. And then, as benign as a naughty uncle, the fat man led her away.

One evening we went to the Sydney Opera, as much on a duty visit to see the interior of this striking and famous building as to hear the opera, which was *The Magic Flute*. The inside of the building and the opera itself were equally disappointing and perhaps symbolic of the Australian failure to come to terms with traditional arts; only in the new, synthetic art of the film have they really succeeded. Inside the segmented shell of the Opera House a kind of metal structure had been built which seemed to exist independently of the building and in which the seats, upholstered in the most repellent of oxblood-coloured cloth, seemed to be suspended. There was a similar dissonance between the music and the performance. I have never in fact valued *The Magic Flute* as much as Mozart's earlier operas; there is a heaviness to it, not only because of its make-believe Masonic solemnity but also because it was composed to fit a Germanic dumpling of a text; Mozart should have stuck to good old Lorenzo da Ponte and his Venetian Italian. Because of these intrinsic shortcomings *The Magic Flute* depends on a superb performance, and the memory of Joan Sutherland in various Mozart roles led us to expect a good Australian rendering, but neither Sutherland nor anyone like her was there that night. The performance hovered in the middle provincial level; I have heard better Mozart sung in a little Bavarian town like Passau at the Prince-Bishop's theatre. The dull German libretto was replaced by a limping Australian one, and the depth of the performance came when Papageno spoke in a rough Sydney accent and made bad jokes about Leamingtons, a kind of local confection resembling what in far western Canada we call Nanaimo Bars.

One day we went up to Paddington, the old respectable working men's district where the terrace houses with their neat white balconies were being refurbished for the use of professionals and stockbrokers. In one of the shopping streets there was an "antique" shop that sold what elsewhere would rank as no more than curios. It was run by a pleasant old Hungarian woman who was just making tea when we entered to buy some trifle, and invited us to join her for a cup, drunk in what she described as her "last real Spode." She was attracted by Inge's vestigial German accent, and described her own early life in Budapest and her flight during the uprising of the 1960s. And then she went into the same refrain as the Polish taxi driver. Never had she yet been accepted by the Australians. Her friends were all Europeans, and life had become for her and for them a second exile; all said with the jests and quips that Hungarians love, but nevertheless very serious — something to be outpoured when the opportunity occurred.

I might have taken her lament more lightly if we had not picked up a taxi outside her shop. The driver was a Norwegian who owned his own little chain of four or five taxis. He was a pleasant man, and when we said that we wanted to go to the Blue Mountains but had no zest for bus tours, he remarked that he too could do with a day in the country, and named us a good price. The next morning he picked us up at our hotel and we drove off westward through one of those outer towns of many thousands of little red-tiled houses, identical in their squares of grass and garden, that surround every city in Australia and make it perhaps the most extensively suburban country in the world.

To anyone who has had the Alps of Austria and Switzerland for neighbours — or the Cordillera of British Columbia — the Blues are very modest mountains, rather rubbly, but with some impressively jagged sandstone crags and precipices falling sheer into deep valleys. Their description was exact, for one saw them through a blue haze rather like the blue tone of some of Cézanne's Provençal landscapes. It came from the volatile oil of the eucalyptus trees that covered the slopes and everywhere exuded the heavy smell of cough tablets.

One very quickly grew tired of eucalyptus forests in Australia. There are said to be six hundred species of this family in the country. Some of them have brilliant red or yellow blossoms and when these stand single they are often splendid. But when one sees many species in a forest it is hard to distinguish them, and the effect is almost as monotonous as that of the plantations of conifers that have recently been established in the Blue Mountains and elsewhere. But blue gums have qualities the pines do not share — among them the power of renewal. Forest fires often happen in Australia; there were two big ones while we were there. Once a fire starts among the eucalyptus, the very atmosphere ignites and the forest becomes a furnace. When the fire is ended, the countryside looks like an area of black death, often many miles of it, and the coniferous plantations remain dead, but very shortly after you seen green shoots emerging from the roots of the native gum trees, and the eucalyptus forest begins to regrow. The bursting of the green among the black then seems striking, and beautiful as a manifestation of life and survival.

The Norwegian turned out to be a widely read and travelled man, so that we had good conversation, and as we drove back into Sydney he remarked that he would like to continue it and invited us to a supper party at his house. He picked us up and took us out to a craggy hillside to which his house clung rather like a swallow's nest, looking down over bosky precipices to one of Sydney's many coves. The guests were all Australians by naturalization, but they came from Austria and Germany, from Hungary and Scandinavia, and there was not a single born antipodean among them. And once again the lesson was brought home, in their conversations, in the tales they had to tell, that Australia, like Canada, is a country of two solitudes, or three if one includes the aborigines. But the division was not that of language, as in Canada, but of origins. Born Australians — dinkum Aussies — do not think of immigrants as New Australians. They themselves are the only Australians, and remain aloof from others as a people whose myths begin not with the convict ships, but with such events as the gold rush and Eureka Stockade (which is why they call themselves Diggers), and they protect their role with curious inverted snobberies of which that against people with an English accent, or Pommies, is best known. If I entered into an argument with an Australian I was always aware that my voice was the first insult.

After leaving Sydney we set out on a big loop of a journey that would embrace all the state capitals, with excursions to lesser places, and we also intended to make a diversion to Alice Springs and Ayers Rock in the desert centre of the country. It was a journey that, like most of our journeys in the past, depended on serendipity, the luck of the road, for I have never been in the habit of taking letters of introduction. But in this respect Australia was a very different country from, say, India, and not serendipitous at all; while the episodes and encounters were perhaps the most revealing points, they came seldom. I had made the mistake of setting off without a mission to give our journey a focus, as I would do later in China by following contemporary Buddhism. I gave up the idea of writing a book on Australia almost as soon as we arrived, and we found ourselves uncomfortably shrinking into disgruntled tourists.

Tasmania was our first destination. We had envisaged it as a green and temperate land, and Hobart as a graceful Georgian city. In fact, as we drove in from the airport, the landscape seemed as scrubby and rubbly as any we had seen so far in Australia, and Hobart itself resembled an English coastal working town like Grimsby; it had neither grace nor space. One was urged to visit the sites of the old convict settlements, but I have no liking for prisons except in the fantasized vision of a Piranesi, and here I suspect I was rather at one with most Australians. I remembered in New Caledonia an exclusive aristocracy of old convict families, but these were mostly the descendants of political prisoners; there is no great credit to being the descendants of pickpockets, and so the Australian consciousness tends to relegate the original convict settlers to that great mass of others including Pommies and immigrants. Since it was the week after Christmas, the hostelries of Hobart were all full, and the only room we could find was in a big casino-hotel on the bay. For nothing better to do, I spent my evenings loafing through the gaming rooms and watching the faces of the gamblers, generally grim and pessimistic but occasionally fired by the euphoria of a run of luck. I kept away from the tables, for I have never wanted to set myself in a position where chance might entirely control me.

As soon as possible we took the plane to Adelaide, and this did turn out, at least in its form, to be an agreeable Georgian city. It was laid out during the Regency by a British surveyor general of the new colony of South Australia, William Light, who seems to have absorbed Aristotelian teachings about the ideal size of a city, since he planned one that could be seen from a high place like the cathedral tower or the roof of the Hilton Hotel in the main square, where we were staying. From end to end, north-south or east-west, one could walk comfortably through the town, with perhaps a pause for beer or coffee on the way, and beyond the square urban area, as precisely defined as a Roman camp, there was a continuous green belt where the playing fields and the rather good zoo lay beside the Torrens River, and there were large areas of parkland for the citizens to walk and cycle. Beyond the green belt, a couple of miles off, the inevitable Australian suburbs began.

At the Hilton we had a large and pleasantly decorated room with a fine view over the city at a good price, and we ate well in one of the three or four excellent Italian restaurants that lay a stone's throw away. Ordinary Australian food, like ordinary New Zealand food, is generally as tasteless as ordinary English food, and one relies on the immigrant chefs. But one thing Australian was superb in Adelaide — the wine. The city lies just south of one of the great vineyard districts of Australia, and even the wine served *en carafe*, which we regularly drank, was greatly superior to any Australian wine that makes the sea voyage to North America. Indeed, the excursions we enjoyed most on our journey were those to the vineyards of South Australia, where the green vines covered the hills, and the buildings were in the style of French wine chateaus and often mellowed by a century of use; even the tall gum trees there were of a species resembling in shape the cypresses of Europe. One realized what tastes and values the Australians had derived from Europe, yet our reaction of pleasure showed how visitors impressed by the aridity of Australian culture grasped at the hint of an older world.

At the same time, in Adelaide I had looked forward to seeing the collection of aboriginal art and artifacts which filled a whole floor of the state museum and was reputed to be the best in Australia. It was a measure of how little — despite their recent surge of interest in white men's history — the Australians value the past of their native people that we should find the gallery cleared of its contents in preparation for a show of LEGO that was part of an educational conference. I cannot imagine such an insult nowadays being offered anywhere in Canada to the aboriginal cultures. But perhaps I am naïve.

In late years there has been some clearing of conscience in Australia regarding the aborigines. They are now fully citizens, their land claims have been acknowledged in a rough and ready way, by large desert areas which no white man wants being returned to them. Adelaide was the first place where we saw a few aborigines, and they still seemed to us among the "insulted and injured," more badly clothed than other people, obviously poor, and caught up like so many of our own native people in the circle of unemployment and drunkenness. On Saturday night there was a great deal of drinking and shouting in Adelaide, and on Sunday morning broken bottles and beer tins were scattered over the pavements, but though I am sure all races participated, it was the aborigines whom we saw sleeping it off in back lanes; it reminded me of scenes of the past in racially marginal Canadian towns like Kenora and Williams Lake.

I found myself drawn towards such of the aborigines as I saw because, as among the Fijians, I sensed a natural goodness behind their conventionally rather ugly features, and looking at them I often wondered whether Neanderthal Man, that strangely wise uncle of our race, had in fact died out completely. Perhaps their vision of the natural world and the world of dream was derived from him. Some people might regard this as a belittling view of the aborigine, but I have always regarded what I know of Neanderthal Man with interest and respect and have regretted his replacement by the destructive and dominative Homo pseudo-sapiens.

Adelaide left its mark on me. I was leaving a tea-shop after fortifying myself with one of those concoctions of strange ingredients known as meat pies in Australia. I went out by a back stairway. The steps were covered with black linoleum and the light was inadequate, so that I misjudged my steps, slipped and fell, and broke my glasses. At that moment, as I floundered on those steps and other hands lifted me and blood streamed like a curtain over my right eye, I felt old for the first time. I was almost seventy-two. Fortunately the broken glass had not gone into my eyes. We patched up the wound with elastoplast. Though I had to go to an optician and get new glasses (this time plastic) I did not go to a doctor to get it sewn up, which was a mistake, for it healed with a scar and a droop of the eyebrow, so that even now my right eye is shaded and somewhat sinister while my left eye looks round and astonished in comparison.

From Adelaide we flew hour after hour over the desert outback to Perth in West Australia. It had been hot in Adelaide, high in the middle thirties centigrade, but in Perth it was touching forty degrees and humid as well. Fortunately, Perth is a town of many modern buildings, and some of them finely designed, so that one would progress slowly down the main streets, walking on the shady side and every quarter of a mile or so heading into one of the air-conditioned towers to get a breather of cool air. In a milder season it must have been a good city for strolling, with its view of the vast blue expanse of the Swan River Estuary. But that January we were defeated by the heat. Yet we appreciated the handsomely designed and very cool new cultural centre, where we saw our first good collection of aboriginal artifacts, arranged in exhibits that showed both their aesthetic qualities, their dreamworld setting and their connection with daily aboriginal life. Perth indeed struck us as the most culturally aware of all the Australian cities. Perhaps that was because of its comparative newness, but perhaps also because its isolation from other Australian cities had made it more self-reliant.

In Perth we abruptly changed our travel plans. Inge announced that she did not think we should really go to Alice Springs. She had a hunch that something would go wrong there, though she could not be specific. I protested, because I wanted to see the great central desert at close hand, monotony, spinifex and all, but experience has taught me to respect intuitions of this kind, and in the end I agreed, and we changed our booking to a direct flight to Melbourne. This led us to another odd encounter with Australian attitudes. We were, it turned out, entitled to a refund of about ninety dollars. "But I may have to give you a voucher," the clerk said. "I'm not sure there's enough cash in the safe." "Surely you'll have ninety dollars there," I said. "Well, we don't keep that much cash around these days," he answered. "There are so many criminals among the new people coming into the country that we have to be careful." But he did produce the money, and I resisted the temptation to remark on the criminal antecedents of so many of the founding fathers of Australia.

As for Inge's hunch, nature amply justified it, and in Melbourne we learnt of the unprecedented rains that fell on the desert centre of the country just at the time when we would have been there. The streets of Alice Springs were rivers on which people progressed by improvised rafts because there were no boats in the desert, and the train to Alice Springs was marooned for days in the midst of vast floods. So we were saved from an experience that would certainly have been adventurous and equally certainly uncomfortable.

Melbourne seemed to us the most civilized of Australian cities, modestly warm after Perth and even in its own way elegant, for the people were turned out more smartly than the folk of Sydney, and the late Victorian and Edwardian buildings in the core of the city were mingled with new buildings and airy arcades that had missed the austerity of the modern age, and whose post-modern fantasies fitted very well with the earlier buildings and seemed to illuminate their solidity with glass and sunlight filtered through palm trees. It was a city for lounging and loitering, for there were great old-fashioned parks with lakes and shrubberies, through which we wandered into town each day from the hotel where we stayed on its edge, another Hilton whose great attraction were its abundant nine-dollar meals in the coffee shop, chalked up each day anew on blackboards and the best restaurant value we had encountered in years. I gorged greatly and drank my fill of the Victoria wines, which were also excellent.

Melbourne was conscious of a tradition in the arts, as well as horse racing, and it had a good art gallery where there was a broad show of Australian works from the great uncouthnesses of Sydney Nolan to an interesting collection of those painters, the best of whom was Oscar Wilde's friend Charles Conder, who left Australia in the late nineteenth century to fulfil themselves in Europe, and produced some highly sensitive works in the impressionist manner.

One day we took a coach trip to the old gold-mine country of Ballarat, riding through vineyards and wheatlands and largely burnt-out forest (Victoria had been badly scarred that year) to the nineteenth-century town of worn down and grimy late Victorian brick buildings that looked no more interesting than British Columbian mining towns of the same era, like Rossland and Fernie. It was, in the same way, grandfather's past masquerading as history, the grimy nest from which a people dislocated from their roots and traditions sprang.

The worst feature of Australian tour buses was the thundering rock music whenever the driver was not delivering his banalities about places on the way. One day we complained about this to a woman clerk in a bus agency, and asked if the music might not be varied or at least toned down. It was what the people liked, she asserted resentfully; if we wanted to travel without music, we should hire our own car. *Vox populi* has an air of compulsion in Australia, where one is even compelled legally to vote in elections.

We turned backward by way of Canberra towards Sydney and Brisbane, our last destination. Canberra was a kind of Ottawa without Ottawa's earlier history, built around a great artificial lake. The best art gallery in Australia was almost unvisited; a couple of girl students played

Bach on their violins to earn pocket money in a shopping mall; a Melbourne woman in a supermarket cried out to us against the barbarous inadequacies of government towns.

Brisbane was muggy and architecturally pompous; food there was the worst in Australia. Yet outside Brisbane we spent perhaps our most contented day in the country. Our time was running out, and we had only one day left to make an excursion out of the city. The choice was between the Great Barrier Reef, which in the beginning of February was crowded with tourists, and the rain forest. Perhaps with a little nostalgia for our own vanishing woodlands, we picked the rain forest, and set off in a little Volkswagen bus that held six passengers and a long-haired young driver who slipped the Clarinet Quintet in his tape deck and never played anything but Mozart except when he talked, which was minimally. I have memory flashes of old farmhouses in tangles of tropical orchard, a cattle station with a broad-verandaed house and the same kind of Hereford cattle one might have seen on a Cariboo range, white wooden churches at crossroads, a village with a pub where we drank beer in the middle of the morning, trees full of white parrots, a big kangaroo — our first in the wild — leaping across the road and into a copse.

The rain forest was dense, damp and dark, quite different from the British Columbian coniferous rain forest, with many kinds of trees I could not identify, lianas looping everywhere, orchids and other epi- phytes, and a dense undergrowth. A great bird noise went on overhead whenever we stopped, but we saw few birds at ground level.

At last we came out on top of the forested hills, and there was a clearing with a big log restaurant and some cabins. We ate an excellent lunch of fish brought up from the reef and sat for an hour on the lawn watching the antics of the wallabies that came hopping from the neighbouring forest and would sometimes stand up to each other and box like European hares. Flights of brilliant parrots, scarlet and blue, yellow and green, flew in and out of the clearing with great noise. It was as near as we ever got to natural Australia, which in retrospect, and despite its vast spaces, seemed to me one of the most urban and — even more — suburban countries of the world.

Chapter 15

EUROPE REVISITED

Unlike most of my earlier distant destinations, Australia failed to stir my imagination any more than it stirred my intelligence while we were there. I had neither the right kind of experience to write a book about nor the right kind of initiative, and I contented myself with a single rather political article in the *Canadian Forum*, which to my astonishment won a National Magazines Award.

It would be more than three years before we undertook another major travel project, to China in 1987. In the meantime, we were content with a yearly springtime trip to Upper Austria and Bavaria, which had become almost our backyards, and we continued them until Inge's mother died in 1987.

The Christmas and New Year period of 1986–87 we spent in Switzerland, starting with Zurich where we walked much and ate well in the nippy near zero air, and going on to Ticino where we had lived twenty years before and staying in "Lugano Bella" of the old anarchist song, and Locarno where Bakunin had lived most of his unhappy last years. We tramped a great deal in the old arcaded towns and in the foothill countryside, using the excellent Swiss railway and postauto systems, and haunting the little Christmas fairs of the old towns, which were now permeated with faraway elements, so that we bought charming little appliqué pictures in cloth and wool by Chilean refugees and a fine Ikat hanging from an Indonesian couple. It was not new experience, except that there is a haunting freshness in every mood of an Alpine setting; rather it was confirming by repetition the continuity of our lives, and so, I suppose, were the short trips of a few days we would make occasionally into the Pacific North West: southern British Columbia (notably our beloved Kootenays) and Washington, Oregon, Idaho and even the highlands of Montana. Every night on these trips, to the great amusement of our friends when we told it, we would stay up till two or three or four to watch the old movies on television in delighted nostalgia, though we would not have had television in our home where it would create a major distraction to our normal working and social life. (Television — I am convinced — is the great atomizer of society in our age, keeping people at home for a vicarious and mostly spurious contact with the world, when they could be out, as their ancestors were, visiting each other, making their own music, taking part in community events.)

I worked steadily through 1984, finishing and finding a publisher for *The Walls of India*; Louise Dennys, after many hesitations, agreed. I wrote *Strange Bedfellows: The State and the Arts in Canada*, which arose out of a much simpler project to prepare a digest of the Massey Report for Carleton University Press. Douglas & McIntyre would publish it in 1985, and it caught the attention of quite a few people in Ottawa, including Timothy Porteous, the retiring head of the Canada Council, who reviewed it extremely favourably, and Marcel Masse, Minister of Communications, who invited me to lunch when he was in Vancouver, and whom I found an interesting example of the Québec political dinosaur, a *bleu* with an almost obsessive feeling that all the Liberal appointees in the Ministry of Communications (the Grits as he called them — an expression I had not heard in the West for decades) were conspiring to frustrate him. Not much came of that conversation or of our hopes that Masse might revitalize the CBC or give real support to the Canada Council, but at least he helped writers by fighting in cabinet for the Public Lending Right payments to writers to compensate for library use of books, and securing them.

I was also working during this period on the translation of Marcel Giraud's immense work (1,300 pages long) of *Le Métis Canadien*. Norma Gutteridge, the pleasant Englishwoman who runs the University of Alberta Press, gently persuaded me to do the vast work, for which I felt qualified by the knowledge I had acquired while writing *Gabriel Dumont* and from my earlier much shorter translations. I agreed to do the work in three years, supported by a generous Canada Council translation subsidy. I had started in 1983, working at it steadily day by day as part of my writing routine. I found the combination of translation and other writing doubly productive. The search for felicitous rather than literally exact equivalents helped to keep in tone the verbal texture of my other writing, and I found the prolonged contact with another mind that translation offered imaginatively stimulating. Giraud had done the research for his book in the Canadian West during the 1930s, but had actually written it while he sat out the German wartime occupation in Paris. It became for him a way of escape from the repulsive present into a past removed in time and distant in space from the Paris where he was living meagrely, particularly as it concerned a people who were struggling to maintain their identity and their vanishing freedom. Perhaps it was this factor of empathy that helped me also to sustain the long task and to make a translation that in the end so pleased Giraud — who wrote to me in excellent English, that he insisted on only one correction. It would appear, two massive volumes, as *The Métis in the Canadian West*, in 1986.

Another task from which I gained a great deal of pleasure over this period was an anthology for Mel Hurtig which we called *British Columbia: A Celebration*. The photographer, Janis Kraulis, took a series of extraordinary photographs showing the variations of British Columbian landscapes and townscapes and its natural life, and I paralleled it with an anthology of writings in English on British Columbia from Cook's companions in the eighteenth century to the younger writers of the late twentieth century, and surprised myself by the richness of the choices. I wrote a longish introduction on the culture of British Columbia (whose strong local patriotism somewhat disturbed nationalist Mel), and dedicated the book to Ethel Wilson and Rod Haig-Brown, my lamented friends who had been the true pioneers of modern writing in the province. Janis and I had a couple of lunches to discover each other, but neither of us tried to influence the other's work, and the harmony that resulted was entirely serendipitous. Mel produced a handsome book, and I was sad when it later went out of print and the collapse of Hurtig Publishers meant that there was nobody to reissue it.

During this period — 1985 and 1986 — I was working also on my second autobiographical volume, *Beyond the Blue Mountains*, which would appear in 1987, but I have already commented sufficiently on that book in the beginning of this volume.

The other activity in which we were much involved in the middle 1980s was the development of Canada India Village Aid, which we ran as an entirely voluntary society, operating by consensus, with no paid staff and no voting, a small and successful example of libertarian organization. We were making contacts with groups in India who operated in similar ways, and notably with Seva Mandir to whom we were introduced by John Friesen. Operating from Udaipur and working among tribal peoples — notably the Bhils, Seva Mandir strengthened our belief in an approach based on helping the people pick their own goals and helping them achieve them; there was nudging, shall we say, but not shoving. Through our contact with Seva Mandir we began to turn away from authoritarian doctor-oriented approaches towards more libertarian approaches based on recruiting villagers to accept training as health workers and then sending them back among their own people. Our first major effort was actually a training scheme of this kind, which produced a significant improvement in local treatment of sicknesses, in public health, and even in nutrition through the encouragement of composting and kitchen gardens. When a drought began in the areas of Rajasthan where Seva Mandir operated, we expanded into the environmental area, forming a partnership between Seva Mandir, which provided the technical services, the villagers who offered their labour, the Indian government which opened its granaries to compensate them, and we who provided the cash for buying the stone and cement (an expensive commodity in India) and transporting it. We built ten dams, each of which served a thousand people and their animals as it filled with ground water and the occasional rain. From the beginning we relied a great deal on the community of the arts, with which Inge and I had close and personal connections, to help us in fund-raising. Toni Onley's act of making paintings in India for us to sell in Canada was only one — though a great one — of these gestures. Through the summer of 1984 we worked on an Indian festival for the autumn. We had the cooperation of the India Music Society, with which we collaborated in importing an Orissa dancer and a noted Indian sitarist; Pacific Cinémathèque, which put on Indian films during the week; the Vancouver Art Gallery which hosted an exhibition of Toni Onley's Indian paintings, and Xisa Huang of the Bau-xi Gallery who did the same for a show of paintings donated by artists from all over Canada, including Alex Colville, Tony Urquhart and Ivan Eyre as well as the current Vancouver masters; finally, we held a great book sale, and with all this and a generous grant from the Canadian International Development Agency (CIDA), we were able to start our training scheme.

The artists, including the writers, continued to support us over the years, and two years afterwards we organized a nationwide poetry competition. Two poets who lived in Vancouver (George Bowering and George McWhirter) joined us in organizing the event and giving a first reading of the thousands of poems, good and bad, that poured in. Margaret Atwood, Al Purdy and I were the final judges, and the whole affair culminated in a poetry reading in 1988 organized by Greg Gatenby at Harbourfront, where Margaret and Al and I read in company with

John Pass, the first-prize winner, and the other five winners. The poetry contest, with a considerable supplement from CIDA, enabled us to build our ten dams in Rajasthan, around which Seva Mandir contoured the land and planted trees chosen for shade and fruit and forage. When he saw the first photographs of the dams, George Bowering said, "Now, that is great concrete poetry." The winning poems were eventually published in *Dry Walls of India: An Anthology against Thirst*, which Howard White brought out and Margaret Atwood introduced.

Two years later the same group, Bowering and McWhirter, Inge and I, would launch a similar competition for anecdotes, led to the idea by an evening drinking Bushmills when the tales flowed free. What we found was that poetry, despite the recent craze for oral readings, remains a written art with thousands of people treasuring manuscripts, while the anecdote is essentially an oral art and — surprisingly — a shy one, for people are rarely inclined to put on paper the tales they tell. So we had a far more limited response than we had from the poets two years before and in order to make a good anthology this time (*The Great Canadian Anecdote Contest*) I had to invite my friends in the literary world, such as Margaret Atwood and Timothy Findley, Ronald Wright and Dorothy Livesay, Julian Symons and Eric Wright, to send us their tales as guest writers. They responded generously, and so a good book finally appeared, with George McWhirter's introduction.

For me one of the splendid features of our work with Canada India Village Aid was the way it created or extended friendships, which I believe was due to the open style of our organization, our persistence in discussion until consensus was reached, and there was never any anger of the defeated at the end of our voteless meetings. Some of the people involved were old friends like Doris Shadbolt, John and Marta Friesen, and the psychologist Toni Phillips. Toni Onley had come in because of our travels together. Russell Wodell, whom I had known years before in connection with a cooperative radio station, eventually became our secretary, after I had abandoned the task, and Amir Mitha, an Ismaili accountant from Uganda, joined us as treasurer after he had worked with us through the India Music Society. Trish La Nauze, a theatrical publicist, came to help with an early book sale and stayed on to become a director and play a major role in India Week. Judy Brown had been one of my students at UBC decades before, and we renewed our friendship in work together. Keath Fraser was a fellow writer who one day approached me with a proposal to prepare an anthology of travel writings, which he would edit and usher through the publishing process. It was to be called *Worst Journeys (Bad Trips for the Americans)* and Keath brought in an amazing variety of writers willing to forego their royalties for CIVA. The book in fact became a best-seller, and up to now has contributed more than $70,000 to CIVA's funds. And finally, there was Sarah McAlpine, whom I had known in her student days when she came to audit my European Literature course at UBC. She became one of the most active workers for CIVA and eventually its president, and she also became, over the years, one of my closest friends, a person of great vitality and variety, loyalty and generosity.

The desire to combine travel with good works was still in the minds of both Toni and me. It was activated when vandals burnt a liberal synagogue in the university area of Vancouver. We stood in the blank empty shell and decided to offer what we had done for CIVA; to go to Israel, for me to write and Toni to paint, and then give the proceeds of the book and the paintings to the rebuilding fund. We would pay our own way and hope to make up with extra paintings and articles in periodicals. The synagogue elders were naturally pleased, though at a difficult moment some of them wanted to approve the book before publication. I refused and, to my surprise, the rabbi, a man of good sense, supported me.

We planned our departure to coincide with the launching of *Walls of India* in Toronto and spent our days there in a succession of radio and television interviews with media blockheads; I also talked to editors and met old friends like Al Purdy and Margaret Atwood, Phyllis Grosskurth and George Galt and Earle Birney. Louise Dennys arranged a lavish dinner, and one evening in Britnell's Bookstore we signed books as people crowded in by the hundreds (Greg Gatenby brought two large bags containing all the Woodcock titles in his library for me to sign on top of *Walls of India*); it was the first time I submitted to such an exercise, and I would not have done it for my own benefit.

In Toronto we went for drinks with the Israeli consul-general, an eminently civilized European, and received the seventh of our introductions to Teddy Kollek, the legendary mayor of Jerusalem, and a great many good hints about hotels and travel. We also had the news that on the evening after our arrival a reception would be held in our honour at the Canadian Embassy in Tel Aviv. We had done our reading, and everything seemed well prepared when we set out for Munich, our first base, where we could visit Inge's mother — now in Passau — and eat some good Austrian food in the inns over the border before leaving Europe. Everything went according to plan until the day before we were due to fly from Munich by an El Al plane to Tel Aviv. We had arrived in Munich the night before. At lunchtime Inge and I saw the headlines of a German newspaper. The Israelis had bombed Yasser Arafat's head-quarters in Tunis; people had been killed, though Arafat survived. We were sure there would be reprisals, and an El Al plane flying out of Munich so soon after the Israeli strike seemed a highly possible target. We mulled the matter over all afternoon and then, when the four of us sat down to dinner in the Franciskaner Hof — eel that night followed by excellent plum dumplings with litre steins of Munich beer — we discussed our plans.

I was willing to go and take the risk, because I wanted to see a new country, and towards the state of Israel I had an ambivalent attitude, partly admiration and partly anger, that I wanted to work out by direct witness. I also felt that at my age to worry about physical risks was somehow undignified. I had lived a good life, and if I went out with a bang . . .

The rest, the younger ones, thought differently and, apart from stating my attitude, I did not try to influence them. They felt the risk and did not want to take it. The cause of the synagogue was quickly abandoned, and we planned instead, since we had come so far, to introduce Toni to the painting possibilities of Europe by travelling through Switzerland to Provence and then through the Pyrenees into Spain, and then back through France into the Rhineland, taking a plane home from Frankfurt and avoiding the big cities after we left Munich. For Inge and me it was a revisiting of places that had meant much to us in the past, and it turned out — though we did not think of that — to be a last pilgrimage through old haunts.

We headed southwest from Munich through the gentle Alps of Upper Bavaria to Lake Constance, where the turning leaves of the vineyards bordered the water with gold, and crossed by ferry to Switzerland's ancient eastern cantons, staying in the old Santis Hotel in Appenzell and going on to Grindelwald for a couple of days in sight of the Jungfrau.

Toni found painting in the Alps difficult after British Columbia's ranges; I think it was hard to adjust to the quick changes of light and colour on the rocks. So we went on through shabby old Interlaken and along the Thuner See to Spiez where we turned off into the Gruyère country. It was the day when the cattle were being brought down from the Alps where they had been grazing all summer among the flower-strewn pastures, and all through the morning we would be held up by little processions of peasants and their animals, the men and women in their colourful local costumes, the animals garlanded with flowers and their bells tolling and tinkling as they walked. The lead cow, which wore a large and heavily sonorous bell suspended from its neck with a wide embroidered band, had a special headdress shaped like a lyre rising above its horns. The villages were full of people in their various *trachts*, and we could hear the boom of the long alpenhorns as the cowherds played them in the squares outside the churches; we were reminded of the great trumpets of the Tibetans.

We reached the benign and balmy shores of Lac Leman at Vevey and drove along the lakeshore, stopping for an excellent pasta meal at Nyon, and skirting Geneva to spend the night in a Novotel at Chambéry. The next day we drove around the edges of Grenoble to the Route Napoléon, and stopped at Aix so that Toni could see the country that had inspired Cézanne and piously do his version of the Montagne Ste. Victoire. A couple of days later we were in Arles, with its echoes of Van Gogh, and I compared the present tourist-oriented city with the relatively unspoilt antique city I had known in the 1930s. Symbolic of the loss of innocence was the Graeco-Roman theatre, which then lay in an open park through which people wandered freely, and freely used the ancient benches of the theatre to lounge and doze or to sit eating al fresco lunches. Now it was enclosed within turnstiled fences and almost empty. It was no longer, after two millennia, part of the city life. The same applied throughout the Provençal countryside. There was a turnstile at the Graeco-Roman site near St. Rémy, and up at Les Baux the splendid old street of half-ruined medieval mansions with great fig trees growing within them had been roofed again and inhabited by curio shops and fast-food eating spots, with a turnstile at the upper end to cage off the rocky little plateau and the old castle-palace where the troubadours had sung. Everywhere petty commerce prevailed.

From Arles we headed westward through Nîmes and Montpellier and Béziers and then inland to Carcasonne, Viollet-le-Duc's little masterpiece of romantic restoration that, with its neat masonry and the candle-snuffer roofs of its towers, looked like a magnified toy. Thence we went on towards the Pyrenees through the arid valleys of La Corbière. On the hilltops stood the ruins of castles whose lords, in the twelfth century, were heretical Cathars — belated gnostics — against whom Simon de Montfort waged a murderous crusade at the bidding of Pope Innocent

III. Their castles were besieged and the inhabitants were burned in grisly mass bonfires. In these bleak grey valleys, under a lowering autumn sky, it was easy to believe an aura of tragedy from that terrible past still hung over the landscape. I think we were all relieved when, at a little spa called Aix-les-Thermes, the road began to climb in great loops through the chestnut forests towards Andorra. Spain was just ahead, and I idly quoted a remark of Proust, the gist of which is that it is unwise to go back to places where one has been happy. But none of them took it seriously.

The pass rose over eight thousand feet into the clouds, out of which a little frontier post loomed; an Andorran in a green uniform waved us into his tiny country. Then the road levelled. As it tipped towards Spain we drove suddenly out of the mists and the sun shone brightly on the tan-coloured mountain pastures and the first ski hotels of Andorra.

It seemed a good omen, but in the end Proust turned out to be right. Even Andorra was not what I had remembered. Only a generation ago it was a spartan little mountain country that lived by cattle and sheep rearing on the high pastures of the Pyrenees and by smuggling. Its hostelries were dismal inns. Now the hillsides were dotted with ski resorts, and the winding valley bottom that forms Andorra's only artery had become a long ribbon of hotels, customs-free emporia, banks and jewelers' shops jostling each other, with the cars of the newly rich Andorrans filling most of the parking space.

Andorra was only a beginning. In the next two weeks, as we went south through Aragon and Castile towards Toledo and then into Andalusia and the western marches, we realized that Spain too had changed in ways of which the Michelin guide I carried gave no idea.

Spain in the mid-1980s, a decade after our last visit near the end of Franco's reign, was undergoing revolutionary changes in three directions: a belated industrial revolution, a rapid population shift from country to city, and a growing annual flood of tourists that had now reached forty million.

In a land that survived until recently by exporting its agricultural products and allowing foreigners to extract its mineral assets, new factories with inadequate pollution controls were appearing like miniature Sudburies where there had once been quiet market towns. The growth of industry made travel far less comfortable. The Spanish railway system is astonishingly primitive still and largely taken up by military traffic, for despite the end of the dictatorship the army remains a strong, ominous presence. The greater part of agricultural and industrial transport was using a highway system constricted by the many mountain ranges. Mostly, as we edged from place to place during our two weeks in Spain, we were caught in long snakes of traffic whose pace was determined by ill-maintained trucks belching black smoke, so that by the time we went back over the Pyrenees, all of us were suffering from minor respiratory troubles and ragged tempers.

In many parts the very look of the land had changed. Rural areas I remembered as well populated fifteen years before were now inhabited mainly by old people. Farming was largely mechanized, the young had fled into the towns in search of employment, and the urban areas had grown in what to the outsider looked like unplanned confusion. One approached old cities whose medieval walls and church towers had stood not long ago as landmarks in a wide open countryside, and found one's way barred by besieging rings of factories, warehouses and raw, new utilitarian apartment buildings set in vistas of rubble and garbage.

One of the great sights of Spain used to be the splendid eleventh-century walls of Avila, which stands on a plateau over four thousand feet above sea level. "The walls are complete," said Michelin. "They dominate the landscape from afar." Alas, they no longer did: a new town was arising outside the walls, and the tide of building had already blotted out what was once the most dramatic view of the city — from the west, seen as one drove over the mountain pass. Mérida was another example — an ancient place where many buildings constructed by the Romans two thousand years ago are still standing. When one entered Mérida in the past, one's view was dominated by the tall arches of the aqueduct that long ago brought the water into the Roman city. This time I had to look hard before I saw those elegant arches, dwarfed among a cluster of jerry-built apartment blocks. There had been no attempt to fit the ancient and the new together in a planned environment.

Almost alone among the larger cities we entered on this visit to Spain, Toledo had avoided the fate of being overwhelmed by its own growth. It too had grown, but intelligent planners seem for once to have taken control, and instead of chaotic suburbs crowding the access to the old city, industrial and residential areas had been built in the hills some miles away and well out of sight. The original Toledo, with its cathedral and its churches and its ancient walls, still clusters on the hill around which the river Ebro flows, spanned by bridges built by Arab kings one thousand years ago. As Toni recognized when he made his own luminous watercolours of the place, the cityscape had changed very little since

Domenikos Theotokopoulos, the man the Toledans call El Greco, painted it four centuries ago.

I never did find out why Toledo had made so much more graceful an entry into the modern world than other Spanish cities, for my time was taken up with one of those misadventures about which Michelin had not warned us. Inge and I had gone into the cathedral, and were walking, towards the exit, discussing that splendid El Greco painting, *El Espolio*, which we had just seen, when I was tapped on the arm.

A little man stood there, dressed in the pale blue shirt and grey trousers that seemed like a summer uniform among Spanish clerks; he had a camera around his neck and carried a little tote bag; his companion, garbed in the same respectable way, stood beside him. "Look, señor," he said with a plummy Madrid accent, "Your jacket!" And indeed, streaked down the back of my coat was what looked like an ample bird's dropping. The little men came forward solicitously, opening their tote bags and pulling out tissues, which they offered us. I took off my jacket and Inge put her handbag on a little step at my feet where we could both see it and started to clean the coat as best we could. We wiped off much of the mess, and the little men walked off, to turn a moment later and point excitedly at the roof. "Look!" they shouted. "The pigeons!" We looked, seeing no pigeons, and when we looked back, Inge's bag was gone. By now the little men had vanished and it was hopeless to hunt them down in the cathedral's maze of chapels and entrances.

We were naturally angry at our loss, for Inge was carrying several thousand dollars in cash, since our synagogue friends in Vancouver had suggested this so that we would be prepared to profit by sudden fluctuations in the value of the Israeli shekel. Her traveller's cheques were replaced quickly by American Express, and fortunately I had her passport in my pocket at the time. The insurance company paid adequately for Inge's lost jewelry. But the cash was irreplaceable. Yet perhaps it was mostly our pride that was affected. We had boasted that for decades we had travelled the earth and had never been robbed. We had begun to think ourselves immune, and now we had been caught. Yet at the same time my anger was mingled with an appreciation of the professional skill of the thieves. It was a well-crafted, self-assured deception, and as a craftsman of another kind I admired it.

In this incident the Spanish authorities won generally failing marks. The police helped us in no way except to show us an album of inappropriate mug shots and give a paper we could show to American

Express. The clerks of Air Iberia, the only airline with a local office, refused point-blank to get in touch with KLM on our behalf to replace our stolen plane tickets. And, in the end, before we left Spain, we were shaken down anew, this time by the agents of the state.

We had swung southwest through Granada, whose contrasts of rich and poor seemed to have grown more startling than ever and westward to Arcos de la Frontera on suddenly empty country roads — the Spain we remembered — through dazzlingly white little Andalusian towns like Olvera and Algodonales, filled with bright flowers and each dominated by its castle of golden stone and its massive baroque church.

Arcos is one of the most beautifully set towns in Spain — a tangle of ancient alleys, steep narrow streets and old whitewashed buildings, built on a high spur of rock where there is no room for the jerry-builders to get a foothold. The town square is right on top of the rock, surrounded by the castle battlements, the richly carved church of Santa Maria and the big eighteenth-century House of the Corregidor, which as been turned into a parador.

For me the main attraction of Arcos — and the reason why I have gone back — is the high and precipitous cliff on whose edge the parador stands, with the rapids of the Rio Guadelete glistening far below. The cliff is inhabited by great colonies of birds: black jackdaws and silvery grey pigeons and elegant little pink-and-grey falcons. To sit taking one's drink of an evening as the sun falls reddening through the dust-haze towards Jerez and the river below turns into a silvery ribbon catching the last of the sky's light, and to watch the aerial gyrations of these birds who live in such miraculous harmony, is to me one of the great experiences of Spain.

We headed northward through Extremadura and across into northern Spain and the environs of Burgos, once a great Francoist centre. Manners did not seem to have changed greatly in that area, as we found when we fell foul of the Guardia Civil. Toni was driving up a long gentle hill, with a broken median line, when the truck driver in front signalled us to overtake. Toni and a French driver before him did so; as the two cars sped ahead of the truck, the line changed from broken to solid, and there the jackbooted Guardia were waiting. They charged each driver the equivalent of $100; there was no way of evading payment, for they arrogantly impounded drivers' licences and car papers until the "fines" were paid in cash. It was a deliberate trap; how much of the "fines" found their way into official coffers we could only speculate.

We decided to head immediately out of Spain, and it was after dark when we crossed into France and reached Bayonne, a good hotel and an excellent meal of local fish. The next day we started on what turned out an artistically oriented crossing of Europe. We drove to Montauban (for the Ingres paintings) and to Albi (for the great Toulouse-Lautrec collection) and Moulins for the famous Madonna, and Colmar for the wonderful old town itself. Then we crossed into Germany, found our way through Freiburg and the Black Forest to Bavaria, where we rested for a couple of days at Oberdorf in the mountains, and then on to Munich to renew our plane tickets. We continued north to Regensburg for the great cathedral (here I had to buy a sweater I still use, for the winter winds had started), on to Würzburg for the marvellous Tiepolo frescoes, and finally to Frankfurt and our plane home.

Chapter 16

BETWEEN JOURNEYS

Our last great journey was still ahead when we returned from Europe near the end of 1985, but we were already preparing for it — our first visit to China. In fact, I and my friend Paul Huang, who founded the Bau-xi Gallery — the best in Vancouver — had been talking about it for a long time. He had been born in China, spoke both Cantonese and Mandarin, and seemed in every way the best companion one could wish. During the years of Mao's ascendancy I had been disinclined for political reasons to go; I doubted greatly in any case if the Chinese at that time would welcome me. But now, in the early years of Deng's ascendancy, it seemed as though the rigidities of the Chinese system were being relaxed, and my long-sustained general interest in Chinese culture was revived: the desire to connect with another ancient civilization. Besides, as rather obsessive travellers, we saw it as another great country to add to our list of destinations — for I have more than a little of the special imperialism of the travel writer. Paul introduced us to the cultural consul in the Chinese Consulate General in Vancouver, and immediately he agreed to explore the idea of a trip there under the auspices of the Ministry of Culture, if we partly paid our own way, which seemed to me a reasonable arrangement.

Meanwhile, during 1986, as we waited for the Chinese bureaucracy to digest our proposal, and Paul kept contact with the local officials, I was involved in a number of tasks that did not show immediate results.

One of them was the consequence of the visit to Vancouver of Andrew Franklin, one of Penguin's London editors. I had worked with Franklin on a new and enlarged edition of my *Anarchism*, which actually appeared in 1986, and he wanted to discuss new ideas with me. I talked of my proposed retranslation of Proust, but he said Penguin were content with the Kilmartin adaptation of the old Scott Moncrieff translation. I considered the old translation Edwardian in spirit and often inaccurate, sentimental where Proust was ironic, soft where Proust was hard, and felt it was time for a new version for the late twentieth century, but I failed to convince Franklin. My feeling was that Penguin had too much money invested in the old Proust to experiment with a new one.

Franklin himself had two suggestions — a new translation of Alexis de Tocqueville's *Democracy in America*, and a *Social History of Canada*. I was interested in the Tocqueville project, and put some time into it, but it did not work out. However, the *Social History of Canada* did; it was to be published by Cynthia Good at Penguin Canada and distributed in the international Penguin network. I enjoyed restating Canada's history according to my regionalist ideas. The book appeared in 1988, and would be one of the best-selling of my books because it hit the college market.

I was working on the *Social History* during 1986 and also finishing *Beyond the Blue Mountains*, the second volume of my autobiography, to which I have already referred in this volume. It would be published in 1987, as was a third volume of my essays on Canadian writers, *Northern Spring: The Flowering of Canadian Literature*, which I gathered together in 1986.

I became involved in anarchist writing once again during this period, not with my old comrades in London around the Freedom Press, whose attitude still struck me as conservative and trapped in outdated revolutionary delusions, but with a German group in the Ruhr who ran an excellent magazine called *Trafik* that reached out to all the libertarian possibilities in our society, whether through environmentalism, culture and the arts, or feminism. For me they represented far more than *Freedom* did the regenerated anarchism of our time, and apart from articles by me in their magazine, they published my first book ever to make its initial appearance in a language other than English. *Traditionen der Freiheit* consisted of a group of essays on various aspects of anarchism drawn partly from past publications and partly written especially for this collection. The Trafikers were also talking of publishing a German version of my *Anarchism*, but up to now it has not materialized.

And then, during this period, there were the excursions into film scripting, rather than filmmaking, for by no means all I wrote in this genre reached the screen or the eye of a television camera. During the early 1970s I had indeed written the series of scripts for the films on the South Seas which I researched in 1973, and these had appeared very successfully on CBC television, and later I had done the scripts for two films on the Doukhobors that Gordon Babineau produced under the joint auspices of the CBC and the National Film Board.

But these were exceptional triumphs, for I quickly found that film writing was quite unlike any other genre, and not merely in form, since it was written in the hope rather than the certainty of production, and it provided a means to earn money, which film companies seemed lavish in dispensing cash for ideas they could not generate themselves, provided one was not expecting the equivalent of publication. I know writers who live in this way, writing and revising scripts that are never metamorphosed into films and earning a living without ever seeing their names on the screen.

It was a frustrating process for any writer who really gains his fulfillment from seeing his work in some effective communicable form, print or film, but for a while I played my own small part when I needed a little money. A British-Spanish consortium paid me $12,000 for a mere chronology of Orwell's life during the 1930s in connection with a film on his role in the Spanish Civil War, a film that was never produced. Another group paid me $2,000 for a sketch of life on the Sepik River in New Guinea that might be used in an "exploration" film; again, I heard nothing of the film. For a period the National Film Board was offering me $800 apiece for two-page ideas; I did about half a dozen of these, none of which was ever used, and then began to feel it was somehow undignified to be misapplying my talent for communication to paid non-communication.

But there was one enterprise that I took more seriously. In 1980, at the Vancouver Film Festival, one of the productions was *Shadows in the Wind*, a film by an Iranian producer, Bahman Farmanara. Bahman was present in person, to tell of the problems of filmmakers under the new Islamic regime, and a few days later I met him at a small party given by John and Marta Friesen. He was a man of broad cosmopolitan culture, and a bright, mobile mind, and I liked him immediately. A few days later he rang up and asked to come and see me. He had the hint of an idea for another feature film, to be done in Canada, though the germ of the tale he gave me came from a Persian story about a man and a woman and a wolf. He thought we might call the film *Lupus*. I liked the idea, felt challenged by the medium, and agreed to write a script for no payment down, since I realized that Bahman had very little money. It was the first time I had done anything so quixotic. I added it to my other tasks, working at it slowly, and over a period of years we tinkered at the script and tried to raise the financial support to produce it. We never did, and though Bahman, who has now gone back to Iran, still talks of it, I have become reconciled to *Lupus* never materializing in its original form. So I have now decided to use the idea for a somewhat unorthodox novel to be called *Stories of Wolves*, on which I am now working parallel to this autobiography. The ground theme of the abandoned film and the developing novel is the revival of a dying village through the return of the son of the dead owner of the derelict mill, but it is really the fate of the returning prodigal that provides the driving obsession of the novel, for he is a former revolutionary disillusioned by methods of violence who is attempting to return to a career of gradually ameliorating society yet is haunted by guilt for his betrayal of the cause he had followed for many years as a rebel leader in South America.

Meanwhile, as 1986 drew to a close, we were well advanced in our negotiations with the Chinese authorities. China at that time seemed in a relaxed and welcoming mood, and the authorities in Beijing were willing to help us go anywhere we wished in China. I had wondered whether they would know about my record as an anarchist, and how that might affect their welcome to me. I realized that they had in fact a good knowledge of my background through a curious circumlocutory gambit that began with the cultural consul in Vancouver and followed me through China. "Of course, we know you are the Canadian Ba Chin," he said to me, and everything was encompassed in that phrase. For Ba Chin was a great Chinese survivor, an old anarchist with whom I had been in correspondence during the 1940s when he lived in pre-revolutionary Shanghai. He was a popular novelist as well as an advocate of anarchism, who had dropped the name of Li Pei Kan under which I had originally known him for the *nom de plume* of Ba Chin — the first syllable of Bakunin's name followed by a sinicized version of the last syllable of Kropotkin's name. I was in a way used to this kind of identification, since the Doukhobors have long been calling me the Canadian Tolstoy. Ba Chin had undergone all the great purges, but somehow had emerged unscathed and still an anarchist. To receive his name seemed a good omen for our journey.

I had one special wish, and that was to see the Gobi Desert and the Caves of the Thousand Buddhas at Dunhuang, which lay along the Silk Road by which ancient communications between China and western Asia had moved. It was still under close police supervision, and we would need a permit, but no difficulty was raised about that. So Paul and Xisa,

Inge and I set about planning our trip. We would fly to Hong Kong and then by Chinese plane to Beijing, and leave there as quickly as possible, first for Datong to see the great rock-cut Buddhas at the Yungang caves, and thence to the old monastic centre in the mountains, Wutai San, and thence via Taiyuan to Xi'an, which had once been the T'ang capital of Chang'an, and thence fly to Lanzhou, from which we would enter the desert and reach Dunhuang. It was deliberately a trip into what I regarded as the land of Yang, the arid, rigorous North China on the edge of Mongolia, as opposed to the Land of Yin, the moist and feminine south of the country. We knew that in the north so much that was connected with the early history of Buddhism would have survived. The south and the southwest we hoped to visit on a later trip.

We did not want to go as guests of the state or of some semi-official organization. I had writer friends who had done that and had been forced into rounds of factory and farm visits in the constant company of local writers, a breed I may love individually but collectively find as annoying as any other kind of mob. The party would consist only of the four of us and Lieng, the teenage son of Paul and Xisa, who would prove a great asset, since most Chinese are fond of children. We would be accompanied by an English-speaking representative of the Ministry of Culture, who would make all the necessary arrangements on the way.

There was — this was China of 1986–87 — no hint of a wish to censor or even to know what I might say, and there was no attempt to put prohibitions on where we might go, though I imagine there would have been difficulties if we had asked to see the regions where atomic testing went on or the areas where there were still rehabilitation camps. The general attitude then was "See what you like. We have nothing to conceal from the world." We paid our way with a not inexpensive daily charge, which left us feeling independent, and which in the long run turned out to be quite economical, for it included not only the travel between place and place and the food and lodging; we were also free to make considerable excursions at no extra charge, to go to the opera whenever we wished, and even tiny details like admissions and guides to museums were paid for. All we needed cash for were the bottles and cigarettes and occasional gifts that we bought at the tourist emporia in the towns.

Chapter 17

CHINA

We left for China in April 1987. The daffodils and bluebells were blooming in our Vancouver garden, and we realized we would be missing the best of the year's seasons at home, and that, as indeed happened, we would find a vegetable chaos when we returned. But the prospect of making our own sense out of the great enigma of China overwhelmed these domestic considerations in our minds.

We flew over clouds most of the way from Hong Kong to Beijing, and it was less than an hour before our arrival that we began to see the close pattern of paddies and orchards that was Chinese soil, and to descend over the fields and the long French-looking avenues beside the roads. The airport was large and new, and surprisingly few planes were standing there. As we were walking along the concourse towards the customs and immigration desks, Paul pointed out to me the banners printed in red lettering that hung across it. They welcomed the "Inaugural" delegation from the German Democratic Republic, in Chinese and in English, not in German. What subtle insult to a client state of Russia was contained in that usage?

The customs officials, one of them a charming young woman who spoke excellent English, were friendly, and all seemed to be going well except that nobody from the Ministry of Culture was there to welcome us. Then we noticed two men gesticulating through the glass wall of the corridor behind the customs desk and pressing against the glass a sheet of paper on which I could faintly read the word "Woodcock." When we dragged our suitcases through the customs area they met us in the hall, a short middle-aged man and a tall young man with a most un-Communist mop of hair. Chen Suyin, the short man, was head of a bureau in the Ministry of Culture; Zhou Ziyi a junior officer. A hostility between bureaucrats had prevented them from coming into the customs area.

Ziyi was to be our "friend" on the journey. We liked him at once and

171

never had any reason to change our minds. They took us, with apologies to a third-rate hotel with a bad kitchen and an even worse bathroom, all the time making excuses that the good hotels were packed. Since we intended to stay only two nights at Beijing, we did not complain; we only felt apprehensive — unnecessarily as it turned out — about the hotels we might encounter in the hinterland.

That evening we went to an acrobatic theatre, where the stage propaganda of past decades had vanished and everything was straightforward balancing and tumbling and juggling, and the decor and costumes were in sentimental colours and Ching bad taste.

It was more interesting to walk in the little streets behind Tiananmen Square where the working people were doing their shopping. Watching the couples wandering in the dim light with their purchases in string bags and their kids licking ice cream or hugging little bags of hard-boiled sweets, it seemed like Saturday night in a north of England industrial town of my youth. Engels, whose great portrait stood nearby in Tiananmen Square alongside Marx and Lenin, would have felt at home there.

Our one day in Beijing we decided to divide between a morning trip to the Great Wall, and an afternoon wandering in the Forbidden City. The journey to the wall began through flat country like that through which we had driven coming from the airport. Brown fields where men were ploughing, and sometimes standing upright on little harrows dragged behind the seeders to press them into the ground; fields of springing blue-grey winter wheat; the ubiquitous plastic greenhouses from which, as the sun rose, the farmers were rolling back the great mats they had pulled down to save the plants from the chance of a late night frost. Peasants were cycling towards the city with large baskets arranged pannier-wise on their back wheels, or sometimes with enormous piles of greens or onions balanced precariously on the carriers. The free market was clearly flourishing.

We crossed a coffee-coloured river where willows wept over the banks and flat-bottomed boats were being poled along. Beyond it the hills came into sight, arid but terraced and planted with young trees in a reforestation project. Little gold-roofed and red-pillared pavilions, new but wholly traditional, stood on some of the hilltops, and in the small walled yards of the hill farms maize was being raked out to dry. Up the steepening grade of the railway two big black steam locomotives, panting out great plumes of black smoke, slowly dragged a train. The inner line of the Great Wall, broken and unrestored, clambered up and down the contours on each side, and beyond it the hills became more wild and beautiful, for there were valleys whose sides were covered with wild plum trees in a cloud of white blossoms.

The wall itself, the outer wall, was grand at a distance, like a great elevated stone causeway sweeping away over the mountains, which here had become steep and majestic, but when we climbed on to it at Badaling Gate it seemed entirely diminished by humanity. Chinese trippers and foreign tourists mingled in a chaotic concourse between the parapets. We even encountered two of our friends from Vancouver tramping along the great sloping pavement behind the flag of their tour group. We had said to them before we left home, "Perhaps we shall meet *in* the Great Wall," meaning the luxury hotel in Beijing where they stayed but which we never saw; we did not expect to meet *on* the Great Wall; clearly the chance that brought us together was not particular about its prepositions.

I did not get my sense of grandeur back until I stood on the parapet gazing out over the receding blue vistas of the mountains beyond, once the land of Huns and menace, and listened to the wall's own voices, the musical chink of the masons' hammers trimming stones for the endless restoration task, and the plaintive petulant wailing of the Bactrian camels that were kept standing for people to mount them and be photographed.

The Forbidden City is a vast monument to a cruel and mediocre age. The emperors of the Ching dynasty, after their Manchu soldiers had destroyed the great Ming palace complex, rebuilt it in its present form; the Manchus had even less feeling for Chinese culture than the Mongols, and virtually none of the artistic sensibility that so often distinguished members of earlier native dynasties like the T'ang, the Sung and even the Ming. Pottery, painting, sculpture, all fell into a derivative decadence, and no literature was produced under the Ching that rivalled the great work of the T'ang poets.

The city impressed — and then depressed — us with its vastness. There are said to be, though I did not try to count them, eight hundred buildings with nine thousand rooms, linked by lanes with high blind ochre-coloured walls and monotonously repetitive stone-paved courtyards. The Forbidden City, with its largely wooden construction, has always been susceptible to fires, and there are very few buildings that really date much farther back than the late eighteenth century, so that the complex represents the worst and least inspired period of Chinese building, when ancient plans were adhered to, mainly for ceremonies or geomantic reasons, but the ancient graces had been lost.

Yet it was not so much the visual monotony, the sense of mechanical designs unrelieved by the flashes of imagination, that made us eager to depart. It was the melancholy atmosphere, the sense of lost and meaningless lives that hung over the place despite the hundreds of Chinese trippers and Caucasian tourists who were wandering through it. All the time one was reminded of the double isolation in which the inhabitants had lived before the gates were thrown open in 1949, from the emperor down through his wives and concubines and courtiers, down to the thousands of wretched eunuchs and handmaids who acted as servants at various levels. To outsiders, the city had seemed a fortress as impregnable as Kafka's Castle, the centre where power resided. But to those inside, it was a prison of protocol and convention, and most of them lived lives as deprived and detached from the real world as those of the most enclosed monastic orders. Yet this was a retreat from life without the consolation of heavenly hope, a situation in which people were abused or killed at whim. The sterile atmosphere of a world cut off from the real world bred its own aberrations, and the cruelties were the products of minds that had grown awry in isolation.

As often afterwards, I was surprised by the ambivalence of Chinese attitudes towards monuments to the imperial past like the Forbidden City. It had been carefully protected and restored, and now a permanent team moves through the city, keeping its buildings in good repair. The artifacts from the imperial collections that survived the successive plunderings of the Japanese and of the Kuomintang in 1949, when many fine works were transported to Taiwan, are well cared for. People are encouraged to visit the city, which has become a kind of public park where country folk wander with their cheap mass-produced cameras, somewhat awe-stricken by all this evidence of the splendour power can give. Even at the height of the Cultural Revolution, no serious attempt was made to carry out a final looting of the Forbidden City. It was left alone in the same way as Mao's power was left alone, for in reality the Cultural Revolution was a manipulated movement that only got out of hand when its victims were either people whom Mao or his associates wanted to diminish or destroy, or people who were so powerless politically that they could safely be made out to be personifications of the evil past. The real symbols of the past, like the Forbidden City, often went strangely untouched.

The next day we set off, with Ziyi alone, from the main Beijing railway station, a Soviet-style memento of the past days of Russo-Chinese brotherhood. The train puffed its black smoke over the plains beyond Beijing and up through low mountain ranges where fragments of the wall clambered over the slopes, and on into Shansi, over a yellow plateau of arid earth dotted with herds of tiny sheep and the ruins of the watchtowers that had once given warning of the Huns invading from the north.

Socialist democracy demands that there should be no first- and second-class compartments in Chinese trains. Face is saved by providing a "hard" class for most people, and a "soft" class, more comfortable and also more expensive, for the minority. The comfort consisted of cushioned seats covered with well-washed canvas and decorated with antimacassars, which are ubiquitous in China. The conveniences we did appreciate were the gigantic thermos flask, holding about five litres, and the set of lidded teacups. The six hours of our journey were punctuated by the appearance every hour or so of a pink-cheeked teenaged girl in a blue uniform, carrying an immense iron kettle with a canvas cosy, from which she would replenish our thermos. The food in the dining car, as we had been warned, looked too dreadful to be worth experimentation, so we drank tea and ate biscuits and bananas we had bought in the little shops outside the Beijing railway station. And as we sipped Ziyi told us romantic stories about the watchtowers.

An emperor had a beautiful wife with whom he was in love but who never smiled. One day she asked what would happen if the beacon fires were lit on the watchtowers. Anxious to please her, he ordered that the torch be put to the fires, and the nobles came out with their levies, parading before the emperor and his queen, expecting a Hun invasion. But the Huns did not come, and the lady laughed uproariously. A month later there was a real alarm. The fires were lit, but this time the noblemen thought it was another hoax and did not call their men together. The Huns invaded and the kingdom fell. For the first time, as I heard the story, I began to realize how nostalgic Chinese have become, in the late 1980s, for the romantic past that the Cultural Revolution so violently rejected only a few years before.

Datong, our destination, is an ancient place turning modern, with chunks of tamped-earth city wall left over from the Ming dynasty, wide imperial avenues, an old town of narrow streets where the great tiled roofs of ancient temples tower over rows of low shops; on the edge rear up the chimneys and surface works of the big state-owned mines, for this is coal country. Datong also has the last factory manufacturing locomotives left in the world, and a few miles away at Yungang the ancient sacred grottoes, with their gigantic Buddhas carved from the rock fourteen centuries ago.

Outside the station stood a small smiling man in sports jacket and grey flannels beside a Toyota van. This was Meng, the head of the local cultural bureau, and the van would provide our transport for the days we travelled through the Shanxi mountains, to and beyond Wutai Shan. He introduced our driver, Lan, and then took us to a hotel which was several degrees better than its counterpart in Beijing.

The next day we set off for Yungang, past the big collieries and into the countryside broken by little valleys and gulches. There I had my first introduction to the pluralistic economy of China, for coal around Datong lies in surface outcrops as well as in deep seams, and little mines went burrowing into every slope; the road was full of beaten-up trucks and scurrying tractor trailers taking the coal into the city, where it would be peddled around the houses, and into the villages for the peasants. All these mines were run by individuals or small partnerships, who paid a royalty to the state and kept the rest of the money they earned. It was an extension into another industry of the changes in farming by which the great communes of Mao's day were abolished, and the peasants began to till their own strips of land for their own profit. Judging by the number of people involved, the pluralist system seemed to be working as well in mining as in farming.

But the Yungang caves belonged to a different age and a different world. During the fourth and fifth centuries — a millennium and a half ago — there had been a great upsurge of Buddhism in China. It was the time when Fa'Hien, a Buddhist monk, went on his famous journey through the Gobi Desert to India to obtain the sacred Sanskrit books of the religion, which he translated into Chinese; Fa'Hien's successful return after fifteen years of wandering gave a great stimulus to the faith, to which the emperors of the reigning Wei dynasty were devoted. Work was started on the caves at Yungang and at the same time at Dunhuang, far to the west, the other end of our journey. The two places were united by the Silk Road, along which not only merchants but also religious teachers (Nestorian Christians and Manicheans and Jews, as well as Buddhists) found their way into China. They brought with them not only theologies but also art styles, particularly the hybrid Graeco-Indian style from Gandhars, near the Khyber Pass, where the earliest Buddhist sculptures were made. Gradually this hybrid style became naturalized in China and changed into an authentic, native art.

Construction on the Yungang caves began in 460 AD under the patronage of Emperor Wen Cheng, who sent a monk named Tan Yao to organize the work. Tan Yao assembled brotherhoods of lay volunteers, artists and craftsmen and began the great assault on the kilometre-long stretch of sandstone cliff that we saw far down the road as we approached the site. Seventy caves, large and small, were eventually hacked out in a period of about a century, and fifty thousand sculptures were made — figures of Buddhas and bodhisattvas and devis and arhats and other sacred beings, cut from the rock in high or low relief. The largest were great sculptures ten or twelve times the height of a man; the smallest were tiny Buddhas only as tall as a thumb, carved in such numbers and with such repetition that sometimes they would diaper the whole wall of a cave.

We approached the caves through gardens and paved courtyards dotted with pavilions holding massive bronze bells, and small worship halls turned into restrooms and souvenir shops, all crowned with the deeply curved roofs and dark crusts of tiles in which the people of the Ming dynasty excelled; all were much newer than the sculptures in the cliffs. A sound unfamiliar in China immediately caught our ears; the chirping of sparrows, which had become almost extinct during the great bird extermination campaigns carried on in China during the 1950s to the detriment of the country's ecology. In the old sacred places they seemed to have found refuge, and at Yungang they shared it with the sand martins that had built in the cliffs and soared constantly over our heads.

My immediate impression of the Yungang caves was that of an eroded version of the great temple of Karnak in Egypt, for the first set of grottoes — the last to be carved — is protected by an arcade whose tall, massive and irregular columns were hacked out of the rock. In some of these later, more elaborate caves, the walls and ceilings were entirely carved with religious scenes or with almost abstract patterns based on some holy motif like the lotus. They often had a fluid lushness that was rather un-Chinese and reminded me that Buddhist art, like Buddhist religion, came originally from India. In one of the largest caves a complete and intricate pagoda soared up into the darkness, carved out of the living rock. The cave beside it had been scooped out into a dome like the inside of a miniature St. Peter's; the sides decorated with turquoise paintings of Buddha and the ceilings with devis flying in elaborate circles, so that the impression was of flames swirling around the head of the great Buddha, nineteen metres high, who sat under the dome with a dwarf disciple, the mere height of an ordinary man, standing on his gigantic thigh.

Beyond the colonnade stretched the early caves cut out by monk Tan Yao and his helpers 1 500 years ago: the great Buddhas, seated in the lotus position, and the Maitreyas (future Buddhas, seated Western-style on thrones), were carved out of the cliff-face. Once they had been protected by wooden roofs (the sockets for the beams could still be seen) but now they stood open to the sky and sun, and though their colours had vanished, they were surprisingly undamaged and crisp in outline — too solid for the weather to destroy, too massive for the Red Guards to mutilate. The largest of them was almost eighty feet high, and in his massive presence I felt dwarfed mentally as well as physically, like Gulliver with the king of Brobdingnag. It was not the mere size of the image; it was not even the sense of being present at a great moment of artistic transition, embodied in the contrast between the statue's Chinese features and its Greek-style draperies. It was, rather, the same kind of awe at the grandeur of human vision that I felt in the presence of any manifestation of great collective faith — in the Gothic splendour, for instance, of French medieval cathedrals like Chartres and Bourges.

Naturally, I wondered about the feelings of the Chinese who came here; the visitors were all Chinese except for us and one stray Australian girl. I talked to a group of young people in blue uniforms who wanted to practise their English on me. They were trainees for counter jobs in the state airline, and their attitudes varied from bored indifference to curiosity to a pride in their country's past. Other people were more actively responding to their cultural traditions, sitting on the sand of the cave floors to capture in brush and ink the details of the statues. And some had come to pay honour, to bow before the Buddhas and to offer joss sticks and biscuits shaped like half moons and tiny gifts of money — even though this was not an active religious centre like some of the places we later visited, and there were no monks in attendance as there were in the old Huayan temple in the heart of Datong.

The sense of tradition renewed was intensified that evening when Meng took us to the first of many opera performances we attended while in China. It was the local Jing opera, in which the basic story is not cluttered with acrobatics and other diversions as is the case in the Beijing opera. I had expected at least some vestiges of the highly propagandist style encouraged during the Cultural Revolution, when militant operas such as *Red Lantern* and *Taking Tiger Mountain by Strategy* were in vogue. But there were no revolutionary songs, no choruses in the uniforms of the People's Army strutting across the stage with rifles and flags. It was as if the clock of theatre had been put back a whole generation.

The opera was a tale of aristocrats in love during the T'ang dynasty, and the audience of miners in their blue working clothes and market women in their little white sanitary caps listened enrapt as the plangent voices of the elaborately clad and coifed and jewelled singers unfolded the tragic history. The art of engagement had come to an end; we were seeing the art of escape into a romanticized past.

The next day we spent wandering in Datong's old town and visiting the two ancient temples, one of them derelict and deserted and the other thriving and well attended, with gay banners flying and gaudily painted images and hundreds of devotees with a few hovering monks. And that night Meng gave us the first of many banquets on our journey; it included such delicacies as baby eels, stewed scallops, exotic tree mushrooms, prawns as big as small crayfish, and a salad of arbutus fruit, like very astringent strawberries with hard stones in the centres. We imagined this to be his farewell, but next day he turned up, having decided to accompany us to Wutai Shan and down over the mountains to Taiyuan.

We witnessed the turning back to the past in quite different ways on this trip. First there was a long day's journey through bleak ranges and over plateaus of yellow loess, in which the villages, built of mud the same colour as the soil, seemed concealed in the landscape. Some villages in fact consisted of walled-off caves like those outside Granada in Spain. In other ways I was reminded of the Andes, since even the steep slopes were terraced into little fields that must have been worked with spades or hoes, for there was no way a tractor or even one of the little mule-drawn ploughs of the region could have been driven up to them.

In a cleft in the mountains we came to an ancient architectural curiosity called the Hanging Temple. It was a lonely sanctuary that straggled over the cliff-face into which it had been ingeniously cantilevered so that it seemed to hang like a cluster of swallows' nests. It had been built fourteen centuries ago and often repaired, but the original principles of anti-earthquake construction had been maintained. When we first saw the temple we imagined that it was supported on a series of tall pillars lodged in the rocks below. But when we clambered up the narrow stairways, among the May Day holiday makers from the nearest village, to the straggling galleries of the temple, we realized that these timbers merely hung down loosely, and it was only when the building was under strain that they actually settled down into their sockets and supported it. This was the only temple we saw in China dedicated to all three traditional religions: Buddhism, Confucianism and Taoism. The statues of the founders of these cults were exhibited together in one room, and while the Buddha retained his serenity, both Confucius and Lao Tzu, the founder of Taoism, were presented as scowling at each other blackly. They had never agreed when they lived and knew each other 2,500 years ago, since Confucius was a law-and-order philosopher and Lao Tzu a primeval anarchist, and the statue makers had gone to pains to project their incompatibility.

Over more mountains and valleys we came to a little town called Ying Xian, in which all that was left of a once great temple was the oldest and largest wooden pagoda in the world. The Wooden Tower stood more than two hundred metres high and had survived weather and earthquakes for nine hundred years. Preserved in the dry northern climate, it was still a remarkably sturdy building, with its tiled roofs supported on ancient elaborate bracketing, its rooms full of grave wooden statues and Sung murals of ferocious Heavenly Kings, its bronze bells ringing sweetly from the multiple eaves, and the swifts soaring high in the air around it.

The village council insisted on offering an impromptu feast in our honour. I sat with Meng and Lan the driver and some of the local cadres as the cooks got to work, and we talked about local superstitions. Everyone agreed they were returning in strength after the attempts to stamp them out during the Cultural Revolution. The astrologers, in particular, were back at work. And arranged marriages were in fashion again among the peasants, which meant not only that both sides had to build good houses out of the profits of the free market, but that horoscopes had to be exchanged to make sure the families could propitiously unite. I had a feeling, talking to the party men, that they had given up resisting the return to the past. "The peasants want it," one of them said, and in the mystique of Chinese communism the peasants have always been the important class, as Mao Zedong taught; after all, in spite of urbanization, the inhabitants of China's 700,000 villages still make up three-quarters of the country's population. When students rebel the government and the party can brush it aside as the flicker of a butterfly's wing compared with the inertia of a billion people. But when the peasants reclaim their way of life, as they have done increasingly in recent years, it is as if a dragon were awakening, and the snorts of fire from his nostrils have to be watched constantly.

All these anxious matters were forgotten when the cooks were ready, and we settled down to an interminable ceremonial meal of fifteen dishes, most of them too rustic to be familiar to Western connoisseurs of Chinese food. The tour de force was a large dish called Son and Mother — stewed chicken topped with deep-fried hard-boiled eggs, washed down with excellent beer and followed up by a long series of bottoms-up toasts in fiery rice liquor, during which the name of Norman Bethune, the only Canadian of whom most Chinese had heard, was heavily invoked.

Celebrations in Ying Xian delayed us so much that when we reached the deepest core of the mountains and began to climb the high pass towards Wutai Shan the sky had darkened, and snow had begun to turn the rare villages into grey and white checkerboards. The road rose, narrowed and became slippery. At nearly ten thousand feet we topped the pass and began to descend slowly into the deep cold valley of Wutai Shan. By this time the light was going, and the low-slanting rays were hitting a cluster of temple roofs, minute in the distance, on a snow-covered peak to the east. We descended among buildings that were becoming shadowy presences, a great hall looming here, a stupa probing the pale sky there, until we were in the bottom of the valley and driving up to the new hotel a local cooperative had just opened.

It was a good hotel, built by workmen from the area whose families had preserved the crafts of temple building from generation to generation. It had massive tiled roofs, large comfortable rooms, with good softish beds and quilts well stuffed with cotton to keep one warm on the sharp winter nights. The food was good, ten to fourteen courses twice a day, with many Buddhist vegetarian dishes, and Chinese breakfasts of steamed buns, gruel, pickles and sweet cakes.

Daylight at Wutai Shan revealed the amazing splendours of a community that, since the T'ang dynasty in the eighth century, had been one of the four great pilgrimage centres of China, dedicated to Manjusri, the sword-bearing bodhisattva of wisdom. The People's Army used it as an easily defensible guerilla stronghold in their campaign against both the Japanese and the Kuomintang. But the temples survived, and today there are said to be fifty-seven of them, although I did not make a count and suspect that the total includes many small shrines. I had expected to find a dying place interesting only for its past, to walk through ravaged gardens to deserted buildings. I found a living sanctuary that was symptomatic of China's present way of life.

With their elaborately timbered and heavily tiled roofs supported on massive wooden columns from long-vanished forests, the temples stood on hilltops, from which deep stairways cascaded into the valley. Tall pagodas and stupas celebrated the great saints and scholars of the past. The halls of the temples stood in flagged courtyards dotted with bronze incense burners and miniature pagodas and stone sundials. Vermilion-stuccoed walls defining the temple properties clambered over the hill-sides. The first almonds were blossoming in shrill pink, and fresh green buds were beginning to show on the birch trees. As environmental architecture it was all superb, as fine as anything in Japan. The Chinese, of course, claim the Japanese are mere imitators.

The temples had not only survived; they were open and active. There was a large community of monks in grey and brown robes, and sometimes in the maroon robes of Lamaist monks. They were not merely old men from China's past; more than three hundred novices lived in the temples, studying and chanting the sutras before the altars. Among the pilgrims, women and old men peddlers were doing a brisk trade in Buddhist rosaries, which spoke well for the freedom of both commerce and religion.

Few of the people were mere sightseers. It was too cold and too early for that. The visitors had come to pay their respects to the great presences, to the towering bronze or painted stucco statues of Sakyamuni and Manjusri and Maitreya. A company of monks of all ages, wearing sheepskin jackets under their red robes, had come from a remote abbey in Inner Mongolia, and a group of wild-haired herdsmen had accom-panied them. Climbing up one of the staircases we met three gigantic monks from Tibet, and when we greeted them in Tibetan, they replied in the broad accent of Kham, the land of warriors and brigands.

But most of the pilgrims were Han Chinese, and they were of all ages. Frail old people struggled up the tall steps, supported by staffs, to ring the five-ton bronze bells and paste on them scraps of paper with prayers for the living and the dead. Middle-aged women walked the lanes muttering mantras as they counted off the 108 beads of their rosaries. There were also young people making their offerings; I saw one man of about thirty in a Mao-style suit teaching his young children to kneel on the cushions and prostrate themselves to the great gilded images as they spoke their prayers.

In the South Temple the abbot invited us into his parlour. A tall, wispy old man in a burnt-orange brocade robe, he gave us green tea and Danish butter cookies which a Hong Kong pilgrim had brought as an offering. He was wearing a hearing aid patched up with surgical tape, and he told how when the Red Guards came to Wutai Shan he had been forced to kowtow, had been dragged on the ground and beaten so badly over the head that he had lost his hearing. But now he and his fellow monks were left in peace. They even received a small pension from the government, and with what they grew in their garden they could keep going. I had a feeling that most of all he was grateful for survival. Another abbot at Wutai Shan had been killed.

A few days later we were in Lanzhou, the capital of Gansu, the long arid corridor of a province through which the Silk Road ran between Mongolia and Tibet towards the Gobi Desert. We had left the cold valley of Wutai Shan and travelled south through the central Chinese countryside, searching out village temples, visiting cities like heavily industrial Taiyuan, an ancient place where Inge, standing in the window of our hotel room, counted sixty smokestacks within her arc of vision, and tiny medieval towns like Pingyao where we ran into Donald Sutherland making his film on Bethune and talked sadly about his brother, the writer, John Sutherland. We had then gone to the tourist centre of Xi'an, mainly because it was the hub of air routes from which we had to get to Lanzhou and northwestern China. We did not neglect the area's archaeological sites, however: the fascinating neolithic village of Banpo where the house construction and the tools so greatly resembled those used by local peasants to this day; the great processional way lined with T'ang statues at the royal tomb of Qianling; and Xi'an's over-famous pottery soldiers. But Dunhuang in the Gobi Desert was our third main destination, and Lanzhou, a bizarre industrial town that straggled thinly for seventy kilometres along the Yellow River, was our jumping-off point.

At Lanzhou I had my seventy-fifth birthday, and the local officials gave a little party with a great square cake they had made especially, and a banquet with suckling pig and a desert dish of lamb cooked in chafing dishes at the table, and squid stew, and baby eels, and many dishes of noodles and vegetables and exotic fungi, and the year's first tart lichees, with plenty of beer and frequent toasts in sweet heady peach wine and in a fiery rice liquor called Happy Li Po, which was chosen to honour me as a writer; according to the legend Li Po drowned drunk in the Yellow River, beside which we were eating, trying to embrace the reflection of the moon.

During the desultory conversation over the poet's drink, we mentioned Wutai Shan and its pilgrims to a man whose garb and manner marked him as a good party cadre. Of course, he assured us, religion was free everywhere in China. Why, there were nine hundred Catholic churches now open and active!

"But surely Marx taught that religion is the opium of the people," said Inge. Our party man was unperturbed. "Of course, that was only Marx's opinion," he lightly replied, and then went on to talk of the difficulty he himself found in writing poetry when he held such a taxing bureaucratic post. I was left marvelling. For it seemed to me that a crucial stage had been reached when the words of the prophet could be dismissed as an opinion.

In Lanzhou we had a setback to our original plans which turned out to be fortunate. There was a sandstorm in the Gobi Desert, and an exceptional shower had turned it into what was called "yellow rain," so that planes could not fly to Dunhuang. The head of the local cultural bureau suggested that we go by road instead — up the Silk Road; we were delighted at the lucky chance. He ordered out the department's minibus, and early the next morning we set out on two long days of hard travel covering the seven hundred miles between Lanzhou and Dunhuang.

The old caravans had long disappeared from the Silk Road and its sand tracks had been replaced by one of those rough roads the Chinese still make by hand labour like the Indians; it is among other things a remedy for unemployment. Camel trains had come this way until the 1930s, and the mud ruins of the caravanserais still stood at intervals of about fifteen miles, the distance of a night journey by camel or wagon; in those days it took at least two months to cover what we travelled in two days. It was desert country most of the way, golden sand dunes or flat expanses of dark pebbles dotted with tamarisk bushes. The brightly tinted volcanic ridges of the Longshou Shan ran to the north of the road, and Mongolia was over its crest, twenty miles away; to the south the great snowy Qilian Shan rose up more than eighteen thousand feet, shielding the borderlands of outer Tibet.

The Great Wall was our almost constant companion, running for many miles beside the road, and here it was not the trim, restored masonry that one sees near Beijing, but the mud wall originally built by the Han emperors two thousand years ago to protect the Silk Road. It had weathered according to the strength of the prevailing winds, and sometimes there were long stretches of wall seven or eight metres high and four thick, with the watchtowers and gatetowers standing massive and clay yellow over the bleak wasteland. The only settlements were widely spaced oases, though once we passed a great cluster of crumbling ruins where three centuries ago an emperor had been led by a dream to order that a city be built in an uninhabitable desert. Often we were alone with the wall, and I remembered poignantly the sad old Chinese poems about the desolate exile of military service on this forlorn frontier.

We passed through no more than four towns in the whole seven hundred miles, and these I recognized as ancient trading centres on the Silk Road. Wuwei had been Liangshow then, and in one of the many generals' tombs there the famous bronze flying horse, now housed in the museum at Lanzhou, was unearthed. Zhangye was the Chang-ye where the great pilgrim Fa'Hien spent the winter of 400 AD on his long way to India. In the old hotel there they gave us sacks of rice for pillows, and the newly installed bathroom was ankle deep in water for lack of plumbers. But in the back streets of that ancient town we found an old temple with an immense and beautiful reclining Sung Buddha, and stored away behind it a collection of bronze statues, the newest a thousand years old, that had been collected in abandoned desert temples and were totally unknown outside Zhangye.

But such things fell temporarily out of memory — though they were safely lodged in my diary — when we crossed a last desert, white with saltpetre, into the great oasis of Dunhuang, and saw the Magao caves, which are often called the Caves of the Thousand Buddhas.

We left the oasis and travelled further into the Gobi to reach them. A narrow valley with a trickle of water allows a cool grove of desert poplars and flowering elm to grow, and behind it rears up a tall cliff of conglomerate rock that holds back the spectacular dunes known as the Singing Sands. There are about a thousand caves cut into the cliff. Those to the east are unembellished burrows where the old monks lived long ago. Those to the west are the five hundred painted caves.

Most visitors — and there are still not many — are whisked through quickly and shown perhaps a dozen caves. We were lucky enough to gain the confidence of one of the curators — the excellent Mr. Ma — because of some special knowledge about the western end of the Silk Road in Afghanistan and Iran that I was able to pass on, as one enthusiast to another, and so we saw more than fifty caves, and those were the best.

The first caves at Dunhuang were carved out and painted in the fourth century AD and the last during the Yuan dynasty in the fourteenth century. During this thousand years Dunhuang was not merely a centre where hundreds of monks gathered to live the religious life on the edge of the desert. It had another and more worldly aspect, for it was a great junction on the Silk Road. The main highway — if one can apply that title to tracks in the shifting sands — ran west from China towards Turkestan and Afghanistan and Persia and eventually Europe, and the highway that crossed it ran northward from Tibet into Mongolia. Dunhuang, the junction point, was also the place where the merchants and their caravans took on supplies and did their best in other ways to ensure good fortune before they started on the terrible stage across the Taklimakan Desert that begins just west of Dunhuang and over which it was said that one finds one's way by following the bones of animals and men. Offerings were made to the Buddha, and rich merchants would often pay for the decoration of a cave or for the construction of statues. The rock at Dunhuang, which consists of pebbles held together by hard clay, did not lend itself to sculpture, as the sandstone in the Yungang caves had done. The Dunhuang statues were all made from armatures consisting of bundles of twigs or canes bound together with linen thread, over which the bodies would be moulded in mud, and then a fine layer of stucco would be added, and, finally, they would be painted. The paints used were pure mineral tints obtained from caves in the volcanic mountains across the valley and mixed with sheep's tallow; the technique was really a primitive kind of oil painting.

The desert, with an average yearly rainfall of less than an inch, gave the ideal climate for the preservation of these works. The great destroyer was the sand that blew into the caves, which were square structures like the inside of a Chinese house, with pyramidal ceilings and fairly narrow entranceways. The entrance would suffer, and also the altars that faced whatever light and wind came in. And this had some very interesting results. Taken as a whole the caves represent a remarkable anthology of Chinese and Central Asian Buddhist art. The paintings in the earlier caves are often distinctly Indian in character, with broad-waisted, heavy-breasted female deities. Often, also, there were evident Persian influences. Then, about the seventh century, Chinese styles appear, first the T'ang and then the Sung. But often, as perhaps was inevitable in a centre where so many artists congregated over so long a period, there are signs of experimental urges; the bold dramatic outlines of expressionism, elaborate patterns that turn a lotus flower into an abstraction. Since the caves had been maintained over so many centuries, there were often extraordinary combinations of style. A cave would be made in the Sui or T'ang dynasty, and the frescoes in the inner chamber would remain as they were originally painted, with colours often of pristine brilliance. But the sand would have made it necessary to repaint the entrance hall, and so the friezes of lady and gentlemen donors would be portraits done — often with great irony and eloquence — in the marvellously expressive line of the Sung painters. The figures on the altar would sometimes have been blurred by the blasting sand — or sometimes defaced by one of the Moslem invaders who rode into Dunhuang — and then one would find that some rustic craftsman had imposed an expressionless pudding face in white stucco on a splendid moulded body with the elegant draperies at which the T'ang sculptors excelled.

Apart from their artistic interest the caves were a mine of marvellous documentation, a veritable pictorial history of medieval China. There were great caravans of traders making their way around the four walls of a cave in all their variety of man and animal; armies on the march with archaic armour and marvellous banners; scenes of village and palace life worked into ancient Buddhist stories, often with some humour like the representation of courtiers annoyed at having their heads shaved at the orders of a Buddhist king, and a peeping Tom lifting the curtain on a room of naked women. It was a vast anthology of custom and folklore and history, as well as a museum, left in situ, of a thousand years of Asian art. I do not think I have seen, in forty years of exotic travel, a single site so rich in interest as Dunhuang.

During the early twentieth century, after being forgotten for ages, Dunhuang was rediscovered by European archaeologists, notably the famous Anglo-Hungarian explorer of central Asia, Sir Aurel Stein. Unfortunately, Stein arrived just after an old Taoist priest living near the caves had discovered a bricked-up grotto full of rare manuscripts and other documents, including the world's first known printed books. The most recent of them was eight hundred years old. In those days archae-ologists tended to be scholarly predators, intent on gathering specimens for European or North American museums and Stein — like Franz Boas in British Columbia — was in this respect no better than the rest. He persuaded Wang, the Taoist priest, to sell him the best of the documents and shipped twenty-nine packing cases of them to the British Museum, where they have been stored away in the cellars for seventy years and more. French, American and Japanese scholars followed to claim their share of the loot, and the result is that the little museum in Dunhuang, where it all should have remained, has only a tiny remnant of this vast and wonderful library. But fortunately only one statue was ever taken away from the caves, by a covetous American collector, and the Gobi Desert was too far off for the Red Guard to do much damage there.

We returned through Lanzhou and Xi'an, siphoned that way by the air routes, and then went south into the areas of southern China around Guangzhou, which seemed a different country from that we had just left, for here it was all green fields and water, whereas we had come from sand dunes and the dry beds of vanished rivers; here the ancient wooden temples, which the dry air preserved in the north, had long decayed and vanished. But in social terms it was not much different. In the south, as in the north, there was the bustle of the new pluralist China, and perhaps the image that best fits them is one I carry in my mind from a town roughly halfway between the two regions — an image of one of the free markets of China.

It took place close to our hotel, and we were able to observe it at intervals during the day, from six in the morning, when it began, to five in the afternoon, when it came to an end. The city had provided rough plastic roofing over the sidewalks on each side of the streets, but the vendors sold from their own stalls or vehicles. The market extended for a kilometre on both sides of one street and for half a kilometre on each side of a cross street, making in all four kilometres of vendors quite closely packed together. Allowing about 2.5 metres per vendor, there must have been over 1500 people selling at any one time. But, particularly in the vegetable section, where peasants from outside the town sold from their own tricycle trailers, there was a steady turnover of sellers, some leaving when their loads were sold and others moving in, so that probably during the day there were at least 2,500 private vendors in this one market; there were several others in the city.

Every kind of food was sold; vegetables, fruit, meat, fish, bean curd, spices, noodles, oil, eggs (including delicacies like quail eggs), cakes and bread, nuts; there were goldfish and books, shoes and clothing and great bolts of cloth sold by the yard, trinkets and toys. As well as a vast variety of perishable goods, almost everything offered in the state-run department stores was being sold by private dealers, and usually much more cheaply. From morning to night the buyers came in a steady stream. Consumers were satisfied, peasants and craftsmen and peddlers were making money for themselves, people were finding employment, and the traditional Chinese love of trading and trafficking was being satisfied.

Chapter 18

LETTERS, FRIENDS AND OTHERS

Back from China, I set to work writing the account of our travels there, spinning off a few articles on the country as I worked. Appearing as *Caves in the Desert* in 1988, the book would gather good reviews and also the 1988 award from the Canadian Authors Association for non-fiction, a prize of $5,000 and a neat silver medal which Matt Cohen accepted on my behalf in Toronto. I began planning for our next trip to China, this time to the land of Yin with Toni and Yukiko Onley as our companions; it seemed to me the landscapes that T'ang artists had painted might suit Toni's landscape talent.

But from now on my connections with China were troubled. Toni and I had planned a trip that would take us to Guangzhou and thence to Quelin and across to Yunan, and then back through the Yangtze Gorges to Wuhan and the Taoist mountain sanctuaries, and finally via Nanjing to Shanghai, stopping at various sites on the way. Evidently untroubled by what I said in my book, the Chinese Ministry of Culture approved the plan and put its own machinery to work. Everything was arranged and we were on the eve of buying our tickets to Hong Kong when I began to suffer from arthritis so painful that I had difficulty walking, and could not make a journey that would be so largely pedestrian. I had to let Toni and Yukiko go on their own, with great chagrin that I could not be able to complete my view of China. But Toni at least offered some splendid views of his own when he returned.

I had to be content with what, as it turned out, would be my last travel of any consequence, a stick-and-taxi trip to Europe to settle my mother-in-law Gertrud's estate in the company of Inge's brother, Dieter. This took us to Basel and to Gertrud's last home of Bad Fussing in Bavaria. In Basel we went to redeem the family gold, like heavy, greasy-looking chocolate bars, out of the vaults of the Schweizerkredit-anstalt, and I remember the surprising change in Swiss banking practices since I went there with Otto Linzer a couple of decades before. Then a cryptlike solemnity hung over this place of deposited fortunes, large and small, and we were received by solemn men in swallowtail frock coats and pin-striped trousers with the manners of diplomats and an overweening gravity that became absurd when one of them lamented the inconvenience the Swiss people had endured during World War II. Now, in 1988, it was laughing young women in gaudy dresses who welcomed us and lightheartedly did our business for us. Basel itself was disappointing; it had lost the lavish charm it had for us in the days when we first went there in 1946 from war-drained England. Then it was a neat, well-fed, newly painted city with a good deal of the contemporary architecture nobody had been pursuing in England during the war, and its shop windows had paralysed our greed with their abundance. Now all the newness had grown shabby, and Basel seemed what it probably always had been, a smallish industrial town grafted on to a medieval commercial city.

Not long afterwards we went to Toronto on another testamentary mission, our own. We realized that, despite our modest way of living, we would have a considerable amount to leave on our deaths, taking into account assets like our house in what had become an expensive quarter, our art collection, our books. Neither of us had relatives likely to be in need, and we could remember our friends in a series of small gifts. What should we do with the rest? Having worked hard for tribal peoples and refugees in India, we decided to think of our own tribe, the writers. Several times in the past my own writing had been impeded by lack of money, and a gift of two or three thousand dollars would have made all the difference between paralysing anxiety and a sense that the next vital month or so was taken care of. Why not leave our money to help other writers in the same fix? I rang up Margaret Atwood, and she suggested we should work out something with the Writers' Development Trust. We flew to Toronto, met Margaret and Anne McClelland and Nancy Southam of the Trust, and agreed that the WDT should be trustees for the Woodcock Fund, which we would begin at once and which would receive the greater part of our estate. Deeds were eventually drawn up and a jury selected, headed first by Eric Wright and now by George Galt, with Dennis Lee, Silver Donald Cameron, Andreas Schroeder and Lorna Crozier serving at various times as jury members. Up to now about thirty writers have benefited, and though we have never tried to establish quality as a criterion, generally it is serious writers who have applied and in some cases won awards after receiving our help.

On this trip we also had dinner with Wailan Low, Earle Birney's companion, and through her had the last of our meetings with Earle, whose friendship with us lasted from our arrival in Canada in 1949. He had come to visit us at Sooke in our first summer, and this was the beginning of a lasting, sometimes irritable but usually cordial relationship that in recent years had grown more genial until Earle had the stroke that virtually removed him from his world.

We found him in a Toronto mental clinic, physically well, to all appearance, white haired as he had long been, with a kind of animal alertness, but living in a remoteness of his own. We entered a large room where he was sitting at a round table with other patients and some of the staff. Immediately as we entered the room I saw a flash of recognition go over his face, and he stood up to welcome us. He knew us but, it turned out, he no longer knew who we were, and so as we talked to him we found ourselves being fitted into the fantasy in which he moved. He had regressed, it seemed, to boyhood and was concerned with baseball teams, and with his failure to make one special team, of which I was an active member; so, he said in parenthesis, was Wai Lan. We went away appalled by the condition of this good friend and fine poet. And yet we had he sense that he was happy within his fantasy world. The moments when he hovered near the recollection of reality must have been his worst.

At the same time as I had been writing *The Social History of Canada*, I was talking to William Toye of Oxford University Press, that excellent and highly creative editor, about a volume of essays defining the century from 1812 to 1914 as the time of Canada's emergence into a distinguishable society rather than a nation (which of course, despite the efforts of Jacobin state builders like Trudeau, it can never be). I chose the discontinuous essay form which paradoxically I found more adaptable than the ongoing narrative for presenting the parallel continuities of Canadian history in the early years. I began by discussing the myth and reality of 1812 and the situation of Canada at the end of the war in 1814. I went on in succeeding essays to discuss such subjects as class in Canada, rebellion and reform, nationalism and imperialism, the roles of women, the myth and reality of the Indian, relations with the Americans, the population of the land; at the end came two more intimately cultural pieces on "The Visual Imagination and the Mystique of the Land," and "The Liberation of the Literary Imagination." I found it a more penetrative work than my *Social History of Canada*, yet it did not sell nearly as well, and I was forced to the conclusion that readers generally prefer the telescope with its panoramic view of history to the microscope, particularly when it is focused on their own origins.

In the same year of 1989 there also appeared not only *The Marvellous Century*, my book on the ancient sixth century BC Age of Reason, but as well a little book of my essays, elegantly produced by Quarry Press, *Powers of Observation*. For years now I had been writing my essay for each issue of *City and Country Home*, and with the simple device of taking a quotation for my epigraph and beginning subject had ranged over a wide area of reflection on literature and history and life, both past and present. I suppose my pieces served in the same way as the "middle" in the old English journals, and I got a great deal of satisfaction about writing them and recognizing that there was an appreciative audience for them, at least on a periodic level. My liking for the essay form has continued; it outlasted my tenure and Charles Oberdorf's at *City and Country Home*, and even now I have ideas for occasional essays and Paula Brook will often publish them in *Western Living*.

To return to 1989, at this time I had established contact with Bob Hilderley, who ran Quarry Press and was as interested as I in reviving the essay as a respected literary form. There was already a kind of arrangement between him and me and Douglas Fetherling by which Doug would gather together my major essays and Quarry would publish them. The first book in this series was indeed completed, a volume called *Anarchism and Anarchists*, consisting of my less-than-book-length writings on the subject, and that appeared in 1992 through a consortium of Quarry Press, the New Amsterdam Press in New York, and Freedom Press in London. It has sold reasonably well, I think, because of the current sustained popularity of anarchism as a subject rather than out of devotion to the essay form.

But *Powers of Observation*, though it got its share of appreciative reviews, only sold well in Vancouver stores where the customers at least knew about me and were mainly interested in its autobiographical aspects. It never generated the great revival of the form for which Bob and I had hoped; *Anarchism and Anarchists* was reasonably successful because of its special international readership.

At this time too my critical writing for ECW PRESS had broadened out beyond my involvement as introducer of the volumes of *Canadian Writers and Their Works*. In addition I wrote three of the long essays on individual writers, and these were also published as small separate monographs. One

of them was on the novelist Matt Cohen and another on the poet Patrick
Lane; both of them concerned writers whom I knew personally (Matt
Cohen) or respected greatly (Pat Lane), so that they were tasks of pleasure.
The third monograph was rather a work of duty, since it concerned that
strange Victorian Charles Heavysege, a genuine worker poet whose
clumsy but powerful closet dramas, like *Saul* and *Count Filippo*, had
proved unplayable on the stage but had been splendidly adapted for CBC
radio by Norman Newton, who saw them rightly as works for the mind
and ear rather than for the eye, and cherished Heavysege's rough strong
rhythms and often eccentric imagery. When Jack David sent me the essays
for a volume on Victorian writers, I was surprised to find none assessing
Heavysege, though that much less interesting rhymester Charles Sangster
had his essay.

While, unlike more antiquarian critics, I have never considered Heavysege a major writer even in Canadian terms, I still felt that historically
he could not be ignored, and so I volunteered to write a monograph on
him if nobody had done so. My rashness was repaid, and I found myself
tracing his obscure and wretched life as a woodworker and minor
journalist (I never did find any kind of portrait of the man) and ploughing
through the *langweilig* stretches of verse for the strange and striking
images and locutions of which fortunately there were more than I
expected. But in the end it was a task of stubbornness rather than joy,
and I ended up resolved to rescue no more worthy Victorian poets from
obscurity.

Yet another scheme of the ever-inventive editors of ECW PRESS in
which I became involved was a series of "introductions" — meaning
critical and explicatory small volumes — on important Canadian novels.
At first the idea had been that I should write on all the fifty or so books
originally selected, but this seemed too much even for my productive
old typewriter to undertake, and it was agreed that I should do only the
first five and that younger critics should do the rest. I began these little
books in 1988 and the first two, on *Barometer Rising* and *The Stone Angel*
(which I think is the best of the five) appeared in 1989; those on *Surfacing*,
The Apprenticeship of Duddy Kravitz and *As for Me and My House* came
out in 1990. I found these exercises in close analysis stimulating and
fertile, since I never indulged in down-writing (assuming my reader to
be a person whose interest in the subject might be equal to my own), I
let the work explain itself in response to my questioning rather than
applying fashionable critical notions, and I avoided pedantry, writing

always with the stylistic clarity that the man-of-letters tradition as distinct from the merely scholastic one demands, and often surprising myself with what I discovered in a book read with the special awareness that such a task involves — not that I attribute any finality to my conclusions. A good book opens itself to many different insights.

A more personal book that ECW published in 1988 was *The Purdy-Woodcock Letters*. The idea for this came from George Galt, a friend whom Al and I share. He realized that our correspondences were both in the archives of Queen's University, and when he dipped into them he felt they were worth publishing. Though Inge (to Al's great offense, though I am used to such reproaches) accused us both of vanity, we had a sense of our roles in the history of Canadian literature. We were there, like it or not, so we both agreed. We wondered how self-conscious this might make our later correspondence, how much we would act up now we knew we had an audience, but in fact I do not think the existence of the book has changed our relationship or changed the way we write to each other.

George Galt tried the big publishers without success, and then went to Jack David, who welcomed the book, with due restraint, for he published only five hundred copies, so that it sold out quickly and already is a collector's item. It was an odd production, for the actual letters were taken out of the Queen's University Archives and photographed for facsimile publication, so that all the faults of our wretched old typewriters with their often worn-out ribbons showed up. I suppose that made it seem a more authentic document, and I have accepted it as that and as a record of a friendship I have valued for thirty years.

Whenever I look at that volume, indeed, with the archaic appearance that its worn characters gave it, I think about friendship, its constancies and intermittencies so far as my own life is concerned.

There are some friendships that have existed lifelong or almost so. I still keep contact with Lance Godwin, the boyhood friend born in the next-door house in Market Drayton when I was two years old. He failed as a writer (though I once thought him far more brilliant than I) and I succeeded, yet our relationship has been strangely and beautifully lacking in envy or rancour. Julian Symons has remarked — in an article he once wrote on me for the *London Magazine* — on the surprising firmness of our friendship despite our glaringly different attitudes to life, and one could say the same of my relationship with Derek Savage, whose religious views I have never really understood, let alone accepting them, but who is still as fondly my friend as when we met in the 1930s, while my friendship with Roy Fuller lasted unbroken to his death.

On the other hand there have been those relationships, haunted by long intermittencies, that have revived after many years as if there had been no parting. Harold Orlans is an example — an American anthropologist whom we met in London in the late 1940s, introduced, if I remember correctly, through a note from Dwight Macdonald. When we went to Canada he gave me a volume of Henry Mayhew to read on the voyage and started a lifetime interest, and he continued to keep in touch. We even met later in Mexico and in Europe, and then had a difference in Florence one day in 1958 that interrupted our relationship for at least a quarter of a century while Harold went into a career as a researcher with groups like the Brookings Institute. Four or five years ago he wrote to me out of the blue, and since then we have kept in touch as if there had been no interruption in our relationship. For some reason he kept my letters from 1949 to 1958, and these, of which he has recently sent me copies, are some of the few actual documents of my life during a period when I did not yet make carbons of everything I wrote with a view to selling my correspondence to archivists.

Then there has been Khando Yapshi, the Dalai Lama's niece, with whom we established a much more personally close relationship than we did with the Dalai Lama himself, even though he refers to us as his "old friends." We saw Khando quite frequently on our visits to India during the 1960s, and then we did not see her or have much communication for about twenty years until she all at once announced she was coming to see us, and last winter arrived on our doorstep all the way from India, a woman of fifty now but still so marvellously the girl we had known so long ago that it was as if no time had passed. I treasure such reknitted friendships as one treasures traditionally the return of the prodigal son.

My friendship with Al Purdy has evoked some surprise among people who know neither of us very well. The general opinion seems to be that we have very little in common. I, on the other hand, have always felt that we share a great deal.

After all, we both grew up in poverty, brought up by hard-pressed mothers because our fathers had died young. Neither of us went to a university, which meant that we are both autodidacts, members of a small but not undistinguished group in the Canadian literary world, including people like Sinclair Ross, Gwen MacEwen, Alden Nowlan, Milton

Acorn, P.K. Page and Raymond Souster. We are among the people who have never been trapped in the academic backwaters, and both Al with his vast book collections and I have developed a kind of generalized erudition which few university-based literary figures can match. We are, in what I feel is the best sense of the word, self-made men; the way in which Purdy transformed himself from a derivative traditional poet into a highly original colloquial poet, in some way outside formal modernism, is itself a remarkable example of this kind of self-recreation. In this direction we have the greatest respect for each other, which helps to keep a friendship alive, and a loyal friendship, as I remember from one occasion long ago when a well-known novelist publicly insulted me and Al immediately came to my defence in very certain terms.

Our correspondence over so many years — from the early 1960s — shows what is to me an interesting evolution. Al's letters did not change a great deal, except that they got easier as time went on. But mine changed radically. When I first knew Al I was partly dealing with him as editor of *Canadian Literature*, to which he was contributing some good impressionistic book reviews, and there was sometimes a touch of formality in my notes. But after a year they changed, and mine too became the relaxed letters of good friends who did not quite understand why they were friends but accepted the gift.

A final note on the correspondence of writers. I think that in the life of a writer his letters are another genre of prose that has to be considered as part of his total work, since they are written with a crafty eye to style, particularly if they are addressed to another writer. They also, of course, enlighten us about the "regular" life the author lives while he is writing, and for this reason I think there is nothing against and a great deal for the publication of one's letters while one is still alive and working. Some years ago I published a volume of letters to Canadian writers called *Taking It to the Letter*, and looking back on it now, I regard it as an integral part of my *oeuvre*, just as I regard my share of *The Purdy-Woodcock Letters*.

Chapter 19

WALKING THROUGH THE VALLEY

All the work I have been describing in the last chapter was done in the shadow of oncoming ominous events, both in the world outside and in our own lives. There was the matter of China. We had brought away with us a feeling of optimism about the country. It really did appear to be moving towards greater freedom, and the Chinese themselves seemed to enjoy and desire that freedom. Indeed, recollecting once again the time we spent there, I can remember nothing but friendly and easy behaviour on the part of the Chinese, whether they were officials or people we met in the street. They were often curious about us, but one never caught the feeling of hostility. "Red-haired foreign devils" were obviously not on their minds. Somehow the revolution, for all its excess, had left them with a sense of pride in themselves, which independence has never given to the great majority of Indians. China seemed to have reached a stage of *social* democracy even if it did not have political democracy, and the servility that pervades Indian society and virtually forces one into the role of sahib was gone. In China I never felt more than a man among human beings. It is true that when we were in China the hard party men were lying low, and it did seem as though a natural evolution towards a more open and pluralistic society was taking place.

When the great student demonstrations began in the spring of 1989, we followed them from Canada with a daily urgency, and at first, when the marches and peaceful occupations went on without hindrance and gradually drew in larger sections of the population, especially in Beijing, we were delighted and thought we would see a general and peaceful popular uprising against the power of the Communist Party, which for the time being seemed paralysed by indecision. Even when the armies began to close in on Beijing, we drew comfort from the fact that the ordinary people were coming out into the streets to divert them from the student-occupied Tiananmen square, which had now become a symbolic centre, and rumours of dissension among the generals and within the high councils of the party encouraged us to believe that the demonstrations had revealed cracks within the ruling caste that would bring its collapse.

In part we were right. There were men high in the party who sympathized with the student demands for the political liberalization of the country. There were generals who doubted if military action was a suitable response to an increasingly popular movement. Were they not, after all, the People's Army? (There are reports too persistent and recurrent to be ignored that at least six generals were executed at the time for their unwillingness.) And the movement spread as press and communications workers gave their support, spreading in the media the idea of a new epoch and actually taking part, with workers' contingents, in the great marches that increased from day to day as the student occupation of Tiananmen Square continued. Most encouraging was the moral support given by the ordinary people of Beijing, who applauded the marchers and later tried to obstruct the army contingents moving into the city.

The day in June when the army attacked and massacred the students in Tiananmen Square was a day of great shock and sorrow for us. We had not then realized how much our visit to China had attached us to those friends of a journey whose constant refrain was "We only hope it will last," meaning that they hoped the process of liberalization would continue. All these hopes seemed then to be destroyed. Yet even at the time I believed that the show of blind force in Tiananmen Square had created a lasting hatred of the party by people of all classes, in Beijing especially, which must contribute to the dissolution of its power.

I did what I could to make my protest known, writing articles denouncing the coup and letters to the press, and on the anniversary of the massacre limping with Inge and Toni Onley to join the demonstration outside the Chinese Consulate General and planting my candle before the consulate gate in full sight of the television cameras. The reaction of the Chinese authorities to all this was curious. I had a telephone call from the cultural consul wanting to visit me, and I refused to meet him. Afterwards I continued to receive invitations to events at the Consulate General and each Chinese New Year an elaborate paper cutout greeting card; one arrived even in 1993. I can hardly believe that the Chinese intelligence service, which is very active, could have failed to take note of my criticisms. All I could assume was that someone in the Consulate General hoped to maintain links in case better times returned.

I was encouraged in the stand I took on China at this time by the visit of a man I had known slightly as a Vancouver journalist, and whose name I promised not to reveal. X had gone to China with a mild Maoist fever, and had eventually found his way into the China News Agency, the official voice of the regime. Disillusion had set in, and when his fellow journalists came out in favour of the student demonstrators, he too supported them in his reports and marched in their demonstrations. He gave us, with a great deal of emotion, eyewitness accounts of the great processions and of being present on an occasion when the ordinary people of a district came out of their little streets to try and persuade the soldiers not to advance on Tiananmen Square. From his agitated account of those days one got both the excitement of the times and the bitterness of their ending, as he told of a Chinese fellow journalist telling him he would be expected to report to the office, and adding in a whisper, "I can lend you money if you need it." He took the hint and escaped into the Canadian Embassy compound, from which he went by cycle rickshaw to the airport with the rickshaw boys shouting Beijing insults at the soldiers along the way. At the airport he found he did not have enough of the right kind of currency to buy a ticket out, but a Japanese official listened to his plea, realized the urgency of his situation, gave him his ticket on credit, and pushed him on board the plane in the middle of a chattering party of Italian tourists so that his papers were not checked with great care. All this he told with such great vehemence, sometimes going on to his knees and weeping as he spoke, that my convictions of the treacherous brutality of Li Peng and his successful associates in the party were reinforced. I too must remain faithful to those who had so abundantly risked their lives and freedom on an idealistic hope.

Later in the year my crisis was a much more personal one, and it took me to the boundaries of death. I had continued to suffer from arthritis, and none of the treatment I was receiving seemed to be working, for I began to walk with difficulty and was often in great pain, which I eventually learnt to control by quite large doses of coated aspirin. At last, when another winter threatened, we decided to see what a spell of desert climate would do. We remembered how a time in Mexico had cured Inge's arthritis in 1953. So late in October we set out on a long drive south to Arizona, through the interior of Washington and the great and beautiful Yakima Reserve, through the woodlands of Oregon and into

the monotonous desert spaces of Nevada, where we avoided the gam-
bling cities with their gaudy strips and stayed instead at the old state
capital of Carson City and at Boulder City. The vast ammunition storage
areas visible from the road were eloquent evidence of American readiness
to make the first strike in defence of U.S. interests masked as a concern
for world freedom.

When we reached Arizona, we headed for the canyon country, and
settled in at Sedona, in its valley of brightly coloured rocks. It was there
that illness overtook me. Our second day we had gone to the Grand
Canyon and gaped over the cliff edges into its multichromatic depths,
which were as spectacularly and alarmingly beautiful as many others have
painted them; their eulogies make it unnecessary for me to repeat the
conventional phrases of astonishment. Already I was feeling strange in
the legs and tottering a little, so I kept away from the more precipitous
edges. We found a pre-Columbian village far off the main road in Navajo
country, with a kind of ball court, a tamed geyser that had once been the
centre of the community, and a three-storey building of flat stones. It was
desert country, but there we disturbed a magnificent stag feeding off the
low bushes.

That evening we arrived back late in Sedona, and the restaurants were
closed except for a Burger King, whose sodden hamburger nauseated
me. I began to vomit in the night, and next day felt extremely weak. That
day I found I could eat nothing but light things like fruit salad and ice
cream. And my ankles were beginning to swell. By the next day the
swelling had spread up my legs, and rather than having me trapped in an
Arizona hospital, which would probably have beggared us into the
bargain, we decided to turn north immediately and travel to the border
as best we could. Inge performed the task in four amazing, alarming and
exhausting days; during that time my legs swelled up as far as the waist
until I was like a Michelin tire man, with my scrotum swollen like that
of a victim of elephantiasis. I began to fall in the motel rooms where we
stopped at night, and to become incontinent. Most of the time as Inge
drove I was in a kind of dazy doze, so that there is not a great deal of the
journey I remember except towards the end the great sheets of rain
sweeping over Highway 5 as we crossed the border. I suppose we were
taking a great risk in not getting immediate treatment, but I got home
to Canada alive.

My doctor immediately came, and so did a neighbour and friend, a
retired surgeon whom I will call Donald, which is neither his real nor

his full name, for he is the kind of man who does not like his good deeds to be too widely known. There was no doubt what was wrong with me. The symptoms were those of oedema, or plain dropsy, one of the classic sicknesses, from which the great Ukrainian poet Taras Shevchenko died, and also the great pre-Socratic philosopher Heraclitus who, believing in the four elements, had himself buried to the neck in a dung heap, which generated heat which he believed would combat the wetness of his condition. It did not, and he died.

I was more fortunate than Heraclitus. I not only survived, but I escaped hospital thanks to my friend's willingness to walk down the hill almost every day to check on me. I was, he and my doctor recognized, suffering from renewed trouble with my heart, this time a condition called congestive heart failure. It could be alleviated but not cured, and I was put on a course of diuretics and digitalis, while I remember Don using a few volumes of my Britannica to lift up the bottom of my bed so that the fluid would drain gradually out of my legs, which, with the aid of frequent massaging, it eventually did.

I was in bed for almost a month, and then, in January staggered out to see the cardiologist, Melville Shaw, in the Medical Building near the Vancouver General Hospital. Shaw, I had heard, was a man interested in the arts, and it gave me a feeling of being in the right company when I opened the door of his waiting room, saw a fine painting of Jack Wise's calligraphic period and a Toni Onley water-colour on the walls, and a handsome Inuit sculpture standing at the end of the desk. When I went into his office, Shaw shook my hand, said he knew my writings and was glad to meet me at last, though he regretted it should be in such circumstances. He certainly translated concern into action, for he saw me three times in the first week, to make sure that the finely tuned combination of pills he was giving me did its work. He prescribed a low fluid regimen, and rationed me to two ounces of alcohol a day, the only one of his prescriptions I have failed to follow to the letter. Perhaps not on that first occasion, but certainly no later than my second visit, he took Inge aside when I went into his laboratory for an electrocardiogram, and warned her that this was an incurable sickness, and I might well survive only two or three years; seven years would be quite exceptional. That is now four years ago, four years during which Mel Shaw has constantly checked my condition, and I feel — as the dedication of this book will have shown — that I owe him not only the time I have enjoyed but also the ability I have found to work steadily even though in a less formidable way than in the sixteen-hour days I would sometimes put in years ago.

Of course, it took me some time to get back into working form, beginning with a quarter of an hour a day at the typewriter and increasing the time slowly week by week, though I managed to finish my *British Columbia: A History of the Province* in time for publication in 1990. However, the circumstances of my sickness, the inability to spend long periods at the typewriter, did not leave me idle. I read widely, and I went back to poetry, which I could handwrite on a pad without great effort. The reading and the poetry were to some degree connected, for Don Mowatt of the CBC had appeared with the suggestion that I might write a poem for voices to be included in a programme on Tolstoy. Tolstoy has been one of the writers I most respect ever since I first read him in my late teens, and though for a period I did become dominated by that great good-bad writer Dostoevsky, I had returned some time before to my earlier admirations for Tolstoy and Turgenev, the Russian writers for whom I feel the greatest empathy. I set to reading all of Tolstoy over again, and all the biographies I had of him, and when my imagination seemed to be suitably marinated I wrote a collection which I called epic fragments, concerning his life at Yasnaya Polyana, to be spoken by two voices, one representing Tolstoy himself and the other his youngest daughter Alexandra, but embracing the nature of all his daughters. I had always regarded Tolstoy as an epic writer rather than an elegiac writer like Turgenev, and I found that narrative fragments, or passages of developing thought, were more appropriate in interpreting his work and spirit than the elegiac or even the lyric manner. The work was successfully performed by my old radio associate Peter Haworth admirably representing Tolstoy at various ages, and Donna Carroll White representing the daughters.

Inevitably, given its subject and given my own precarious recent experiences, there was a heavy presence of death as the goal of the poem "Tolstoy at Yasnaya Polyana," just as there was in the volume with the same title that Bob Hilderley published at Quarry Press in 1991.

The concern with death was neither morbid nor novel so far as I was concerned. I had faced it at the time of my first heavy heart attack in 1966, when I had recognized to my astonishment — for I had always considered myself a coward — that I did not fear death. My immediate reactions when I knew I was in great danger of not seeing the night through on that occasion were, first, a burning curiosity about what was going to happen, and then some anxiety about the untied ends of my life that I might be leaving for other people to tidy up. I was walking in the valley of the shadow and I feared no evil, and lived the next quarter of a century in this mood, taking necessary precautions, but still travelling far and wide on other journeys than that into darkness and keeping my bags packed in the sense that I became extra careful to finish pieces of work so that not too many uncompleted projects would be lying around when I did depart. Indeed from this time I worked with a new intensity, economizing both my time and my strength.

The second bout with death in 1989 led me into a kind of mythologizing of my situation in an attempt to fit it all into a philosophy of existence. I had long abandoned my Christian roots, the Low Church of my childhood, the High Church of my youth, and, though I had developed a great interest in Buddhism as a philosophy, and many personal links with Buddhists from the Dalai Lama downward, I had never committed myself to Mahayanist beliefs outside the ethical life, and the Tibetan concept of the Bardo Thodol, the self's passage through death, had always struck me as a salutary myth rather than in any way a literal truth.

But I had, shortly before my first heart attack, reached a kind of deist position, expounded in *Dawn and the Darkest Hour*, my book on Aldous Huxley, in which I recognized that atheism was as absurdly dogmatic as any of the religions it attacked, and that to imagine that the world was entirely random in its operations is as foolish as to believe it may be controlled and directed entirely by some deity. There is too much evidence of pattern in nature, from the structure of a snowflake to the rosette of a young thistle plant, and in natural events like the great migrations of birds and fish, for one to be able to posit a universe without some patterning but not necessarily determining consciousness that fights against human perversions of nature, and it is within that sense of the appropriateness of what happens when nature is left to its own that I conceived of death.

I did not do this without constructing my own personal myths. I thought a great deal about the victims of God, figures like the railroaded Judas and Pilate that sensible man, decent for his time, and especially about the cynical conspiracy against Job devised by Jehovah and the dark other. My imagination gave to the forces of existence an angelic shape; I never heard the angels singing in my fruit trees like William Blake, but I did sometimes dream of them, and strangely convincing and sometimes appalling they were. And, in a kind of modified Gnosticism, I saw God and Satan as evil counterparts — Satan being God's enforcer and prison governor, and thought instead of another victim of God. This was Lucifer, the God of Light metamorphosed in holy imagination into a dark force of evil, his very title of Brightest and Best of the Sons of the Morning stolen to attach it to Christ. And death too I saw as a kind of angelic presence haunting the earth in plain clothes, capricious, even corruptible by love and strangely respectful to the creative.

I have never been concerned greatly with the manner of death, though I dread dying as the victim of another person's anger. I can accept the decay of the body, that the most beautiful of us go back to renew the earth as dust or ashes and grow uglier on the way. But, as a matter of pride rather than of faith, I cannot accept the death of the mind. I cry out — metaphorically of course — whenever I think of a fine creative intelligence being removed by some mindless virus and having no survival. And I do not really get much solace that my books *may* still be looked at in a hundred years' time; such vicarious survival does not console me for the indignity of the mind's (or soul's) extinction. Yet I have never encountered any promise or hint of continuing life more convincing than the occasional psychic visitations, which are real enough, but, like the Greek conceptions of Hades, offer dismal hints about the ongoing of consciousness. So I do not fear death itself, but I do not welcome the prospect of the mind's extinction; I agree with my old friend Dylan Thomas's exhortation, "Do not go gentle into that good night!" and perhaps that is why death and aging played such a part in my poetry of the late 1980s.

The poem "Tolstoy at Yasnaya Polyana" leads inevitably from birth to death, that sad lapsing away of the old man as he tried in the end to hasten towards liberation, and death freed him. Halfway through the poem, Tolstoy goes on his famous drive through the wood of his dead friend-enemy Turgenev, and, as I paraphrase him in verse:

My horse moved strongly
and I felt healthy
in body and mind,
and yet I thought
as I do constantly
of death. And just then I knew
on the other side of death
everything would be as good

WALKING THROUGH THE VALLEY

and I understood why the Jews
made paradise a garden.

But all this sense of good in the hereafter seemed to have gone when
Tolstoy, an aged man, made his great departure

   . . . in the dead
   of a night
   that would lead him
   to death.

Apart from the Tolstoy poem, my book included an ironically romantic
verse play of love and death, *Maskerman*, which I had written in the 1960s
(Al Purdy had hailed it at that time on a postcard as a masterpiece of
decadence) but which had never appeared in a volume, and two groups
of what I called "Lyric Poems," which in fact were really elegiac in tone,
entitled, respectively, "Dreams" and "Mirrors."

The play *Maskerman*, about an errant film cameraman and his fatal
choice of women, seems to me now an ironic document, though I find
it as lively as ever, and perhaps the wittiest thing I wrote. It was inspired
by a friend's amorous adventures, and it also fitted like a good pair of
shoes the actor, Ian Thorne, who starred in it under Gerald Newman's
direction. Today, emerging somewhat scarred from a marital quarrel, I
begin to feel it was also written about myself. One's early works may not
be literary prophecies of one's later life, but they do often indicate
tendencies within oneself that may later emerge. But at least, unlike
Maskerman, I was not caught in the undertow of the whirlpool of love
and death; I have not yet submitted to a self-elected destiny.

The "Dreams" among my shorter poems were often of death, figured
in dreams, or about lost friends, or about the awareness of the dead
inhabiting an ambience in which I move. There was one calling up the
dead rebels to witness to Elijah Harper's one-man rebellion, which
helped to shape Canadian history by the fortunate defeat of the Meech
Lake accord. Perhaps the most representative, and the only one I feel
inclined to quote, was called "Guardian Angel."

We often
meet in the street now,
you with your wry
ingratiating smile

(Bell's Palsy in that
drooping mouthline?)
and your limp
that seems to mock my own.

Not the sort of a chap
I'd make a friend of
propping up a bar
with confidences,
or an enemy either!
Why should one love
or hate one's future
or its ministers?
The time for that will come.

Meanwhile you're at work,
quiet,
soaking the air with presence.
Sometimes I feel dizzy
bending over a flower bed
and there's the faintest
touch on my elbow —
support, not grasp —
and you are there, grey and friendly.

It's the trap of course,
getting me used.
One day you'll grasp
as help turns to arrest
and I'll know then
as we go stumbling down
that ashen path
whether I love or hate you.

The mirror poems were related to the dream poems in the sense that
mirrors may reveal us, but nothing in this life is so certain as the glass of
our own perceptions may make it appear.

But all's deception,
the lines of light crisscrossed,

my left my right, zones of
feeling, intelligence,
changing place, my face an unknown other's,
till the camera's eye
probing between mirrors
rearranges all
with other glasses.

Lenses and mirrors,
there's our sum of knowledge.
Only the colours now
are false.

By the summer of 1990 I was back at work again, which means back
at prose, and we were taking short holidays in the northwestern American
states, though I found in Montana at over five thousand feet I began to
suffer from lack of oxygen, to wax incoherent, to feel great exhaustions.
The same disability, a result of my heart condition, now made it
impossible to take long plane flights because of the uncertainty of air
pressures. I was effectively grounded at last, and our great travels were
ended, which I regret and Inge as well, for we travelled far and fervently
together. If the Gods offer punishments for hubris, this is mine. I gloried ✗
so much in my knowledge of strange places.

But at my desk I had still the continents and centuries to consider. I
turned first to translation again, and put Peter Kropotkin's *Paroles d'un
révolté* into English; strangely enough, despite Kropotkin's great repute
at the turn of the century, it had never been translated. I worked on it
steadily, a page or so of typescript a day, and it helped to get my prose
back into trim after the interlude of my sickness. This, of course, was the
earlier activist Kropotkin, who believed in a revolution tomorrow or the
next day and in the need to be prepared for it. Thinking of his advance
from such simplistic thoughts to the grand visions of *Mutual Aid* and
Fields, Factories and Workshops, I could see my own development paralleling
his, from the naïve militant who helped to edit *Freedom* in the 1940s to
the broadly libertarian and undogmatic thinker I believe I have become.

Certainly both the general anarchist idea, and the particular insight of
the later Kropotkin into the extent of voluntary activity even within a
rigid state formation, combined to influence the books I began to write
at this period, *The Monk and His Message* and *Power to Us All*.

The Monk and His Message really emerged from the effects on our view of history of the rapid collapse of the Communist regimes in Europe from 1989 onwards. Up to then the great bureaucratic structures of these states had remained impregnable because people believed them so, not merely the subject people but also the ideologically driven ruling class. What happened was the coincidental weakening of the power of ideology and the strength of civil disobedience used, when fear departed, against governments that had lost their sense of rightness, represented most dramatically in Václav Havel and the Czech resistance, but also in the Leipzig demonstrations and their successors in other German cities. It seemed to me that here we had a challenge to all determinist views of history, whether progressive or eschatological-Hegelian, for here the unanticipated was clearly taking over; a spectre was haunting Europe, but not Marx's spectre.

As my first title I had picked the phrase "The Possibility of the Impossible," imagining it to be original, but then I found that it had been used already by Havel and some of his supporters. However, by this time another current had engaged my interests, stemming from a highly sensible statement by my friend the Dalai Lama for a total neutralization of Tibet that might shift the direction of the history of his country and indirectly of the world. Many people scoffed; the Chinese were established and would not leave. My observation of events in Europe and my memory of China in 1987 made me think here again of the possibility of the impossible.

My conclusions from all these ruminations were (a) that there are in fact no laws of history, that historians pick trends and clusters of events from the chaos of existence, and offer us comprehensible patterns that are determined only by their own perceptions, and (b) that almost since the beginning of the writing of history it has been manipulated by ruling groups or by groups aspiring to rule (Herodotus being the prime exception because he was too early to be corrupted). I was encouraged in this view not only by the statements of contemporaries like Havel, but also by the ideas Tolstoy expressed in *War and Peace*.

I went ahead to write a history of history-making, showing how consistently it had been distorted and the past used to create a false projection for the future. I declared that our freedom as peoples and as individuals depended on shedding our dependencies on ideological patterns and on determined history and accepting the future as a new and open world, and that this was necessary to our understanding of a world where Communism had become marginal. I argued that we have made a metaphor out of the chaos of the human condition and called it history; some have turned it into an imagined force and called it History. In fact it is the sum of our choices (or failures to choose) in a world dominated by chance and change.

As *The Monk and His Message: Undermining the Myth of History*, my book appeared in 1992, published by Douglas & McIntyre, but by that time I was well ahead with another book that applied the viewpoint emerging from *The Monk and His Message* to contemporary and local issues. The botched Meech Lake attempt at a new Canadian constitution, aborted by Elijah Harper's obstinate gesture of raising his eagle feather and saying "No" in the Manitoba Legislature, had been revived in a new form. A referendum on the issue was looming, essentially a simple yes-no proposition committing electors to accept or reject a whole complex plan worked out, mostly in camera, by federal and provincial politicians with a few native representatives, operating behind closed doors. No means of the public making its contribution through a constituent assembly or an electronic dialogue was devised or even suggested. The politicians wanted a deal, and expected the people to give them carte blanche to continue making arrangements among themselves, as in the past. Since I am no orator and by choice have never set out to acquire disciples who will propagate my ideas, I decided to approach the situation in my natural way, by a book that would ideally appear a few weeks in advance of the referendum.

I was opposed to the idea of a new constitution because, as Proudhon said in a similar situation in France in 1848, "it *is* a constitution." I feel — as the shapers of the British polity seem to have done — that the structure of a society is an evolving one and must not be laid down like the legendary laws of the Medes and Persians. Ideally I would still like to see an anarchist arrangement of society, but I recognize that this particular impossibility has not yet become possible, and that one can only offer it as a touchstone by which present arrangements might be judged. On the other hand, I believed that a reshaping of Canada into a true confederation, decentralized and increasingly libertarian, was not a remote possibility, and that people at the time of the referendum should have before them an alternative pattern of society to the one the politicians contemplated to keep themselves in power.

I talked the matter over with Howard White of Harbour Publishing, and though Howard did not agree with my every point, he did promise to publish a book of essays advocating my ideas. I called it *Power to Us All: Constitution or Social Contract*, and it dealt with all the questions of a true confederation of free people, with power springing from the base, not the apex, of the triangle. I talked of regional economic arrangements as an alternative to power deals, of local and municipal autonomy, of the undemocratic nature of Canadian "representative" democracy with its quasi-fascist thirst for "leadership" and its five-yearly elections; I pointed out how by giving the native peoples the sovereignty that is their due we might take some lessons from their traditions of consensual politics. I called for true participatory democracy. I pointed to the natural variousness of Canada, geographically and historically and argued that our complementarity held us together far more than an artificial kind of unity of the kind arrogant and dangerous men like Trudeau and Mulroney have tried to impose. I called for "creative anti-national disunity," for military neutrality and the attack on environmental crime. And I argued that if the present political process did not allow such an evolution, we should be prepared to demand our power through civil disobedience.

I worked on the book well into the late spring of 1992, and then in July I was once again attacked with serious illness. I began to lose my balance and fall; I had terrible shuddering attacks which lasted for as much as an hour. One night, taking a drink at Michael Mercer's, I fell several times and Inge had difficulty getting me home. Our doctor, Bob Menzies, turned up in the middle of the night and put me to bed until further notice, and in those days I lay there correcting the edited version of my book, so that on the fourth day, when I went into hospital, it would be ready for the press. I need not have hurried, for the printer in Manitoba ruined the publication schedule; his binding machine broke down and instead of getting the work done outside he held up the edition so that the book appeared a mere two weeks before the referendum. However, the people had already made up their minds about the politicians, and the No votes gained a majority in the referendum, which was the beginning of a march towards a different Canada.

I was suffering from an acute inflammation of the prostate gland, and the sonar scanner revealed that because of the holding up of urine I was suffering from infections of liver, kidneys and bladder. All these had to be cleared up before I could have the fairly simple prostate operation.

Naturally, like everyone who goes there, I was frustrated in the Vancouver General Hospital, which since my previous stay in 1966 had been turned into a kind of industrial unit with the specialists as managers and the nurses much less caring, efficient and friendly than in the past. The food was appalling, far worse than I had eaten on my journalistic trips in the past to local prisons where I fed with the inmates; but of course it is taken for granted that prisoners rebel physically against bad food, while patients do not.

I went into fever and slipped into passages of delirium, so that I imagined a woman friend who visited me was a lady out of Turgenev. One day I was surprised at the number of doctors who came to visit me; the internal medicine man, the urologist, Mel Shaw my cardiologist, my general practitioner, two old doctor friends; on top of it all, the head of the blood-testing unit, a very efficient Chinese lady, personally took my blood sample. But, doctors being so close about their patients' secrets, it was not until a month after I was out of hospital that Mel Shaw told me as a friend that on that day they had thought they might be losing me to septicemia. But my tough old body stood it all, I recovered, had my operation, and after nearly a month escaped into the sunlight.

Chapter 20

EPILOGUE

I realize, as I write these last pages, that the illness I have just described took place less than a year and a half ago. In the case of *Beyond the Blue Mountains* I let almost a decade pass between the terminal date of action and the date of the book's publication. But as one grows old, life becomes more pressing, time seems literally to pass more quickly the less there is of it left, and there is an urgency about anything one has to say.

I have found among old people like myself an inclination to acquire or to create that often seems immoderate, yet really is a way of testing time and tempting providence. It may be the acquisition of necessities; I remember an old German friend who would keep filling his cellar with cases of toilet paper, pails of mountain honey and cases of red wine, theoretically because it was cheaper that way, but really, I felt, as a kind of ritual to ensure a long life, which he had. Other people I have found collecting books they will never have time to read if they live for decades, or moved by works of art whose vitality, when they acquire them, seems in some magical way added to their own.

I have found the same kind of magic emerging in my own life, in at least two ways. First, I have long sought the company, not of the very young, but of those about a generation younger, who might be the sons and daughters I never had, and in their company rather than that of my contemporaries I find my mental stimulus, and even gain, from some of them, an added inner vitality. There are so many such friends that I hesitate to name them (most have appeared in any case) but I recognize how important their presence has been in the last decades.

And then, of course, there is the writing, in which my sicknesses may have been no more than perhaps necessary times of retreat. Certainly my last period in hospital set me thinking, in the long nights when sleeping tablets did not work very well, along more imaginative lines, and after I emerged I turned back to poetry, and wrote the sequence that will be appearing shortly with Quarry Press in a volume entitled *The Cherry Tree on Cherry Street.* (McCleery Street where I have lived for thirty-four years was once called Cherry Street after the great orchard the first settlers, the McCleery brothers in the 1860s, planted there; the last of the orchard's trees, immense, decaying and at least ninety years old, still stands in our garden.) But then I turned even farther back, to the fiction I had not written after I threw my aborted novel into the Atlantic in 1950. Since I came out of hospital I have written a small number of short fictions, mostly about the world of my childhood, one of which, "Old Borscht," has already been published in *Event,* and two others will be appearing in *Saturday Night* and *The Canadian Fiction Magazine* respectively. I have also been working the concept of my discarded film script *Lupus* into a novel which is nearing completion, and I am planning a much larger novel on a naturalist travelling in South America. Perhaps the most hubristic survival act of all, I am now deep in my translation of Proust's great work, *In Search of Time Lost.* At present, I have roughed out my translation of most of *Swann's Way,* and a section of it is due to appear very soon in *Quarry.* That I should live long enough to complete the whole 3,400 pages of the great work does seem to me improbable, and yet . . .

So I find myself aged and invalid, yet still dedicated to the writing that has sustained me and been my life; resigned, yet even to my own surprise careless about time and what can be done within it, and ready to depart as soon as my life loses meaning for me, which is not yet.

Still, I doubt if I shall be writing much more about my life, or if this volume of memoirs will be followed by another. But I have enjoyed both living and writing about my life and, while I refrain from quoting St. Paul, I consider myself to have been on the whole a fortunate being in a fortunate time and place, though I have tried never to let that blind me to the wretchedness of others. I have hoped for humanity and like many others have seen the realization of my hopes indefinitely postponed, so that I should feel sad beyond measure as I end this account. Inexplicably, I do not feel sad. That Possible on the far edge of Impossibility still stirs my imagination, and the growing consciousness of political and environmental realities among ordinary people offers at least a chance that humanity might save itself and other beings and the planet most of all.

II "BEYOND THE BLUE MOUNTAINS" 1986

II "WALKING THROUGH THE VALLEY." 1994.

I "LETTER TO THE PAST."

"GABRIEL DUMONT: THE MÉTIS
CHIEF AND HIS LOST WORLD."

"WALLS OF INDIA" - (1984)

empathy - P. 45 -

R 107 - cormorants.
P. 16 - pudeur - (Fr.) -
P. 142 - indurated -
P. 153 - postauto -
" 160 - gnostics -
" 164 - paradon -
" 150 - spinifex -
" 152 - epiphyte -
" 181 - stupe -
" 187 - bodhisattva.
" 187 - situ - "
" 204 - "do not go---- etc.
" 207 - hubris -
" 207 - Books ① + ②